The

INSIDERS' GUIDE TO NEW ORLEANS

by
St. Leger Joynes and Jack DuArte

New Orleans   Greensboro   Norfolk
THE INSIDERS' PUBLISHING GROUP

Distributed Nationally by
Insiders Guide
2475 Canal St., Suite 108 New Orleans LA 70119
(504) 821-7757

Dedication

The Joynes Family

(Leger, Evelyn, Rita, Annalisa, and Danielle)

&

The DuArte Family

(John, Antoinette, Carol, John, Steven, and Baron)

REVISED 2nd Edition
WINTER 1982-83

Library of Congress Catalog Number 79-26755
ISBN 0-932338-03-8

PREFACE

This book is the result of a friendship and a common fascination and affection for a city. The chemistry of friendship began in 1975 when a magazine editor-publisher sought out the city's principal restaurant critic to talk about the joys of dining. Hundreds of table experiences later, the two friends began to explore the idea of a collaboration on a guidebook that would be a resource, rather than a throw-away, or one time souvenir. The book had to include more than a cursory enumeration of historic landmarks and famous restaurants. The New Orleans that we authors know deserves a more in-depth, sophisticated treatment.

The book, of course, had to be useful and practical for the two or three day, first-time visitor, but a larger goal was to make the guide a resource for residents of the city itself, and a companion for those frequent visitors who want to share more fully in the city's quixotic spirit. The concept called for an authoritative, and sometimes scholarly approach to New Orleans history and legend. Both of us were keenly aware of the misinformation that is propagated by well intentioned, but ill advised tour guides. Since the past so significantly colors the attitudes and lifestyle of New Orleanians, understanding it is a key to the texture and feel of the city. But we wanted to remove the "history lecture" technique in relating the stories that needed to be told. The solution has been to use an anecdotal style, and to tell the historical saga where it is most meaningful: at its geographical site. The reader will therefore find historic notes in the hotel profiles, as well as extensive chronicles concerning events at the city's major landmarks. Where historic sites no longer exist, or where legend dominates, a separate chapter has been created to give insights on Dixie, Craps, Riverboat Gamblers, etc. The chapter is titled "Legends," but much of its content is verifiable fact.

You will find many strip maps and legends within this edition. Every historic attraction, restaurant, and hotel which is profiled is shown on a map. The map legend provides a cross reference to the page on which the profile appears. An additional reference is available in the index. By reviewing the maps, you can see not only where you are, but what is convenient to your location at the moment. For example, if you are staying at the Chateau Le Moyne in the French Quarter, you can locate yourself on the appropriate map and see the precise walking distance to restaurants and attractions around you.

The restaurant chapter in the book profiles more than 130 establishments. It is the result of a lifetime of critical dining. In a city so famous for its cuisine and its restaurants, we felt that the informational profiles required the further qualification of a three-star rating system. Other books in the **Insiders'** national series do not rate restaurants, but New Orleans is an area that demands it. We encourage readers to review the chapter introduction for an orientation to the rating system prior to searching the profiles.

The initial edition of the **Insiders' Guide to New Orleans** took two years to research and write. We took every tour, saw every historic place, visited every hotel, and ate in every restaurant. Courtesies were extended on admission tickets, and in a few other areas, but for the most part, we paid all our own expenses. None of the text of the book was reviewed or approved by those we wrote about in order to insure the book's editorial integrity.

We trust that our book will lead you to the places that your appetites and budgets dictate. We hope that it will save you time and money every time that you use it. Most of all, we want our book to help you enjoy a city that we love. We want our years of experience to make you an insider in New Orleans, to lead you to the people and the places that appeal to your own personal tastes and interests. Perhaps we will meet you across a table in New Orleans. A lot of good things seem to start that way.

Monty & Jack

Acknowledgements: The authors wish to thank the following for their aid and counsel during the long period of development for the first edition of this book: Madeleine Adams, Barry Blake, Joanna Broussard, Mike Casey, Jerry Clower, Winky and Donna Cocks, Gail Conners, Joe Connolly, Rhonda Daniel, Rachael Daniels, Dennis Delaney, Alan Dreeben, Ted Eisenberg, Lloyd and Vickie Flatt, Joe Flynn, Susan Heyd, Roger and Barbara Jacobs, Charles Jenkins, Walter and Beth Johnson, Mickey Joyce, Charles and Patches Lancaster, Martha Lauck, Juanita Martin, Bernard and Earline Mason, Anne Mrok, Frank Nuccio, Robert Rintz, Dan and Marylee Robinson, Anthony Saragusa, Richard Scelfo, Raymond Schneider, Brent Simpson, Chuck and Rhoda Steiner, Steven and Lori Taylor, Leonard and Sandi Threlkeld, Ed and Valerie Tunstall, Debbie Wills, Max and Ruth Yarnall, Roger Yaseen, and Steve Zimmerman.

Special thanks to: Rene Schiegg, Lisa Sins, and Randi de la Gueronniere.

Photographs: Ellis Lucia and Monty Joynes with major contributions from the Greater New Orleans Tourist and Conventions Commission and the Audubon Zoological Garden.

Production and Editorial Staff: Martha Jones, map graphics and cover; Gloria Magid, Peggy Haile, Linda Giessinger and Sue Nagle, copy editing and index.

ABOUT THE INSIDERS

St. Leger "Monty" Joynes has had an affair with New Orleans for more than twenty years. He married a Cajun, and later returned to Louisiana as the Associate Publisher of **Holiday Magazine** to direct the Holiday Fine Dining Awards. He was responsible for **The Holiday Award Cookbook** in 1975. As an author, he has written hundreds of magazine feature stories, and has co-authored three travel guides which have become regional best sellers. He is also the author of a novel. Monty lives with his two daughters in Norfolk, Virginia. During recent years he has been a seasonal resident of the French Quarter.

Jack DuArte is a native of New Orleans who enjoys a national reputation for his expertise in food and wine. He wrote a gastronomy column for the **Times Picayune** for five years, and was a contributing restaurant editor to several airline in-flight magazines. Jack was the 1977 Man of the Year of the New Orleans Restaurant Association. His other awards include the Les Amis Du Vin Chevalier Award, the Campagnons d'Bordeaux, and the rank of Maitre d'Table from the Confrerie De La Chaine Des Rotisseurs in France. He is a frequent judge at food festivals and cooking contests. He also co-authored the **DuArte-Brennan Guide to New Orleans Cuisine & Dining.** Jack is a member of a Mardi Gras parade krewe, and is the president of a regional wine brokerage firm headquartered in New Orleans.

CONTENTS

MAPS

Saint Louis Cathedral in the early morning

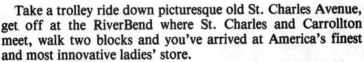
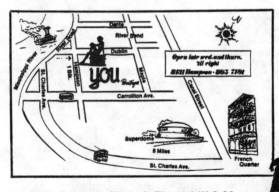

THIS IS NEW ORLEANS

New Orleans is a state of mind. As Warren LeRuth, the great chef and restaurateur likes to say, "You love New Orleans, and she'll love you right back." New Orleans has style born of romantic traditions.

There has been Indian habitation near New Orleans for 2,000 to 2,500 years. The Marksville period natives built burial mounds in the Barataria Basin not far from where Jean Lafitte later hid his warehouses and ships. The Indians venerated the Mississippi River, the great "Father of Waters," and lived off its bounty of game, fish, and shellfish. The first white men passed through the area in 1682 as the La Salle expedition traced the Mississippi from its source near the Canadian border, and laid claim to the Louisiana Territory for France.

Louis XIV, the Sun King, for whom Louisiana is named, sent La Salle back to the river basin in 1684 to establish a permanent settlement, but shipwreck, disease, and Indian attacks led to mutiny. La Salle was assassinated and the expedition to establish a colony failed. By 1698 the English were challenging the French for rights in Louisiana, realizing the importance of controlling the great river's outlet to the sea. Pierre and Jean Le Moyne, brothers who had been successful in the colonization of Canada, were outfitted in Brest, and set sail to explore the mouth of the river and to set up a French colony.

The Sieur d'Iberville, the older brother, and the Sieur de Bienville were successful in establishing villages in Natchez, Biloxi, Mobile by 1712 with a total of 300 colonists. Bienville explored the great river and in a daring bluff turned back English claims to the territory at a place forever after known as "English Turn." With French influence assured, an incredible Scotsman named John Law insinuated his way into control of the French economy and tied its rise and fall to paper shares in Louisiana. In 1717 he sold the royalty of Europe on bogus Louisiana pearl fisheries, gold and silver mines, and an Indian population that would gladly provide free slave labor to its white Christian betters. No mention was made of the mosquitoes, swamplands, hostile natives, and disease that confronted would-be settlers.

In 1718, after the death of Iberville, the younger Le Moyne brother, Bienville, began to oversee the clearing of land for a port settlement on the Mississippi River as John Law's appointed Governor of the Louisiana Territory. Bienville named his new capital city, built on portage shown to him by the Indians on his first expedition, Nouvelle Orleans, in honor of the Duke of Orleans, Regent of France.

To produce labor for the new colony, the unscrupulous John Law gathered criminals, and even "the correction girls" from the notorious Paris house of detention, La Salpetriere. Although the girls were prostitutes and a midwife was sent to accompany them, their offspring go unacknowledged to protect the vanity of proud New Orleanian families.

Where did the fun begin? When did Nouvelle Orleans, a city established on an impossible swampy site, become "the city that care forgot?" Perhaps one of the early territorial governors, the Marquis de Vaudreuil set the tone. Amid the mud streets, and crude buildings, he acted as if he was still in the court at Versailles. He refused to accept the indignity of squallor and disease that inflicted his primitive colony. He brought the gaiety of formal balls, the luxury of champagne, and the fashions and manners of the French court into this unseemly community of adventurers, exiles, and administrators. So what if the ladies came barefoot in the knee deep mud streets to the ballroom, washed their feet, put on their shoes, adjusted their gowns, and then danced the night away. So what if most of the people ate corn mush all week long so that they could set a regal table for guests at the week's end. What was important, even to those early New Orleanians, was that there were moments in life reserved, and completely given over to merriment. Whatever the social status, whatever the cruel fates dealt in the way of hardships and misfortune, there would be good times without regard to the costs. There would be food, and drink, and friends with talk and laughter uninhibited by circumstance.

In 1763 another group of French exiles driven out of Nova Scotia by the English began to arrive in New Orleans. The Acadians were farmers, and they settled along the bayous in the southern part of the state. Their "Cajun" culture with its distinctive music only added to the tradition of "laissez les bons temps rouler," let the good times roll.

The French colony was shocked in 1764 when it learned that a bankrupt France had secretly ceded Louisiana to Spain in 1762. Cousin Louis XV obliged his Spanish cousin, Charles III. After all, a Spaniard, De Soto, had discovered the Mississippi. The French colonists however rejected the first Spanish governor, and had to be occupied by "Bloody O'Reilly," an Irishman in the service of Spain. O'Reilly executed the French resisters, and established the Cabildo as the seat of Spanish authority. Thus the French and Spanish cultures merged, ultimately intermarried, and created the Creoles. True Creoles trace their ancestry to the French and Spanish colonial periods. The Vieux Carre today shows almost exclusively the influence of Spanish occupation because of two disastrous fires, one in 1788 and another in 1794, which destroyed the existing wooden French built structures.

New Orleans in the 1800's became an extravagant city. Wealthy planters who escaped the slave revolution on Santo Domingo helped to cultivate a sugar industry that soon produced fortunes. The port city attracted a sophisticated population who rode in carriages and went to the first opera house in America. Gambling houses were common, and prostitution flourished in elegant townhouses as well as rough riverside shanties.

At the turn of the century, Louisiana became French property again under the hand of Napoleon, who had visions of establishing a strong

French presence in North America. But the fortunes of war changed, and when the English pressured Napoleon on all fronts, he abruptly sold the Louisiana Territory to a surprised Thomas Jefferson administration in 1803. It was the biggest real estate deal in history, and because of a unique set of circumstances, the city passed from the Spanish, to the French, and finally to the Americans within the space of ten days.

Americans poured into their new acquisition, and the antagonism between the cultured Creoles and the rough and tumble Americans became so acute that each set up his own municipality with Canal Street as the dividing line. The separate communities were forced to unite in December of 1814 as the determined English landed a substantial invasion force and attempted to take the city. General Andrew Jackson and his army of Creoles, Free Men of Color, Jean Lafitte's pirates, Kaintock rivermen, and uniformed American soldiers gave the English army one of its worst historical defeats. The victory seemed to propel the city into its most glamorous and prosperous age, the "Golden Age" of 1825 to 1860.

Consider the irony: New Orleans began as a French colony out of the scheme of a Scotsman; it became Spanish at the hands of an Irishman; and the English almost won it in the end except for the generalship of an American.

The Golden Age

Many visitors to New Orleans come to the city looking for the vestiges of its halcyon, pre Civil War days. The wealth generated by sugar and cotton, and the importance of the river port made the city the most prosperous and exciting city in America during the period. The image of great plantations supported by the institution of slavery, of regal mansions and elegantly dressed ladies and gentlemen, and of river boats that became floating palaces are well etched into the American romantic consciousness. Although the opera house that they patronized is gone, and the grand hotels and restaurants of the period have been replaced by those of a more modern era, there are enough surviving and restored treasures of the Golden Age for us to glimpse at the grandeur of their lifestyle.

In the French Quarter, the Garden District, and along the River Road, the townhouses, mansions, and plantation homes which are open to the public attest to the richness of the past. To walk these paths is to step back into time, where in the presence of antique witnesses the imagination can conceive, and even believe that formal luxury coexisted with bawdy houses; that gambling on crops or the turn of a card was a reasonable way of life; that dueling was a heroic defender of Honor; and that voodoo thrived as a religion. It was an age when the Irish and German immigrants arrived, and joined in the labor force to dig canals and to die by the thousands to Bronze John.

The beginning of the War Between the States at first seemed like another extension of the South's romantic spirit. Especially for New Orleans, rich, vibrant, and extravagant in all its moods, the adventure of war was a fancy uniformed duel concerning a difference of opinion about economic lifestyles. Torch lit parades, first class soldiers of the Washington

Artillery whose ancestors had defeated the British at Chalmette, and a real native hero, General Pierre Gustave Toutant Beauregard, fired the city's enthusiasm. The thrill of early victories was arrested however in the capture of New Orleans in April 1862, and then held in the vice like grip of Union General Ben Butler. The occupation of Federal troops lasted until 1877. During the war years the port was sealed, and the commerce of king cotton and sugar died. With it died an age of refinement built on an impossible dream.

The post war years were mean ones for the citizens of New Orleans. The slave based economy was ruined. The river traffic gave way to the emerging railroads. Reconstruction was a chaotic period of hate, violence, corruption, and anarchy as white supremacists battled a Republican carpetbagger government for control of the city and state.

The Modern Era

The force that brought New Orleans into existence, the force that ebbed and flowed through its history, in victory and defeat, in poverty and wealth, again was the dominating element in its rebirth and emergence into the modern age. The Mississippi. The Father of Waters. It still carries the commerce of the heartland of America, and its great port, New Orleans, opens the door to trade with the rest of the world. The fortunes of world wars, so much a catalyst in the initial history of the city, again made the port a vital center of interest and activity. By 1945, at the end of World War II, New Orleans was second only to New York as the most important port in the nation. Today, the city skyline and its shipbuilding, cargo wharfs, and oil industry support facilities attest to the economic success of the modern city.

In the process of becoming rich again, however, New Orleans did not lose, or forget, its cultural legacy. Something of the Creole spirit not only endures, but flourishes. It is a quality that you can actually taste in the cuisine. It is a character trait that is not only apparent during the Carnival season. It is not a Mardi Gras affectation. It is something stored in genes, and passed through generations. It is a talent for having fun. It is an affection for things beautiful. It is a veneration of things old and traditional. It is a curiosity about chance, especially if horses, cards, or dice are involved. It is a drive to wear a costume, and join a parade. It is a passion for the cooking arts, and a taste for beverages alcoholic. It is a propensity toward friendship and hospitality. It is a thing natural to New Orleanians that most people have to work at to achieve.

The French Quarter

If you want to catch the spirit of New Orleans, you begin in the French Quarter. The Quarter is the Vieux Carre, the "old square" where the city began with Bienville in 1718. It is the city's most precious asset, and its age, narrow streets, and row house construction make it vulnerable. Its quaint and distinctive character is zealously guarded by the Vieux Carre Commission, a body that carries the force of the Louisiana Constitution as well as the Code of the City. All work undertaken on the exterior of any building in the Quarter requires a permit. Any painting, repair, lighting, tree planting, courtyard improvement, etc. must conform to specific standards to preserve its historic architectural qualities. Commission inspectors are deputized by the New Orleans Police, and they are taken seriously by property owners. There is currently a moratorium, for example, on any further construction of hotel rooms in the Quarter.

If you can only spend a few hours in New Orleans, spend them in the French Quarter around Jackson Square. The roof tops connect like Paris, and there are artists and entertainers on the streets. The lush verdant courtyards, concealed from the busy sidewalks, are gracious in the Spanish style. Art galleries, antique shops, jazz clubs, strip joints, award winning restaurants, and elegant hotels fascinate the senses. The historic streets reveal their legacies in ornamental iron balconies, carriageways, and architectural wonderments. It is a place unlike any other place in the world. Music spills out of unsuspecting facades. You walk, you stop to eat the special foods, and sample the original drinks. "Yes of course," you realize, "this is obviously the city that invented Jazz."

THE STATE OF LOUISIANA

The original Louisiana territory, which President Jefferson acquired from the French in 1803, comprised all or part of 17 different states. The "Pelican State" today includes 48,523 square miles in 64 "parishes," instead of counties. Their names reflect the early French and Spanish colonial occupations. The state flower is the Magnolia, and its capital is Baton Rouge. The state was admitted to the Union in 1812.

LOUISIANA'S TEN FLAGS

1541	Spanish colors of Leon and Castile
1682	French Fleur-de-Lis
1682	British Union Jack
1763	Bourbon Spain
1769	French Tri-Color
1803	U.S. Flag of 15 stars
1803	West Florida Lone Star
1810	Independent Louisiana
1861	Stars and Bars of the Confederate States
1861	U.S. Stars and Stripes

RESOURCES FOR INFORMATION

Louisiana Office of Tourism
Dept. LTX, P.O. Box 44291
Baton Rouge, LA 70804

Publishes a free 32-page color brochure about state attractions.

Louisiana Travel Promotion Association
P.O. Box 64654
Baton Rouge, LA 70804

Publishes an 80-page full color **Louisiana Tour Guide** which includes suggested driving tours, maps, sightseeing, and accommodations information. Free.

Greater New Orleans Tourist
and Convention Commission
334 Royal Street
New Orleans, LA 70130

Publishes an annual Visitors' Guide of about 64-pages reflecting the tours, restaurants, shops and services of its membership.

THE WEATHER

The average mean temperature in New Orleans is 70 degrees. The hot, humid months are July and August. The near subtropical climate yields over 60 inches of annual rainfall, so it is wise to carry an umbrella.

PERSONAL SECURITY

The caveats that go with visiting any major American city are applicable to New Orleans. If you are alone, it is better to take a cab than to walk dark, unfamiliar streets. Never flash your cash or jewelry and use the courtesy of your hotel safe rather than leave valuables in your room for long periods of time.

It is not recommended that you visit the older cemeteries except in a group. St. Louis No. 1, for example, is a maze that invites ambush by the often violent bandits who scale the back walls to rob unsuspecting visitors.

It is not recommended that you explore the French Quarter alone, or as a couple, in the early morning hours, especially after a night of cabaret. Stay on the major lighted streets if you must walk, and always use a cab when in doubt.

Seeking the favors of ladies of the night is a dangerous avocation. Your place or theirs, the stories of rip-off and worse are too commonplace to deny.

Do not leave intoxicated friends alone late at night. They are easy targets for mayhem, and will often use poor judgment in where they walk and to whom they talk. Stay with your group of friends whenever possible. Any "walk on the wild side" will be at your own risk.

AUTO TOWING IN THE FRENCH QUARTER

The French Quarter tow trucks are notorious. There are about thirty of them assigned to the Quarter, and they actually cruise around looking for parking violators. The drivers can snatch and tow, and they do so with alarming quickness. There is a reason why the police are tow crazy in the Quarter: fire. Any fire in the Quarter is an all alarm situation because of its antiquity and population density. The narrow streets, however, do not lend themselves to modern fire fighting equipment. An illegally parked car could prevent the engines from turning corners. If your car is towed, you can pick it up 24 hours a day at the 400 N. Claiborne Auto Pound. The tow and ticket is going to cost about $50. Every ticket doubles during Mardi Gras. It's an automatic $100 for blocking a parade route.

EMERGENCY MEDICAL CARE

821-3232

The New Orleans Police Department operates the Emergency Medical Service. Paramedical units fully equipped and trained for heart attacks and other emergency situations are within ten minutes response time to major hotels and tourist areas. Most EMT's (Emergency Medical Technicians) agree that the Charity Hospital Emergency Room is the best place to be transported to in a life-endangering situation.

The city bills for the emergency service. $30 for first aid, $75 if transport to a hospital is required. Certain supplies and equipment utilization charges may be added.

The St. Charles Avenue Streetcar.

GETTING AROUND

MOISANT NEW ORLEANS INTERNATIONAL AIRPORT

Over 5 million passengers use this facility annually. Its scheduled airlines serve virtually every major metropolitan area in the U.S., plus destinations in Mexico and Latin America.

Here are the airlines serving the city and their local telephone numbers:

AMERICAN AIRLINES	523-2188
AVIATECA	522-1010
CONTINENTAL AIRLINES	522-2161
DELTA AIRLINES	529-2431
EASTERN AIRLINES	524-4211
LASCA AIRLINES	525-1695
NORTHWEST ORIENT AIRLINES	566-1100
QZARK AIRLINES	831-5752
PAN AMERICAN WORLD AIRWAYS	529-5412
PIEDMONT AIRLINES	454-2668
REPUBLIC AIRLINES	525-0423
SASHA HONDURAS	729-4528
SOUTHERN AIRLINES	523-5683
TACA INTERNATIONAL	729-4551
TEXAS INTERNATIONAL	581-2965
TRANS WORLD AIRLINES	529-2585
US AIR	837-3457

UNION PASSENGER TERMINAL

1001 Loyola Avenue   **Map, pg. 105**   586-0027

The Union Passenger Terminal serves Amtrak trains, and both Greyhound and Trailways bus lines. Its location is convenient to the Central Business District.

PUBLIC SERVICE TRANSPORTATION

New Orleans has one of the best public transportation systems in the country. It is especially attractive for the out-of-town visitor. You can do most of your sightseeing by bus or street car. Please have exact change when boarding.

STREET CARS

Transit service on the St. Charles line has been called "the oldest continuously operating street railway in the world". The complete route is 13 miles long, and the round trip from Canal Street to S. Carrollton and back takes about an hour and a half. Service on the line began in 1835. Now 35 cars, each seating 52 passengers, provide a colorful link with many New Orleans attractions.

Exit at Jackson Avenue or Washington Avenue for a walk through the Garden District. Audubon Park, Tulane and Loyola Universities, and many other attractions, restaurants, and hotels are on its route. Avoid the working people rush hours, and you can usually find a seat.

FRENCH QUARTER MINI-BUS

These olive and mahogany painted, 19-passenger mini-buses are dressed to resemble the street cars that traveled the Quarter's narrow streets in the early 1900's. The service, begun in 1974, has a peak hours route running mostly on Bourbon and Royal Streets, and an off peak route which uses Dauphine and Chartres as a base for making turns onto St. Peter and St. Ann. We recommend a 20 minute round trip on the mini-bus for a quick orientation of the Quarter and its sights.

PUBLIC BUSES

Buses running in the bus lanes in the middle of Canal Street provide inexpensive transport to such attractions as City Park, the cemeteries, and the Lake Pontchartrain lakefront and beach. The Magazine Street bus, which can be caught in the middle of Audubon Park, is a good alternative to the streetcar on St. Charles for the return trip to Canal Street after a tour of the Zoo.

Any bus heading away from the river will take you to the Metairie Cemetery area. Another short bus ride will take you to City Park. The Lake Vista bus on Canal Street will give you a tour of the lake shoreline. Don't be shy about asking drivers, or local people at bus stops, about directions. Schedules and line routes are posted.

CENTRAL BUSINESS DISTRICT SHUTTLE

This triangular route serves the Rivergate Conference Center and the Superdome along a Poydras and Canal Street axis. Buses go in both directions, and run with a high frequency. The service is especially useful for the convention delegate, and a help to the tourist who wants to explore the International Trade Mart waterfront area and the Superdome on the same outing.

AIRPORT LIMOUSINE SERVICE

722-7691

This is a 24-hour service providing modern van transportation between the airport and New Orleans hotels. Drive time in non-peak hours is about 18 to 20 minutes. Deplaning passengers should allow about 45 minutes for baggage pick-up and the ride to their hotels.

Passengers returning to the airport should reserve limousine service 24-hours prior to departure from their hotels. Allow 90 minutes prior to the flight for pick-up, delivery, and processing at the airport. The fare is $6.00 per person, one-way.

CAR RENTALS

The major car rental firms serve the International Airport and have other locations in or near the Central Business District. Reservations are recommended.

FIRM	TOLL FREE	LOCAL
American International	800/527-0202	467-3151
Avis	800/331-1212	523-4317
Budget	800/527-0700	525-9417
Hertz	800/654-3131	568-1645
Holiday	800/237-2804	522-2992
National	800/328-4567	525-0416
Thrifty		729-5573

TAXICAB SERVICE

Service from the International Airport will cost over $15. Cab stands are located near major hotels, and cabs are generally easy to hail. Here are the major local companies and their 24-hour service number:

Checker/Yellow Cabs......................525-3311/943-2411
Metairie Cabs.....................................835-4242
United Cabs.............................522-9771/524-9606
White Fleet Cabs..................................948-6605

TOURS BY LIMOUSINE

For those who desire, and can afford, the privacy and convenience of a hired limousine, there are several experienced operators who can provide service. The companies generally use late-model Cadillacs (or vans for larger partiers), provide 24-hour service, can provide multi-lingual tour guides, and accept major credit cards. They will tailor a city, plantation, or night club tour to the customer's wishes. Rates vary from about $17 to $23 per hour. There is usually a minimum.

JACCO Tours **CAJUN COUNTRY**

BAYOU BOAT RIDE & PLANTATION TOUR

Swamp Parade

Acadian Culture • Cajun Fisherman
• Pirogues • Wildlife, Alligators &
Exotic Birds
• Sugar Cane Villiages
Swamp Gardens
Marsh and More

The most memorable experience and the highlight of your visit to Louisiana. We'll cross to the West Bank of the River and show you the South you expected to see, where senic Bayou's are 3,500 years old and Indians have lived since the time of Christ. We'll drive the old Choctaw trail, through the Lafourche-Delta Swamp. Visit a Cajun Village, meet the friendly people who still speak 17th Century French, and be escorted by a native fisherman-trapper by boat into a peaceful subtropical terrain compared to the Amazon, where the first Tarzan movie was filmed and Lafitte buried his treasures. Eat real Cajun cookin' (crawfish etoufee, alligator sauce piquante, etc.) Drive along the banks of the mighty Mississippi, ride a ferryboat. Personally visit the oldest Plantation home in the Lower Mississippi Valley.

DEPARTS DAILY — 9:00 A.M. - 6 HOURS Air Conditioned Mini Bus

568-0141

MR. JACCO YOUNG one of New Orleans most beloved and respected sons is delighting both locals and visitors with his Swamp and Cajun Country Tours featuring a bayou boat ride, plantation tour, acadian culture, cajun fishermen, pirogues, wildlife, alligators, exotic birds, sugar cane villages, swamp gardens and much, much more truly your most memorable experience and the highlight of you visit to Louisiana.

ALL MAJOR CREDIT CARDS ACCEPTED

• *You are picked up and returned to the hotel.*

AAAA Tours, 936 Athania Pkwy., Metairie   834-2133
Bonomolo Limousines, 7272 Endston Ct., N.O.   947-4162
New Orleans Limousine Service, 3119 Jackson Ave.   588-2118
Linda's Limo 505 Live Oak, Metairie   835-2738

MEDICAB OF NEW ORLEANS

P.O. Box 445, Gretna 70054   367-7720

Medicab will plan special tours for the wheelchair person or the disabled requiring specialized service. It provides transportation for non-emergency medical and recreational trips.

AIRPLANE TOURS

Lakefront Airport   246-6543

The Piper Flight Center offers private charter tours of the city and its environs. Here's the way to get a bird's eye view of all the sights along the lake and river.

Three passengers can hire a plane and pilot for $67 an hour. Give the Flight Center about a day's notice to arrange your flight.

TOURS BY BUS

Touring by bus is a safe and convenient way to see the highlights of New Orleans. The driver or an accompanying tour guide provides an entertaining narrative on the sights. Reservations may be made by phone, or at kiosks located in most hotels. Buses pick up and return tour passengers to most hotels. Check for specific times. Prices quoted for the tours are subject to change.

GRAYLINE OF NEW ORLEANS

1793 Julia St.   525-0138

New Orleans In Three Centuries Departs 9:30 and 1:30. Three hours. $10 per person. Tour includes French Quarter, Garden District and St. Charles Avenue, Downtown and the riverfront, Bayou St. John, City Park, Lake Pontchartrain, and a stop at St. Louis Cemetery.
New Orleans After Dark Departs 8:30 p.m. except Sunday. Four hours. $25, all inclusive, per person. Includes a drink, cover charge and gratuities at each club. The tour begins with cocktails and view from the Top of the International Trade Mart. The next stop is a French Quarter jazz club, followed by the floorshow at the Blue Room of the Fairmont

Hotel. The evening ends with cafe au lait and beignets at the French Market Cafe du Monde.

River Road Plantations Departs 10 a.m. 6½ hours. $23 per person. Lunch not included. This guided tour covers 125 miles. The River Road route passes fields of sugar cane, and the remains of plantation homes along the river. Oak Alley and Houmas House, two restored antebellum homes, are visited. The lunch stop is at a country restaurant when Cajun specialties may be sampled. The return trip is via the shores of Lake Pontchartrain with views of its cypress swamplands.

Paddlewheeler and City Sights Departs 11 a.m. 5½ hours, $15 per person. This tour combines a two-hour harbor cruise on the Mississippi with Grayline's New Orleans In Three Centuries city tour.

DIXIELAND TOURS

4861 Chef Menteur Hwy.   283-7318

Covers Entire City Departs 9, 2 and 8:30 p.m. About 3 hours. $10. This firm has been conducting tours for more than 25 years. In addition to new buses, it operates 14-passenger vans. The city tour covers all the major districts and landmarks on a 50-mile route.

After Dark Departs 8:30. Returns about 2 a.m. $23. Visits three night clubs, and ends the evening at Cafe du Monde for coffee and beignets.

Plantation Tour Departs 10 a.m. Mon.-Sat. About six hours. $22. Takes River Road route to San Francisco and Houmas House plantations. Don't forget your camera.

SOUTHERN TOURS

7801 Edinbugh St.   486-0604

Covers Entire City Departs 9 and 2. 3½ hours. $10 per person. This tour covers about 50 miles, and includes a lively commentary on the city's landmarks and legends. Cameras welcome.

After Dark Departs 9 p.m. Four hours. $23 per person, all inclusive. Includes name-entertainer show at the Blue Room of the Fairmont Hotel, jazz club in the French Quarter, and a third night club before the traditional coffee and beignets in the French Market.

Southern Plantation Tour Departs 10 a.m. Mon.-Sat. Six hours. $22. Does not include lunch stop at Cajun restaurant. Travels along the levee of River Road to the San Francisco plantation house, and Houmas House, two outstanding restorations of the antebellum period.

JACCO TOURS

728 Dumaine   568-0141

Cajun Country Bayou Boat Ride & Plantation Tour This is an all-day (six hours) tour which departs the French Quarter hotels at about 9 a.m., and it combines a visit to one of the major New Orleans area plantations with a unique excursion into Cajun Country.

The "Cajuns" are famous for gumbo, jambalaya, crayfish boils, hot pepper sauces, unique fiddle band music, and rowdy card games. Their motto is "laissez les bon temps roule" or "let the good times roll." Their culture and language is French, and their history began as French colonists to Nova Scotia.

The Jacco Tour, conceived and operated by Cajuns, takes you to Lafourche Swamp where Cajun fishermen and trappers still work in a sub-tropical environment suitable for the location of a Tarzan movie. The visit includes stops at Cajun shops and an authentic Cajun restaurant. A ferry crossing of the Mississippi, and the plantation tour completes the full day.

RIVER CRUISES

Cruises on the riverboats which ply the Mississippi River out of New Orleans are the best way to appreciate this port and its great river highway. The 2½-hour cruises pass under the Greater New Orleans Bridge and head upriver against a 4.5 m.p.h. current past the commercial wharfs lined with ships from all over the world, past the Garden District to Audubon Park. Downriver, the boat rounds Algiers Point, the sharpest turn and the deepest water on the river, past the Industrial Canal that connects with Lake Pontchartrain, to Chalmette, where Jackson stopped the British at the Battle of New Orleans. Longer excursions cover about 40-miles of water ways, entering the Algiers Lock, paddling up the Intracoastal Waterway around Crown Point into Bayou Barataria, the hiding place of Lafitte the pirate and then back past Hero Cutoff into the Harvey Canal, a busy industrial and shipbuilding area, to the Harvey Lock and the Mississippi again.

Riverboat cruises can be reserved at many hotel and motel desks. Check with the seller or steamboat company to confirm seasonal schedule changes and prices.

NEW ORLEANS STEAMBOAT COMPANY

2340 International Trade Mart   586-8777/524-9787

Natchez Sails 11:30 a.m., 2:30 p.m., and 6:30 p.m. Two hours. Adults $8.50. Children 6-12, $4.25. Luncheon, dinner, snack bar, and beverage services available on all cruises. The Natchez is the largest all-steel

The Delta Queen is perhaps the most luxurious way to travel on the Mississippi River today.

sternwheel steamboat built in this century. Its wheel is 25-feet in diameter, and propels the 3-deck, 285-foot vessel from its wharf across from Jackson Square. Her steam calliope makes music for up to 1600 passengers. As in all steamboat excursions, a lively narrative accompanies the trip.

Cotton Blossom Zoo Cruise This new cruise attests to the fact that the Audubon Park Zoo is becoming a major visitor attraction. Three departures daily take passengers from the Canal Street Dock upriver for a landing at the Park. The Zoo Cruise is a great way to enjoy the sights of the River and visit the zoo in the same outing. Departures begin at 9 a.m. Call for ticket prices and full scheduling.

Bayou Jean Lafitte Sails 11 a.m. Returns at 4:30 p.m. Adults $9.50, children 6-12, $4.75. This sternwheeler makes the Bayou Cruise to Barataria. It has three decks with both open and closed observation spaces. When the excursion boats are not running their regular schedule, you may see them on the river with private parties. Many convention groups charter the river steamers for the evening. Departs from the wharf near Jackson Square.

President Sails Friday and Saturday nights at 10 p.m. from the Canal Street Wharf located behind the Trade Mart. Boarding for the Moonlight Dance Cruises begins at 9 p.m., and the cruise ends at midnight. Styles of entertainment change. Big Bands, Rock & Roll, and Jazz groups are scheduled, and there is often a star personality featured as a headliner. Admissions depend on the status of the entertainment. Reservations are recommended. The President is a unique vessel. It is the largest tour boat on the Mississippi. It was a side wheeler packet steamer named the "Cincinnati" until it was converted into an excursion boat in 1933. The five deck vessel is now powered by diesels, and equipped with radar. The top deck is high above the water line and is a romantic place for strolling under the stars. The concert and party decks are enclosed and air conditioned. A cash bar and light refreshments are available.

THE VOYAGEUR

Foot of Canal Street   523-5555

The Voyageur makes two cruises daily. The River, Plantation & Bayou Cruise sails at 10 a.m. and stops at Chalmette National Park before entering the Algiers lock for the ride to Barataria. The cruise returns about 3 p.m. Adults $7, children 6-12, $3.50.

The Harbor, Plantation & Battlefield Cruise sails at 3:30 and returns at 5:30 p.m. A 30-minute stop is made at the Chalmette battlefield. The "plantation" in the tour is the Beauregard House at Chalmette which serves as a park information center. Adults $3.50, children 6-12, $1.75.

QUEENS OF THE RIVER

International Trade Mart   522-3492

The Delta Queen and her sister vessel, the Mississippi Queen, two of the grandest paddlewheelers ever built, cruise the Mississippi and Ohio rivers from New Orleans to Cincinnati with major stops in St. Francisville, Natchez, Vicksburg, Memphis, Evansville, and Louisville. The luxury steamboats offer 3, 4, 7, 10, 11, and 14 night cruises to various destinations along the great river. Cabin and stateroom accommodations are available on three decks, and the food and nightly entertainments are highly rated.

The white wedding cake superstructure of the majestic steamboats recaptures the golden age of the river when elegance and style were a gift of a land rich in cotton and sugar crops. The river route passes the plantations and the battlefields of the legendary mid-19th century. For a few days, the traveler can be suspended in time, and transported to this rich historical era.

For details on the schedule and itinerary of the Queens, see your travel agent, or call or write The Delta Queen Steamboat Co. in New Orleans, or at their home port office, 511 Main Street, Cincinnati, Ohio 45202.

Attention
CONVENTION CHAIRMAN

As the chairman of your upcoming New Orleans convention, you have many responsibilities. Before its meeting date, you have got to "sell" New Orleans to your group in order to encourage convention participation. Once the convention begins, you also want to make sure that everyone enjoys New Orleans as their meeting site.

The Insiders Guide to New Orleans can make both "promoting" your convention and "satisfying" your delegates easier. As you can see, this book is the most complete guide to New Orleans you can buy. It contains "everything" your convention goers need to know to enjoy the city. From restaurants to historical attractions, the book is not only a convenient and practical guide, but it is also a valuable reference book and souvenir. It will be used and appreciated by all who receive it.

Convention chairmen have found that they can use his unique book in several ways.

First: They are offering **The Insiders Guide to New Orleans** at the immediately preceeding convention to excite their group about the upcoming convention in New Orleans.

Second: They are giving the guide as a premium for "early bird" convention registrations, and direct mailing it to participants as an aid in making their convention plans.

Third: They are placing **The Insiders Guide** in their registration kits, and completely eliminating the need to gather and stuff assorted attraction flyers and brochures.

The Insiders Guide to New Orleans retails for $4.95 in bookstores nationwide, but convention chairmen can purchase the book in bulk quantities at a significant discount. The books can be delivered free to your convention headquarters in New Orleans. For national and international conventions requiring thousands of guides, inquire about the creation of a "special edition" for your convention.

The authors, St. Leger "Monty" Joynes and Jack DuArte, are also available for convention program appearances. Their entertaining presentation may include a colorful slide presentation, or even a wine tasting. Monty talks about the unique history, and the legends of New Orleans and gives the inside on what to see among the attractions. Jack extols the virtues of New Orleans style cuisine and recommends the great and small places to find it. Both share their opinions on the current nightlife scene, and tell where the jazz is the best. Monty and Jack can then be available for questions about the city they know so well, and to autograph copies of their book.

Inquiries concerning bulk purchases of **The Insiders Guide to New Orleans** and/or appearances by its authors should be addressed to: The Insiders Publishing Group, Suite 108, 2475 Canal Street, New Orleans, La. 70119.

Leo Meiersdorff
"Internationally famous — uniquely New Orleans"

#504 "Small Jazz Poster" 20" x 26".
A Color Poster of an old New Orleans Jazz Hall

#505 "Large Jazz Poster" 23" x 31".
A Color Poster of a New Orleans Jazz Parade.

In a world where imitation has always been the most sincere form of flattery, Leo is often copied but never duplicated. His jazz and culinary paintings and drawings are his best known works because they have received the greatest world-wide attention and distribution.

After years of study and experimentation, he has mastered his craft. Leo has flashes of inspiration which he immediately captures on paper. If not satisfied, he may destroy the entire sheet but he will seldom rework his lines of colors.

A native of Berlin, Germany, Leo derives most of his inspiration from the people, music, food and ambience of New Orleans' French Quarter where he resided for more than a decade.

Leo Meiersdorff's work is extensively used by the television and movie industries. As a graphic artist and art director, he has worked on major network productions. Since 1974 he has been voting member (Grammy Awards) of the National Academy of Recording Arts and Sciences and has designed numerous album covers for leading jazz musicians.

For information about his other posters and graphics, please contact:

CUNNINGHAM ENTERPRISES, INC.
734-B ORLEANS AVENUE
NEW ORLEANS, LOUISIANA 70116
PHONE: (504) 566-1034

THE LEGENDS OF NEW ORLEANS

A legend is an unverifiable story handed down by tradition from an earlier time that is popularly accepted as history. Legends drive serious researchers crazy because they often conflict with the few facts available, and always splinter into variations. New Orleans clings to its legends. They are perhaps the hallmark of the city's romantic personality.

Here then is a collection of facts and legends that offer insight into the personality and character of old New Orleans. Feel free to become part of the historic process yourself, and tell these stories to others in your own manner.

AUDUBON . . . John James Audubon (1785-1851) was the artist and ornithologist whose monumental work, **Birds of America**, established him as America's most celebrated naturalist. The Audubon Society and Audubon Park are named in his honor. Audubon was attracted to Louisiana because more than half of the known species of birds in the United States have been recorded within the state. More than one-third of the 435 hand-colored plates in the American series were done in the state, and Audubon had a studio in New Orleans on several occasions, one at 505 Dauphine, and another at 706 Barracks.

Audubon was born in Santo Domingo (now Haiti), but he claimed Louisiana as his home. His father was a French naval officer, his mother a Creole. He was educated in France, and then settled in Pennsylvania where he married. His wife supported him while he roamed the woods sketching, and yes, shooting birds. In his lifetime he did more than a thousand life size hand-colored figures of birds in nearly 500 species.

BANQUETTES . . . Some New Orleanians still refer to their French Quarter sidewalks as banquettes. The term translates "little benches" and is a carry-over from the days when the paved walkways had curved streetside edges, resembling benches, to protect the pedestrians from the overflowing garbage and sewage in the streets.

THE BRASS BAND FUNERAL . . . This nineteenth-century custom is rare, but still practiced today. In an earlier era, a lodge brother who belonged to a burial society (a type of funeral insurance) would receive his full benefits. The hired marching brass band usually met the funeral party at the lodge hall and played marches on the way to the funeral home. Young Louis Armstrong (prior to 1920) played in such a marching band. With lodge members in front, followed by the band, the hearse, and the other mourners, the procession goes to the church to the accompaniment of hymns. The band takes a break outside the church, and then plays dirges, and the traditional "Nearer, My God to Thee" en route to the·

cemetery. At the gate, the band parts, "turning him loose." They may play a hymn at graveside.

Leaving the cemetery, with the brother's soul relieved of its worldly burdens, the band breaks into "When the Saints Go Marching In" and other "hot" tunes. Former mourners open their decorated umbrellas and begin to dance behind the band as it entertains its way back to the lodge hall. They are called "the second line," and they encourage people on the street to join them.

GENERAL BEN BUTLER . . . Captain David Farragut commanded the Union campaign against New Orleans in 1862. His fleet fought past Fort Jackson and Fort St. Philip that guarded the Mississippi, then ran the batteries at Chalmette to demand the surrender of the city. Although Confederate troops chose not to defend it, Mayor John Monroe defied Farragut's demands even when the city was threatened with bombardment. The crisis was averted when Commander Porter negotiated the surrender of the remaining New Orleans river forts, and General Ben Butler marched his troops down the gangplanks on May 1st to begin the long occupation by the Union.

Butler soon became infamous as a Yankee tyrant. When his officers were scorned and insulted by New Orleans ladies, Butler issued an order which rallied the South in hatred, and even caused the English House of Commons to denounce him. In plain language, his order said that any woman who insulted a Union officer in New Orleans would be treated legally as a street tramp (read prostitute). Butler hanged a harmless citizen, William Mumford, for tearing down the Union flag from the former US Mint building, and he sent the brave Mayor Monroe off to prison. A number of Episcopal ministers who refused to pray for President Lincoln were ordered exiled from their churches. Butler was replaced in December, 1862, but his ruthless and corrupt regime of less than eight months would make his name forever after loathed in New Orleans.

MOTHER CABRINI . . . America's first Catholic Saint was born in Italy in 1850. She came to America in 1889 and began work among the Italian immigrants of New York City. The deplorable circumstances of other immigrants in New Orleans caused her to come to the city for the establishment of a school and settlement house. She worshiped in the St. Louis Cathedral during her stay in New Orleans. Her likeness now looks down at the pews in the Cathedral where she often knelt. Mother Frances Xavier Cabrini became an American citizen in 1909. Before her death in 1917 she was responsible for opening 67 schools, orphanages, and hospitals in the United States, and for the development of a flourishing order of 1500 nuns, the Sisters of the Sacred Heart. She was canonized as "the saint of immigrants" in 1946. A woman frail of body, her spirit and accomplishments are well remembered in New Orleans.

THE CAJUNS . . . Their "capital" is Lafayette, and their country, some 22 parishes in Southwestern Louisiana, is called Acadiana. They are famous for gumbo, jambalaya, crayfish, hot pepper sauce, unique fiddle band music, rowdy card games, and "laissez les bon temps roule" (let the good times roll). They are immortalized in Henry Wadsworth Longfellow's epic poem "Evangeline" as a passionate people forever separated from their homeland. Their history began in the early 1600's as French colonists to Nova Scotia, a region called Acadia. For more than 100 years they were isolated farmers, a closed society of devoted Catholics. Then abruptly in 1713, Britain won control of Canada and harassed the Acadians to renounce Catholicism in favor of the English king's Protestant religion. In 1755, tired of their refusals, British troops seized their homes and herded them onto ships to be deported. Many families were cruelly separated. Many died in the crude conditions of the deportation. The ships deposited them along east coast American colonies, and in the West Indies. Some were returned to Europe.

New Orleans, then under Catholic Spain, with its French roots, accepted many of the Acadians and gave them land grants to the outlying bayous of Louisiana. By 1763, the Acadians were planting new roots, and a "Cajun" culture began to emerge. Even today in a parish like Evangeline, 90-percent of the population is French speaking. Attending a fais-dodo, a house party with a live band, in Cajun country is like being in a foreign land. The food, the music, and the speech is unlike any other place in the world. The Frenchman at the bar speaking a different French is probably from Paris or Quebec. There is an active cultural exchange being organized by the respective countries to recognize and preserve the Cajun culture. Some of the great chefs in New Orleans are Cajuns, and nearly every menue in the city has been influenced by them in some way.

THE CASKET GIRLS . . . In 1727 the French colony at New Orleans lacked order or discipline. The civilizing influence of women was missing, for unlike the English colonists, the French had not built their settlements around family units. In August, six Ursuline nuns arrived to serve the hospital and to establish a school for girls. In France, marriageable young girls of good character were recruited for the colonies. They became wards of the Crown, and were placed under the protection of the nuns until they could be married. Before their passage to Louisiana each girl was given a small trunk, or casket, containing a basic wardrobe. It would be the only dowery that these girls from poor families could offer, but that did not prevent them from receiving many proposals. Years later when New Orleanians traced their ancestry, they proudly claimed the Casket Girls. There were other women, of course, in the colony, including a shipload of prostitutes from a French prison, but no one chose to acknowledge that they were capable of producing progeny. French Creoles always traced their roots the Casket Girls.

CEMETERIES . . . Burial in a swampy ground can be a grisly occupation if not an impossible task. Many parts of New Orleans are below sea level, and with its heavy annual rainfall, the city would be flooded without constant drainage and the pumping of water out of the city into the lake. Burial above ground thus became an early custom. The old cemeteries are like small walled cities of tombs, some of them elaborate and custom designed. Double and multiple family vaults are common. After a year and a day, a vault may be reopened and reused; the remains of the prior deceased removed to a lower vault among the remains of others so that the top vault can receive the newly deceased. A family vault can thus accommodate many generations. There are also examples of large compartmented tombs built by burial associations to provide space for their members. Fraternal organizations often established burial associations, and erected monuments to their lodge or vocation, **i.e.** fire or police. Provisions for the poor were made in the outer walls of the cemeteries. These oven vaults were probably named for their shape, although the hot southern sun obviously baked the remains in the brick enclosures. The rows of vaults were rented, and a new occupant could take possession after two years.

In the early cemeteries tombs were erected haphazardly. The crowded grounds now appear to be a series of random pathways, a maze. Some of the older tombs are in poor condition, and you can see the plaster-over-brick method of construction, or a tree growing from a tomb roof. The All Saints' Day holiday, November 1st, is still taken as seriously in New Orleans as it is in France. The tradition of honoring the dead calls for religious Catholics to bring flowers, pull weeds from crevices, and to whitewash the tombs. The cleaning up and repairs precede the Holy Day. Then families gather at their respective tombs to present flowers, and to receive friends and relatives who come to pay their respects.

CHRISTMAS BONFIRES . . . The people along River Road above Laplace collect scrap during December and build huge bonfires on the levees. On Christmas Eve the fires are lit to light the way for the Christ Child. You can see the fires, and hear the firecrackers, on Christmas Eve along the River Road routes 44 and 18, and perhaps be welcomed to join the party at a local restaurant.

THE COCKTAIL . . . In the early 1800's, an apothecary named Antoine Peychaud hosted fellow Masonic Lodge members after their meeting in his shop at 437 Rue Royal. Peychaud had arrived in New Orleans with the French planters who fled the 1793 slave uprising in Santo Domingo. He brought with him a recipe for compounding a liquid tonic, he called bitters. He mixed the bitters with Sazerac-de-Forges French brandy and served it in an eggcup to his friends. The drink became very popular, but Americans found it difficult to say "coquetier," the French word for eggcup, so they pronounced it "cock-tay," and then "cocktail." The Sazerac Coffee House made Peychaud's cocktail famous. Through the years from 1859 to 1949 the Sazerac Bar and its Sazerac cocktail were big business. In 1949 the Roosevelt Hotel (now the Fairmont) obtained the franchise to the bar and moved it to the hotel. Peychaud's bitters are still made by L.E. Jung and Wolff Co. of New Orleans.

KING COTTON . . . In the years before the Civil War, Louisiana ranked 2nd in per capita wealth in the nation. The port of New Orleans was the greatest cotton port in the world. Of the $185 million in port receipts reported in 1860, $109 million was attributed to cotton. Cotton bales came downriver on steamboats from plantations north of the sugar cane belt. Much of New Orleans' golden age was built on the wealth of cotton commerce.

CRAPS ... Bernard Marginy has been called the greatest Creole of them all. He spent for pleasure with a haughty disregard for the cost. His father had entertained the Duke of Orleans, the great-great-grandson of the Prince for whom the city was named, while the Duke was exiled during the French Revolution. The Duke later became King. In 1800, when his father died, Bernard was the richest 15-year-old in America. While in England, the young Creole learned a dice game called "hazards." He brought the dice home, and soon taught his New Orleans friends this clever game of chance. The derisive name Americans gave to the Creoles was "Johnny Crapaud" or crapauds because the Frenchmen ate frog legs. When they saw the "frogs" huddled around the new dice game, they called it Johnny Crapaud's game. The tongue of the frontier shortened crapaud to craps when Americans began to play the dice game themselves.

By the time Bernard Marigny was 20, he had rolled his way to $1 million in losses, and began to sell his plantation. The subdivided lots became the suburb of Faubourg Marigny, and the streets were laid out at a 50 degree variance to streets in the Vieux Carre and thus had separate names. Marigny had his mansion at what is now Elysian Fields and Decatur. One of the main streets, and he named them all, was Rue de Craps. An 1850 ordinance changed most of his colorful street names, however. The great Creole was by then reduced to the status of a humble clerk in the office of Mortgages and Conveyances. He died a natural death in 1868 in a state of poverty. At 83, it was said that he had a happy disposition and no regrets for the fortune he had lost.

CREOLE COOKING ... The influences of this unique cuisine are French, Spanish, African, and Latin American. Its history began when Governor Bienville asked his cousin and housekeeper, Madame Langlois, to school the angry women of his colony on the preparation of native foods. They were sick to death of serving corn, and wanted wheat. With the help of Choctaw Indian squaws the ladies learned to make cornmeal, hominy, and grits from corn and were soon serving cornbread with wild honey. The secret of filé, a powdered spice made from sassafras, and the making of vinegar from citrus fruits was shared. Stuffed roast squirrel, and fish baked in herbs began to grace early 18th century tables. In the 1760's the Spanish settlers introduced the pungent seasonings and condiments that they had enjoyed in Mexico and the Caribbean countries. The Acadians arrived during this period. French in spirit, and pioneer at heart, their farm women had a special talent for making common provisions, and game, into delectable dishes. Cooks trained in the chateaus of France and the castles of Spain also added their skills to the emergence of the Creole table during the colonial periods. After 1803 the Americans came and in the years of building, especially the age of the great plantations, the Creole pot was stirred by a tradition of Negro mammies in the kitchen. They assimilated the national influences that preceded them and added their own talents for seasoning and preparation. Their fresh vegetables from a seasoned pot pleased both field hand and master. In wealth, or in the poverty that followed the Civil War, they still created a distinctive array of dishes.

Today, both in great restaurants, and in great home kitchens, the history of New Orleans can be traced on the table before you as you enjoy Shrimp Creole, Seafood Gumbo File, Chicken-Okra Gumbo, Remoulade Sauce, Jambalaya, Sauce Piquant, Crayfish Etouffee, Herb-Baked Oysters, Fish Courtbouillon, Red Beans and Rice, Dirty Rice, Eggs Hussarde, Bananas Foster, Pecan Pralines, Cafe Brulot, Bread Pudding with Whiskey Sauce.

DIXIELAND ... Following the Louisiana Purchase, the influx of English-speaking Americans ran into a French speaking Creole society. In recognition of the bilingual trade that developed, the Citizens Bank of New Orleans in 1837 issued its ten-dollar bank notes with French on one side and English on the other. The French word for ten, Dix, was prominent on one side of the bill, and frontier rivermen began to mispronounce it. The notes became well known as Dixies, and Louisiana became Dixieland. Until the Louisiana constitutional convention of 1921, all official matters requiring due publication appeared, by law, in both French and English.

ENGLISH TURN ... Iberville returned to France after exploring the New Orleans area, and left his younger brother, 18-year-old Bienville, to further explore the Mississippi. One day in September 1699, Bienville with two canoes and five men encountered a 12-gun English corvette in a bend of the Mississippi just 12-miles downriver from the portage at New Orleans. The English ship, which had wintered in Carolina, had colonists on board and was looking for a site to establish a colony on the Mississippi. Two other English ships lay beyond the mouth of the river. Surprised, out manned, and out gunned, Bienville demonstrated amazing audacity by telling the English captain that the French had already established several colonies on the Mississippi and that a French fleet was prepared to repel the English if they did not leave the area. It was all a bluff, but the Englishman, who had once been a prisoner of Iberville after an encounter at Hudson Bay, yielded to the young Frenchman and turned his ship around. If the English had pressed their advantage, the history of New Orleans might have been English instead of French. The French thereafter called the turn in the river Detour Des Anglais, and English turn it is still called today.

SAINT EXPEDITO ... A coffin-sized crate arrived at a New Orleans wharf one day stripped of its shipping instructions. Although the crate was stamped "expedito", it could not be rushed to its final destination. For over 40 years, the crate remained in a dockside warehouse unopened and unclaimed. Finally when the warehouse was being emptied for demolition, the box was opened and a statue of a figure dressed in the helmet and robes of a Roman soldier was discovered. It was offered to the "burial chapel", Our Lady of Guadelupe Church at 411 North Rampart Street. Seeing the saintly figure, and the word "EXPEDITO" stamped prominently on the container, the dutiful parishioners installed the new Saint Expedito in their church. He is still there today, stationed to the left of the main altar. Figurines of the Saint are on sale in the church gift shop. Many local people believe that Saint Expedito answers prayers, and answers them without delay.

FLATBOATS AND KEEL BOATS ... Before 1825 when the steamboat came into general use, flatboats and large keel boats (most 18 feet wide and 70 feet long) carried the goods and passengers of the Mississippi River. Up river or down, the journey was hard and often dangerous. The men who rowed and poled these craft were a rough breed. Their strength, tempers and appetites are legends of excess. The Creole society of New Orleans saw them as savages.

Flatboats with 26 men at the oars could battle the river current while ascending from New Orleans and make Louisville, Kentucky in three to five months. Many boat operators found it easier to sell their cargos and their boats when reaching the port city and take their chances on the equally dangerous overland journey back home. Bandits, river pirates, and Indians proved hostile factors in any type of travel. Up river or down, men on boats had to be prepared to shoot or knife fight their way to safety.

Even after more than 200 steamboats were plying the river trade, flatboats were still abundant on the river. In 1832, more than 4,000 flats arrived in New Orleans. And as late as 1845, with nearly 500 steamboats on the river, 2,700 flats came downriver. Many of these boats were broken up to provide lumber for the antebellum building boom.

THE FREE LUNCH ... In 1837 the major business in New Orleans was done in the exchanges, or auctioning houses, where cotton and other commodities changed hands. The heaviest trading hours were from noon to 3 p.m., and most businessmen had to give up their lunches. Then Philippe Alvarex, manager of the St. Louis Hotel Bar, came up with an idea to stimulate his bar business: a free luncheon buffet for the price of a toddy. The quick lunch idea spread all over the United States, and became an American institution until the prohibition era.

THE GERMAN COAST ... John Law, desperate to lure colonists to the Louisiana colony, promoted it to poor German families of the Alsace-Lorraine with fabulous tales of wealth. Perhaps as many as 6,000 emigrated during the 1720's, but only about 2,000 survived the hazards of the trip to being turning a swampy wilderness into farmlands. The place where many of them settled on the Mississippi a few miles above New Orleans became known as the German Coast. The industrious German farmers developed into the food suppliers of the growing port city.

THE HAUNTED HOUSE ... The building at 1140 Royal Street has offices on the first floor, and apartments above, but it was once the sumptuously decorated home of Madame Delphine Lalaurie, a classic demonic split personality. She was married three times, and the mother of five. She was a beauty from the Creole aristocracy, and after her third husband built the house on Royal she entertained lavishly. Lafayette, and the cream of society were feted by this sparkling, cultured hostess. But above the party rooms was a dark secret she shared only with her devoted butler and coachman, Bastian. In the attic, chained by their necks, were mutilated slaves, the victims of her pathological sadism. Once Delphine had been fined for the "accidental" death of a slave child who had fallen from the roof into the courtyard. A neighbor had testified seeing someone behind the child with a whip. Then in 1834, a slave started a fire in the kitchen rather than be returned to the attic. Volunteer firemen came to put out the fire and a crowd gathered to help the cultured lady save her precious furnishings. She tried to prevent them from entering the attic, but they broke down the door when they heard the cries from inside. When the crowd learned of the torture chamber, there was a riot. Suddenly her carriage burst from the driveway with Bastian driving the horse and Madame LaLaurie escaped and was never seen in the city again. Her husband, a doctor, removed his wife and children to France. The burned house was restored and went into the hands of other owners. Stories are told, however, of clanking chains, and screams in the night, and the apparition of a child on the roof. Superstitious people avoid the house after dark believing that it is haunted by victims of Madame Lalaurie.

THE IRISH CHANNEL . . . If yellow fever, cholera, and dangerous construction jobs had not killed off many of the 101,000 Irish immigrants who came to New Orleans between 1820 and 1860, there would be more Irishmen here than in Boston. In 1850, 20-percent of New Orleans was Irish. The Germans came in big numbers, too, (about 150,000 in the same period), but many of them moved to upriver farming communities. The Irish Channel, which lies along the river, above the Business District, and below the Garden District at Magazine Street, has always been a neighborhood of the working class and the poor. The area has never been totally Irish, but in the era before the Civil War, its immigrant population changed the composition of New Orleans from predominantly black to white. Today, being from the Irish Channel still connotes a certain toughness, a sense of being street wise.

JAZZ . . . The Blues and Ragtime were being played in the saloons and bordellos of Storyville. Outside "spasm" or "skiffle" bands composed of boys playing homemade instruments played for coins on the street. The century had turned, and a new form of music was emerging from a fusion of influences. Musicians began to use their instruments like individual voices. They were "jassing" around in Dixieland, making "razzy dazzy" music. In 1917, a white band calling itself The Original Dixieland Jazz Band made a Victor record. The recording of "Original Dixieland One Step", and "Livery Stable Blues" sold a million copies, and Dixieland (traditional) Jazz was introduced to the world.

Some of the influences on jazz came from the drum beats of West Africa which were expressed in the chants and work songs of slaves. Free men of color learned classical music, and Creoles loved a parade with brass horns.

Voodoo and the wild music celebrated at Congo Square made contributions. Music had always been a vital part of the city's culture, from opera to banjos made from gourds, and Jazz is its unique legacy.

THE KAINTOCKS . . . They were from the wild frontier territories of Kentucky and Tennessee. They developed the keelboat and turned the Mississippi River into their personal highway. Their favorite pastime was fighting, and the best man on each boat wore a red turkey feather. When the feathers crossed, it was rough-and-tumble, an anything goes combat to decide who was the greater bully. Their New Orleans hang-out was The Swamp, a collection of saloons in shacks, dance halls and brothels in shanties, and gambling dens and flop-houses in an island of iniquity. The Creole society was horrified by the uncivilized Kaintocks. If these were Americans, they wanted no part of their new fellow countrymen.

JEAN LAFITTE . . . When Louisiana's first governor offered a $500 reward for the capture of Lafitte, the spirited boss of Barataria retaliated by publicly offering $1,500 for the person of Claiborne himself. Legend has made Lafitte a pirate, but he is more appropriately described as a broker or pirated merchandise and illegally imported slaves. His warehouses in the forbidding bayou swamps of Bartaria housed plundered goods that his ships won in pirateering or in trade. The merchants of New Orleans provided a willing market for his contraband. He was called a bandit, pirate, and worse by the government, yet he was an educated man and even employed the legal counsel of Edward Livingston, the man who secured the steamboat monopoly for Robert Fulton. Lafitte was not a swashbuckler in the sword and flaming ship tradition; he was rather a businessman who sold plundered goods at bargain prices. To his great credit, he rejected the offers of the British to join them in the conquest of New Orleans, and brought his men and arms to the side of General Jackson. His decision cost him his Grand Terre warehouses and the loss of his ships. New Orleans was safe and he and his men were pardoned for past crimes by the President, but Lafitte was bankrupt. He and his brother became undercover agents for Spain, drifted from New Orleans to Galveston, and eventually were lost to history.

JOHN LAW . . . He made France speculation crazy about the riches to be gained in the Louisiana colony. He promised, he exaggerated, and he lied extravagantly to loosen the pockets of investors. He was a Scotsman who gambled and won, duelled and killed, and charmed his way to the top of French society. He used his forceful personality and skill with figures in banking and won the confidence of the French Regent. In 1717, he acquired the charter for Louisiana and a 25-year monopoly on its trade. Bienville was named the administrator in the colony for the new company. Law sold stocks all over Europe with the backing of the French crown. When volunteer immigration did not meet the needs of the colony, his consolidated Company of the Indies drew from the jails and prisons the dregs of French society to join the hard-working, honest colonists who had responded to Law's dream-like pictures of the new land. German immigrants and slaves were introduced to the colony under Law's charter. During his promotion of Louisiana, the population rose from 400 to 8,000. Law eventually became the comptroller general of the Royal Bank. He invented the issuing of printing-press money, notes not backed by gold but by the real estate of Louisiana, and when his land scheme failed there was a run on the Royal Bank which bankrupted France. Law fled for his life in 1721 having led an entire country to ruin over a mosquito-infested swampland on the Mississippi.

THE LEVEE . . . New Orleans lies in a double saucer shaped basin, with Metairie Ridge between the two depressions. On one side is the Mississippi River which rises to more than 18-feet above sea level at flood stage. On the other side is the huge Lake Pontchartrain which reaches 10-feet above sea level at flood tide. Much of the city itself is below sea level, and without the system of levees, spillways, and pumping stations, the area would be inundated. Until 1859 when the first mechanical pump was invented, New Orleans was constantly a wet place to be. From 1893 to 1904 a comprehensive drainage plan was implemented. Drainage water flows by gravity away from the river toward the lake, and then the 21 pumping stations take over to force the water out of the delta basin into the lake. The stations can pump a total of 25 billion gallons a day; water enough to fill a lake 10-square miles by 11 feet deep. Pumping station Number 6 has the largest pumping capacity of any single unit in the world. New Orleans must be pumped constantly in order to stay dry.

THE BATTLE OF LIBERTY PLACE. . . At the foot of Canal Street, in a small circle between the Trade Mart and the Rivergate, is a monument which commemorates a battle between the forces of the Crescent City White League and the Republican "carpet-bag government" of Governor Kellogg. On September 14, 1874, 500 Metropolitan Police with six pieces of artillery attempted to dislodge the White League from its armed barricades on Poydras Street. The League had called the city to arms to dispell the Republican government and to restore white supremacy. Although the League lost 16 killed and 45 wounded, it carried the day. It took the election of 1876, however, before white rule was restored by political compromise. The monument was erected in 1891 with only the date of the battle and the names of those who died. In 1932, inscriptions pertaining to white supremacy were added. Then in 1974 the city added a disclaimer of the previous sentiments inscribing that they were "contrary to the philosophy and beliefs of present day New Orleans."

THE JENNY LIND VISIT . . . In 1851 the great showman P.T. Barnum was the impresario for the most celebrated singing voice of the age, the Swedish Nightingale, Jenny Lind. Their arrival in New Orleans was coincidental to the completion of Madame Pontalba's elegant townhouses so an apartment was furnished for the singer, including a silver name-plate on the door. A crowd estimated at 10,000 greeted her, and she stayed for a month, giving 13 concerts. Barnum collected $87,600 in ticket sales alone. Miss Lind presented $1,000 to the Volunteer Firemen's Association, and they responded by staging a parade of fire equipment and uniformed men under her balcony. A bouquet of flowers was raised on a long staff from the hands of the parade marshall to Miss Lind, and she curtsied and waved as the men passed in review.

The new Pontalba houses could not have been promoted in any grander style, and the Baroness was not above auctioning off the contents of Miss Lind's rooms to souvenir hunters.

HUEY P. LONG . . . The "Kingfish" was one of the most remarkable phenomena in American political history. In a period of 12 years, 1923 to 1935, he rose from obscurity to become the virtual dictator of Louisiana, and a serious candidate for the U.S. Presidency. He was a former door-to-door salesman who used the hopes and prejudices of the poor to gain total power in his state. In the end, he controlled every city and state job, the state police, the machinery of election, and the state legislature. For two years, he held both the Governor's seat and a seat in the U.S. Senate. His puppets then occupied the statehouses in Louisiana and Arkansas. He avoided impeachment, and investigations into his illegal conduct. In the 1932 Democratic National Convention he supported F.D.R. but was accused of attempting to steal the national spotlight. He was already running for President. His "Share-Our-Wealth" campaign numbered 9 million members in clubs around the country. A secret Democratic poll indicated that Huey Long might have the balance of power in the 1936 Presidential election. But on Sunday, September 8, 1935, while Long was in Baton Rouge dictating to the state legislature, a young doctor assassinated him while he was leaving the capitol building. Then, as now, there are only two opinions concerning the Kingfish: love and hate:

THE LOUISIANA LOTTERY . . . Operating from 1868 to 1893, the Louisiana State Lottery Company was the greatest gambling venture ever authorized by law in the history of the United States. The lottery, in fact, was a private profit making license that lasted for 25 years. Except for $40,000 due annually to the state for the support of Charity Hospital in New Orleans, it was tax exempt. The rich proceeds went to a private syndicate headed by Charles T. Howard. Howard and his associates bribed the carpetbaggers and uneducated Negros in the chaotic Reconstruction Louisiana Legislature to enact a bill that created a monopoly for their lottery company. With the great wealth generated by the lottery, the company influenced every aspect of the political, economic and social life of the state. It bought politicians, and intimidated the largest banks and newspapers. Although the company seemed benevolent to charitable causes, its generosity was only a public relations sham to cover the fortune it was exacting from the economy. Savings deposits, for example, dropped by over one half between 1880 and 1890. The priviledged few stockholders received a dividend of 170 percent in 1889. Annual profits averaged between $8 million and $13 million. There were daily, monthly, and semi-annual drawings. The high stakes drawings attracted ticket buyers from all over the country. The lottery had branch offices in New York, Chicago, Washington, and other large cities. The semi-annual drawing was worth

$600,000 for a $40 ticket. There could be several winners, however, because tickets were fractionated into 20 parts. The lottery company hired two old Confederate Generals, P.G.T. Beauregard, the "great Creole and hero of Sumter", and Jubal Early to guarantee the public an honest drawing. The white haired former generals conducted the lottery drawings, for which they received a salary, for 16 years. When the lottery charter came up for renewal, John A. Morris, acting for its syndicate, offered the state $1.25 million a year to recharter the lottery. The recharter bill passed the legislature, was vetoed by the governor, overridden, and went to the state Supreme Court. It finally went to the people as a constitutional amendment in the election of 1892 and was overwhelmingly defeated.

MARGARET . . . The only inscription on the monument in Margaret Place (Camp, Prytania, and Clio Streets) is her first name. Her family immigrated from County Cavan during the years of Irish starvation and oppression. She was orphaned at nine, married, moved to New Orleans in 1835, and then lost her husband and child within the same year. Demonstrating great inner strength and faith, she began a life devoted to the poor and needy.

Beginning with no other resources than her limitless energy and a keen business sense, she built a large bakery house, and then expanded into dairy products. The Sisters of Charity of St. Vincent de Paul especially benefited from Margaret's great charity, but her spirit was generous to all. Showing courage, she became a Civil War heroine by defying the Union occupying general, Ben Butler. When she died in 1882, her total estate was left to charity. The impact of this illiterate, remarkable woman was remembered in 1884 when the marble statue by Alexander Doyle was erected by her city. It was the first statue of a woman erected in the United States.

THE MISSISSIPPI DELTA . . . The delta is an extension of the land caused by the flowing of a massive river toward the sea. The clear crystal spring waters of the river's beginning carve the soil out of the land as it builds, widens, and becomes a forceful liquid ribbon on the face of a continent. The river becomes Ole Muddy. "It's a treat to beat your feet on the Mississippi Mud." Between your toes, the sediment is the consistency of a slippery paste. For millions of years the unruly river played a network of traces in the earth, flooding as an annual rite of spring, and leaving bayous and swamps and waterways in its wandering path. Finally, near the end of its run, it gave up the weight of the soils it borrowed from almost a dozen states and created new land called the delta. New Orleans is a part of this delta, now built up nearly 100 miles from the river's escape into the Gulf of Mexico. The city is on borrowed land, land delivered in the steady passage of a mighty water for more than a million years.

MOSAIC WALL TILES . . . The names of French Quarter streets changed from French to Spanish during the time the colony belonged to Spain (1762-1803). In commemoration of this Spanish heritage, the Spanish government provided for colorful mosaic tiles to be embedded in French Quarter walls.

NAPOLEON'S RESCUE . . . In 1812 Napoleon lost 500,000 men of his Grand Army in the retreat from Moscow. When the European allied armies took Paris, Napoleon abdicated as Emperor, and was allowed exile on the island of Elba in 1814. In 1815, he escaped from the island, and when the news hit New Orleans, Mayor Nicholas Girod, excited by the prospects of Napoleon coming to Louisiana, took the stage at a play he was attending and declared that the Emperor would be given the mayor's house as a residence. Napoleon, however, returned to Paris, made himself emperor again, and then lost all at Waterloo in June of the same year. He was imprisoned by the English on the rocky island of St. Helena.

Girod, in an effort to supply Napoleon for his Napoleon House, formed a syndicate in 1821 for the purpose of organizing a rescue from St. Helena. A fast seagoing schooner with Dominique You (Lafitte's pirate lieutenant) as captain was purchased, and there is some evidence that Napoleon was aware of the planned rescue. He died, however, before the schooner was ready to sail.

The house at 500 Chartres is the one Girod is said to have built for Napoleon, but the record is not clear. Dr. Francisco Antommarchi, who delivered the Napoleon death masks to New Orleans, used Girod's Napoleon House in 1834 as an office. Today a casual bar and restaurant occupies the building.

THE QUADROON BALLS . . . The placee system of pairing light-colored young women with well-to-do young white men was a fixture of ante-bellum social structure. Mothers carefully groomed their daughters for presentation at the lavish Quadroon Balls. When a young man chose a mistress from among his dancing partners, he would strike a bargain with the watchful mother. The quadroon women were reputed to be very beautiful. In 1788, Spanish governor Miro ordered that these women should no longer "walk abroad in silk, jewels, or plumes." The census of that time numbered 1500 "unmarried" women of color, all free, living in little houses near the ramparts." Since the quadroons were not prostitutes, and remained faithful to their sponsors, it can be concluded that 1500 men in a city of less than 8000 were keeping these unique women. The sons of these second families, the free men of color, were so numerous by 1815 that they formed a regiment and fought at Chalmette in the Battle of New Orleans. These gens de couleur owned plantations and slaves, and often sent their children to schools in France.

RIVERBOAT GAMBLERS . . . Gambling seems to have been bred in New Orleans since the time of Bienville. Fortunes were made in business based on speculation on bills of exchange, real estate, currency and merchandise, so perhaps it was natural to speculate further on the turn of a card, or the roll of dice. In 1823, six gambling houses were legalized on the condition that each pay $5,000 a year towards the support of the Charity Hospital and the College of Orleans. The art of the gambler reached its apex, however, on the great floating steamboat pleasure palaces of the plantation eara. Rich planters and their families cam to New Orleans via the river every winter for the social season. The passenger lists also included merchants, bankers, speculators, foreign travelers, and a few well-dressed gentlemen of another calling. Their trademarks were smooth civility, courtly manners, and a silver tongue that could be intellectual or witty. Their fingers were especially nimble at cards, and their minds knew the odds on all kinds of wagers. The best of them made 40-year careers on the Mississippi relieving passengers of cash, jewelry, luggage, and even the deeds to plantations. When the Civil War broke out there were enough professional gamblers in New Orleans to form their own military company, the Wilson Rangers. They were no native sons, however. They made a great show of riding out of town to drill only to find the shade of distant trees to continue their card playing.

SHOTGUN HOUSES . . . The ornate gingerbread woodwork says Victorian, but there is nothing fancy about many of these narrow houses that were built before the turn of the century as inexpensive rental units. Because the rooms are in a row, without hallways, the theory is that a shotgun could be fired through the house without hitting anything. Shotgun singles and doubles can be seen in many old neighborhoods throughout the city. In the French Quarter, they are especially in demand for renovation at very inflated prices.

SLAVERY . . . Colonial empires used slave labor and 18th Century France was no exception. The first shipment of 147 Negro slaves arrived for Bienville's New Orleans colony in 1720. Four years later the French court enacted the Code Noir, or Black Code, which regulated the conduct of masters and slaves. The code required slaves to be instructed in religion, and to be free from labor on Sundays and Holy Days. Cruelty was forbidden, yet a slave would have his ears cut off and his shoulder branded for running away once, hamstrung for leaving twice, and be put to death for the third offense. The slave could hold no property. Not even free men of color had political rights, although they could own property, including slaves. The Black Code also called for the expulsion of Jews from the colony, and the prohibition of any religion other than Catholicism.

The slave insurrections in the West Indies made slave owners fearful, so they restricted slaves from meeting together and established curfews.

America forbade the import of foreign slaves following the Louisiana Purchase, but Jean Lafitte and other illegal slave traders made a fortune producing slaves for auction in New Orleans. The St. Louis Exchange Hotel (now the site of the Royal Orleans) was a place where many slave auctions were held.

By 1860, slaves were so important to the cotton and sugar plantation economy that half of the total Louisiana population (700,000) were slaves.

THE ST. CHARLES HOTEL . . . It was the first great American hotel, and it quickly became the social center of New Orleans in its most extravagant period. Built in 1836, its five story Corinthian portico dominated the city. Elegant shops were on the lobby level, and the huge octagonal marble bar was the most fashionable place in town to enjoy a hot toddy. Nearby, the St. Charles Theatre was its equal in lavish decor, and could be compared with the best houses in Europe. Architect James Gallier made his reputation on the design of the hotel. It was destroyed by fire in 1851, and rebuilt twice during its long history. During its winter seasons, 800 guests were lodged in the grand hotel. Sadly, the hotel was demolished in 1977 during a wave of downtown redevelopment. The site at 200 St. Charles became a parking lot.

THE GREAT STEAMBOAT RACE . . . . It attracted international wagering when it was announced that the "Natchez" and the "Robert E. Lee" would race from New Orleans to St. Louis. The race began on June 30, 1870, and the crowds gathered all along the levees of the winding Mississippi to see them pass. Up-river towns relayed the progress of the race by telegraph to the world. Above Memphis, the "Natchez" ran into fog, and grounded when her pilot could not see the bars and turns of the unpredictable river. The "Robert E. Lee" was met in St. Louis by 30,000 people. The winning time was 3-days, 18-hours, and 14-minutes.

STORYVILLE . . . From its earliest days as a port city, New Orleans was well known for women plying the world's oldest profession. A French officer in 1744 complained that there were not ten women of blameless character in the entire city. In 1817, a girl "notoriously abandoned to lewdness" was fined $25. In 1847, the wayward women were sent to the workhouse. By 1857, the city tried issuing licenses to madams and their girls; a form of taxation personally administered by the mayor. In 1897, in an attempt to prevent the rich bordellos from moving into respectable neighborhoods, Alderman Sidney Story offered an ordinance to restrict such establishments to a single area. The experiment in controlled, legal prostitution (and gambling) was nicknamed "Storyville" to the chargrin of the alderman In hotels and train stations a visitor to the city could purchase the **Blue Book**, a kind of Yellow Pages directory which listed and advertised the houses, the specific girls, and the entertainments. Lower Basin Street was its main street, and Tom Anderson, a Louisiana state legislator and member of the Committee of Affairs of the City of New Orleans, was its "mayor." His Arlington Annex Saloon, Miss Josie Arlington's palace, and Mahogany Hall were popular places in a red-light district that advertised 700 prostitutes.

"Good time is her motto. A visit will teach you more than pen can describe. Don't be misled until you have seen Jessie Brown and her ladies. Everybody must be of some importance, otherwise he cannot gain admittance." These are samples of enticement from the **Blue Book**. Many of the Storyville houses were lavishly decorated, fashionable brownstones that offered dancing and musical entertainments in addition to good whiskey and the girls (See: "Jazz"). The district operated "wide open" for 20 years. In 1917, as America entered World War I, the Secretary of the Navy took exception to the vice area that was so available to his men and forced the closing of the most famous red-light district in America. None of its landmarks remain.

STREETCAR NAMED DESIRE . . . Tennessee Williams put this trolley line in the American vernacular when he used it for the title of his famous play. Williams wrote the play from his apartment on St. Peter Street off Royal. The streetcar named "Desire" once passed along Royal Street from 1920 until 1948. Most French Quarter streets once had streetcar tracks. A streetcar with "Desire" showing in its destination window is on display at the rear of the Old Mint building. The only operating cars are now on the St. Charles Avenue line serving uptown New Orleans.

THE SULLIVAN-CORBETT FIGHT . . . In 1891 Louisiana was the first state to legalize prize fighting. A 10,000 seat arena, the Olympic Athletic Club, was rushed to completion for the staging of a match between John L. Sullivan, undefeated champion of the world, and James "Gentleman Jim" Corbett, a challenger from California. Sullivan was a legend who boasted, "I can lick any man alive." The fight on the humid September evening, 1892, was fought in a roofless amphitheatre. It was the first heavyweight match under Marquis of Queensbury rules, and the Boston brawler, Sullivan, was outboxed by the well-trained Corbett for 20 rounds. Finally, exhausted, Sullivan's guard fell, and Corbett knocked him out in the 21st round. The Olympic Athletic Club has disappeared from Royal St., but the Sullivan-Corbett match remains one of the greatest fights in history.

SUNSHINE BRIDGE . . . The bridge crosses the Mississippi about 70 miles up-river from New Orleans near Donaldsonville. River Road plantation tours cross this monument to Louisiana politics which runs from one cane field to another. Louisiana governor Jimmie Davis built the bridge, and he actually wrote the song "You Are My Sunshine."

VOODOO . . . The Black Magic of Voodoo arrived with 10,000 refugees who fled Santo Domingo in the West Indies following the 1790 slave uprising. One-third of them were blacks, and their religion was a strange mixture of Catholic saints, African gods, and secret rites that were wild, and often obscene. The superstitious of all races sought the little charms, or gris-gris (gree-gree), the colored candles, the powders, and the potions to win lovers, harm enemies, and prejudice life in their favor. When the cult was banned in the city, the voodoo worshipers moved to the wooded swamps of Bayou St. John near the lake.

The Voodoo Queen who is still remembered is Marie Laveau (1794-1881), a free woman of color who was a hairdresser to the rich, mother of 15 children, and nurse to the wounded at the Battle of New Orleans before giving herself to voodooism and becoming a witch. Marie Laveau popularized voodoo, and used the slaves of the rich to build a knowledge of family secrets, love affairs, and fears which served her well in her supernatural trade. Her tomb in St. Louis Cemetery No. 1 is still visited by members of her cult who believe that their prayers will be answered if they mark her tomb with brick dust. There is recent evidence that more complex voodoo ceremonies are still secretly carried out in New Orleans graveyards.

FAMOUS WRITERS . . . Until the Civil War most of the literature in Louisiana was written in French, and reflected French romanticism. The city's greatest English language literary traditions stem from two periods, the mid-19th century, and the 1920's. Most of the writers were not natives, but rather were attracted to New Orleans for its color and lifestyle. In the 1920's the French Quarter offered a stimulating and socially tolerant atmosphere equaled only by Montparnasse in Paris, and Greenwich Village in New York. There are more than 50 Vieux Carre homes and cafes associated with prominent authors.

Lafacadio Hearn's Gallic-styled novels of the 1880's form the bridge between the old and new cultures. **Walt Whitman** was in the city, and worked briefly for the **Crescent**, a newspaper, in 1848 during an important period in his creative life. **Samuel Clemens**, who was on the river between 1857 and 1861, also wrote for the **Crescent**, and took the name **Mark Twain** for his by-line. **William S. Porter** used the name **O. Henry** while a reporter for the New Orleans **Item**.

The novels of **George W. Cable**, especially **Old Creole Days** (1879), first romanticized New Orleans to a great national audience. His French Quarter scenes put **Madame John's Legacy**, and the **Haunted House of Madame Lalaurie** into popular legend. His advanced social consciousness, however, earned him the enmity of the very people he sought to immortalize.

In 1921, the **Double Dealer**, a literary magazine published in New Orleans for only five years, attracted the work of such moderns as **Sherwood Anderson, William Faulkner, Ernest Hemingway**, and **Thornton Wilder**.

Anderson allowed his Pontalba apartment on Jackson Square to be a gathering place for artists between 1922 and 1925. **Lyle Saxon**, who lived on Royal Street and wrote Louisiana history and folklore, also hosted visiting writers. Faulkner, **John Steinbeck, Thomas Wolfe, Sinclair Lewis**, and **John Dos Passos** were among those who visited. Many rented apartments in the Quarter for various periods of time. Faulkner lived at 624 Pirate's Alley in 1925 while writing his first novel, **Soldier's Pay**, and supporting himself as a tour guide. Dos Passos wrote parts of **Manhattan Transfer** while living at 510 Esplanade in 1924. In 1935 another important literary publication, **The Southern Review**, was founded by Louisiana State University professors **Cleanth Brooks** and **Robert Penn Warren. Tennessee Williams** came to the Quarter in 1939, and eventually became a part-time resident, living at 1014 Dumaine. John Steinbeck married his wife Gwen in Lyle Saxon's apartment in 1943.

There are hundreds of poets, novelists, and artists who have walked the French Quarter. **Gertrude Stein** and **Erskine Caldwell** had their New Orleans experiences to relate. The novels of **Robert Tallant** and **Frances Parkinson Keyes** often deal with the city and its history. The playwright **Lillian Hellman** and novelists **J. Hamilton Basso, Truman Capote**, and **Shirley Ann Grau** are native New Orleanians.

YELLOW FEVER . . . It comes on quickly. Headaches, then fever, and the skin and eyes turning yellow, the swollen face a hideous red and orange. Then the profuse hemorrhages, the black vomit, and death, often in two or three days. For more than 100 years, the hot weather brought Bronze John and terror to New Orleans. Yellow Jack, the Saffron Scourge, the viral disease known by a hundred names, began in epidemic proportions in 1793. Ships from South America and the West Indies probably introduced the fever year after year. The disease is spread from infected persons or monkeys by mosquitoes.

The mosquitoes swarmed each season, but doctors looked to the open gutters, the polluted swamps, and the humid summer vapors for a cause. They bled their patients, or forced them to eat calomel, a mercurous purgative. The worst yellow fever epidemic in 1853 killed five percent of the New Orleans population. Although 30,000 fled the city, 7,849 died, and some 27,000 others were ill. The epidemics seemed especially hard on the immigrant working class. In digging the New Basin Canal (1832-38) 8,000 German and Irish workers perished to fever. After severe epidemics in 1854, 1855, and 1858, the mouth of the Mississippi was blockaded by the Union in 1861. The economy of the city was strangled, but Bronze John was isolated from the port city for the duration of the Civil War.

The plague-ridden summers demonstrated the unselfish heroism of many New Orleanians. Rich or poor, friend or stranger, Christian philanthropy was extended to many fever victims. Epidemics followed no pattern. After a decade of few deaths to yellow fever, and only one victim in 1877, the season in 1878 killed over 4,000 and infected 24,000 more.

Walter Reed indentified the mosquito as the vector of yellow fever prior to the 1905 outbreak in New Orleans, but it took more deaths to mobilize the city to action. The campaign against mosquitoes became a citizens' war and the scourge of Bronze John was finally ended that year.

HOW TO BECOME AN INSIDER

You can become one of the insiders by sharing your greater New Orleans travel experience with us. What you write to the authors of this guidebook will be weighed seriously in the editing of a revised edition.

Tell us about the good and the bad as you follow our recommendations. If enough of you are disappointed in a restaurant or hotel, and our investigation confirms your experiences, we promise to drop the offending place from our book. Your opinion has power as far as we are concerned.

On the positive side, share the happy times with your fellow travelers. What places provided exceptional service, or helped you in an unusual way? Where did you find a new place, or a great value?

Now that you have used our book, help us to refine it and make it serve you better on your return visit. We welcome your cards and letters with comments and suggestions.

MONTY and JACK

Suite 108, 2475 Canal St., New Orleans, LA 70119

Louisiana Superdome

DAILY TOURS

Every Half Hour—9:30 am to 4:00 pm
(EXCEPT DURING SOME SUPERDOME EVENTS)
For Tour Information—Call 587-3645

Stadium Club
In The Superdome

OPEN TO THE PUBLIC

WALKING THE FRENCH QUARTER

After years of walking French Quarter streets, there are values to share about the methods of seeing and experiencing. One should be uninhibited to look up to roof lines, to stand and study, to cross the street to get a better aspect to develop a freeze frame of memory in the mind.

Practice looking to both sides, exploring architectural details, and the characters you pass in the street. Be prepared to refocus in all directions without preconception. Try to set off without destination. Follow the trail of your instincts and curiosity. Wander without specific purpose, for the experience only. Learn to pause without concern for time. Be open to the meeting of strangers, and to the exchange of conversation. If you can do these things, you will begin to approach the Romance flavor of the Creole lifestyle and mentality. You will become a part of the Quarter.

Many of the memorable sights in the quarter are the ones you discover for yourself. It's a carriage way that has been converted into a narrow art gallery. The flagstones lead to a courtyard. You look up and there is a collection of decorated funeral umbrellas open on a decaying balcony.

The Quarter is a single black youngster working a crowd in Jackson Square. He is dressed in a white teeshirt, and his jeans are rolled up to expose his black tap shoes. He taps a little to attract a crowd and then get members of his audience, kids and adults, to form a line while he taps and chants the "old ham bone". They try to imitate him with mixed success. The boy quickly passes a cardboard box for gratuities to the first row of the hundred people who have paused to watch.

The pigeons in Jackson Square have special friends who allow them to land on their heads, arms, and shoulders. The "pigeon-lady" carries a perching stick, calls the birds by name, and seems to be training them by hand feeding. She talks to them, instructs them, and they follow her and do her bidding. It's another free show.

The street artists who border the tall Jackson Square iron fence, and work the alleyways around the St. Louis Cathedral are painting bayou landscapes, wild flowers, French Quarter scenes, and portraits of children and adults who are posing seriously hoping for a favorable likeness. Nearby, in the shade of the Lower Pontalba, an old cowboy with a guitar is singing Western songs. He seems as interested in talking as in singing. Across the square, Jude Acers, a U.S. Senior Chess Master, sits behind a chess table on the street playing all comers. Individuals playing him have one of the best people-watching seats on the Square.

JACKSON SQUARE

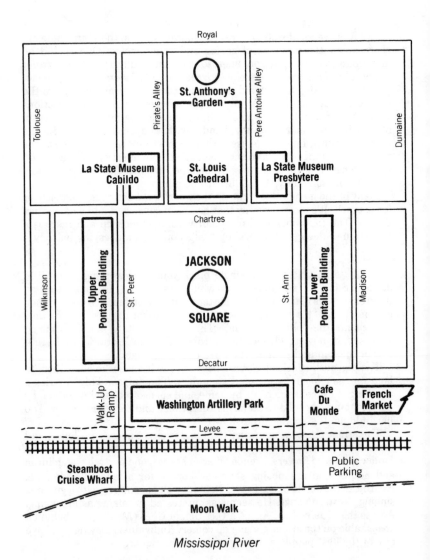

Royal

Toulouse

Pirate's Alley

St. Anthony's Garden

Pere Antoine Alley

Dumaine

La State Museum Cabildo

St. Louis Cathedral

La State Museum Presbytere

Chartres

Wilkinson

Upper Pontalba Building

St. Peter

JACKSON

SQUARE

St. Ann

Lower Pontalba Building

Madison

Decatur

Walk-Up Ramp

Washington Artillery Park

Cafe Du Monde

French Market

Levee

Steamboat Cruise Wharf

Public Parking

Moon Walk

Mississippi River

It is not necessary to know who lived in what house, or the exact date of an event to enjoy the feeling of the French Quarter. Your enjoyment can be more meaningful, however, if you appreciate the historical significance of the buildings on Jackson Square, and follow the profiles and background information researched in this book.

You can see for yourself from the new paint, and the perfection of the elaborate trim where Creole cottages have been carefully restored. You can note the antique houses which have been cut up into apartments, and are showing their age and disrepair. There are other properties being gutted because their rotting floor can no longer support habitation. Next year, if you return, the exterior facade will be 19th century, but the interior will be completely modern. There are still horse head hitching posts dating from the days of mud streets and carriages. And your eyes will stop abruptly on a few houses in the Quarter tht just don't belong. They are the architectural heresies that were built before the city got organized to perserve its heritage.

Wear your most comfortable walking shoes, and prepare your senses for an extravaganza as you walk these uneven streets.

JACKSON SQUARE

In 1712, three years after New Orleans was founded, the French military engineer Adrien de Pauger laid out the center of the new city around a public square, or Place d'Armes. The parish church was placed in the center of the symmetrical plan. It was to be flanked by a presbytere, or church rectory, and a corps de garde or police station. Prior to the Louisiana Purchase in 1803 when the official religion of the colony was Roman Catholic, and public Protestant worship was forbidden, the square was in fact the heart, and the soul, of the new city.

If you can only be in New Orleans for a short period, Jackson Square is the best place to absorb its traditions. The square and the buildings which dominate it on three sides comprise one of the most important historic sites in the United States. To understand the legacy of New Orleans it is necessary to fully appreciate the significance of the Cabildo, the St. Louis Cathedral, and the Pontalba Buildings.

Opposite the Cathedral, across the expanse of the landscaped square dominated by the statue of General Andrew Jackson, is the great river, flowing with the heartland waters of America. A few steps away is the French Market where trade began with the Indians nearly 300 years ago.

There is dark roast coffee and beignets to be savored in an open air cafe. You will be entertained by street entertainers, and watch quick-study portrait artists practice their art along the perimeter of the tall iron fence. The restaurants, the shops, and the bells of St. Louis blend into the panorama that shows all the color and excitement of an international living room. There is a joie de vie here that is perhaps unsurpassed by any other place in the United States.

ST. LOUIS CATHEDRAL

The Basilica on Jackson Square has been a church site since 1727. The early parish Church of St. Louis was dedicated to Louis IX, the sainted King of France, and was a substantial edifice. French Govenors Périer, Bienville, Vaudreuil, and Kerlerec, and Spanish Governors Unzaga, Galves and Miro worhsipped in the original church which stood for six decades. From its earliest years the church had an organ, a choir, and a belfry. Prominent persons were buried under the floor of the colonial church.

The Good Friday fire of 1788 destroyed the original church along with 856 other buildings in the new city. The second Church of St. Louis was the gift of the wealthy Don Andres Almonester y Roxas, a native of Andalusia, who built his fortune in New Orleans by land speculation and building. Don Almonester combined ambition for public honor with an inclination toward charity. His fervor to rebuild the church was associated with his desire to obtain a title of Castile from the Spanish King.

The flat-roofed building flanked by bell-capped hexagonal towers was dedicated as a Cathedral on Christmas Eve 1794. Almonester received his knighthood in 1796 and had a place of honor in the Cathedral until his death in 1798 at age 73. He is buried in a crypt under the floor of the church.

Pére Antoine

One of the legendary figures associated with the church is Father Antonio de Sedella. Pére Antoine presided over the Cathedral during a period of rebellion against ecclesiastical authority by its trustees. The Capuchin priest was loved by his parishioners, but from 1805 until his death in 1829 he was without the blessing of his church superiors. He wore only a coarse monk's dark brown habit, and was well known for his benevolence among the poor. His funeral service was one of the largest ever recorded in the city.

The Victory Mass

General Andrew Jackson participated in a victory pageant after the Battle of New Orleans in 1815. Thereafter on January 8th solemn ceremonies at the Cathedral commemorated the saving of the city. The Te Deum is traditionally sung as it was in the 1815 mass. The bell, which still rings out the hours from above the Cathedral clock dates from 1819. It is inscribed in both French and English: "Brave Louisianians, this bell whose name is Victory was cast in commemoration of the glorious 8th January 1815."

The St. Louis parish church and then the Cathedral remained the only Catholic church in New Orleans for more than 100 years. It was the center of Catholicism, the only religion permitted, and city life through the French and Spanish regimes. It was a full 30-years after the Louisiana Purchase before another Catholic church was established for the Anglos. St. Patrick's on Camp Street dates from 1833.

Heroic Funerals

In 1824 Pere Antoine conducted a funeral service for Napoleon Bonaparte at the black-draped Cathedral. The admirers of the French Emperor in the city were so numerous that it seemed a natural expression of their honor and grief.

Another grand funeral ceremony with the deceased in absentia was held in 1834 for General Lafayette. The Revolutionary War hero had visited the city nine years previously and had been entertained royally by New Orleanians.

The Cathedral Rebuilt

Throughout the long history of the Cathedral, the building itself has suffered from the elements and required major repairs. The state of decay, the growth and prosperity of the city, and additions to the Cabildo and Presbytere in 1847 which showed the church in lesser scale prompted a rebuilding effort by Cathedral trustees.

The primary architect of the church as we see it today was J.N.B. de Pouilly who contracted for the rebuilding in 1849. Attempts were made to save certain walls from the original church, but these proved structurally inadequate. For all practical purposes, the old church was entirely demolished.

There were many delays including the collapse of the uncompleted central tower during construction. Both the original architect and the builder were dismissed. Finally, on December 7, 1851, two years behind schedule, the new Cathedral was dedicated with great ceremony. The day included military parades, 21-gun salutes, and a mass that lasted four hours. Archbishop Blanc, the fourth Bishop and first Archbishop of New Orleans, presided over the dedication. In the years following, he greatly expanded the Catholic ministry in Louisana. Some 47 churches were dedicated during his 25 years as prelate.

The Don Almonester church of the 18th century could have been placed inside the 19th century Cathedral with room to spare. The spire of the 1851 church according to De Pouilly's design was an airy, spidery tracery of wood and ornamental wrought iron. It was encased in a weather-proof covering of slate in early 1859.

Cathedral Art

The numerous murals and symbolic decorations in the Cathedral today are renaissance in style and baroque in execution. The chancel ceiling painting is "Sacrifice of the Divine Lamb". Alexander Boulet painted most of the original works, but by 1872 the Boulet murals had deteriorated to such an extent that Erasme Humbrecht was employed to repaint them. He retouched, repainted, and altered some of the paintings on the vault and above the lateral chapels. His new work included "St. Louis King of France Announcing the Seventh Crusade" which can be seen above the main altar.

The murals, painting, and artifacts of the Cathedral invite a long visit for those who have an appreciation of liturgical art. The more casual visitor will sense the symmetry of the large church and the historical and religious legacy that permeates its sanctuary.

Mother Cabrini

A shrine of special interest is the figure of recently canonized Mother Frances Xavier Cabrini. She actually worshipped in the Cathedral during her residence in New Orleans, and her likeness now looks down at the pews where she often knelt in prayer.

Heads of state and other notables continue to recognize the status of the Cathedral. Charles De Gaulle, President of France, made his only public act of worship during his U.S. visit here in 1960.

The Cathedral Becomes a Minor Basilica

In 1964, Pope Paul VI elevated the St. Louis Cathedral to the status of a Minor Basilica. Basilica honors are bestowed only upon churches with singular antiquity, and historical importance which are also significant centers of worship. There are only five major basilicas (all in Rome and Assisi), and 15 minor basilicas in the United States. The New Orleans church ranks as the second oldest cathedral church in the U.S. Although the name of the church was restored to the more popular "St. Louis Cathedral" in 1966, it still retains its minor basilica status as "The Basilica of St. Louis, King of France".

Visitors Welcome

The Cathedral welcomes visitors, and tours of the church are conducted daily by informed laypersons except during mass. Donations for the maintenance of the historic building are solicited. The Cathedral is an active parish with some 3000 parishioners. Reverence and respect for worshipers during your visit should be observed. For the current masses, call 525-9585.

ST. ANTHONY'S GARDEN

This garden of oaks, sycamore, magnolia, and paths lined with boxwood hedges is in the shadow of the St. Louis Cathedral on Royal Street. The little square was once a reported duelling site, but it became a church garden in 1848 when it was deeded to the Cathedral trustees.

The white marble obelisk topped by a funerary urn is in memory of 30 French seamen, crew members of the Steam Corvette Tonnerre, who died in the quarantine of New Orleans in August 1857. Victims of yellow fever, the men were buried at the Quarantine Station 70 miles below the city. The ship's survivors, supported by contributions from New Orleans citizens, erected the monument at the Station. Fifty years later, with the Station decayed and the monument broken and covered by underbrush, it was discovered by the French Vice-Consul. The remains of the sailors and their memorial were moved to St. Anthony's Garden, and after a solemn ceremony in the Cathedral on July 14, 1914, the remains were interred in a vault under the monument. The story is another example of the city's emotional tie to its international legacy.

THE CABILDO

The site of the Cabildo was first used as a police station and criminal courtroom with a substantial prison in back of it. A murderer in the early colonial days might be led through the streets in a cart, then brought to a scaffold on the Place d'Armes, broken on a wheel and left to die. Mercy consisted of being strangled first before the blows and public display. The first corps de garde was probably completed in 1725. A new coprs de garde was built in 1751, and parts of its walls are incorporated in the present building.

The first Cabildo building dates from 1769 and the Spanish administration of Don Alexandro O'Reilly, an Irishman in the service of Spain. The French rule in Louisiana officially came to an end in 1762 when Louis IV of France ceded the territory to his cousin Charles III of Spain, but the actual claim of Spain was not enforced until 1769, seven years later. The news of the transfer was kept secret for almost 18-months and it took another two years for the Spanish to attempt to take possession of its new colony. The French colonists revolted against the Spanish envoy in 1768 only to run up against Spain's mercenary general, Alexander O'Reilly.

O'Reilly arrived in New Orleans with 2,600 Spanish troops on order to quell the resistence of the French Superior Council. He arrested the leaders of the revolt, abolished the council, and tried and executed five men by firing squad. O'Reilly then established a Spanish Cabildo for the government of the city and caused the new town hall to be constructed on the site of the corps de garde.

The Illustrious Cabildo

The Illustrious Cabildo or City Council first met in the new building in 1770. In addition to the council chamber, and antechamber for "citizens requiring justice," the Cabildo also housed the city archives. The great fire of March 21, 1788 destroyed O'Reilly's Cabildo, the parish church and presbytere or rectory, the police station, the armory, and the public jail.

Another disastrous fire struck the city in December of 1794, again destroying the corps de garde and the royal jail. The new Cathedral, still under construction, was providentially spared. Funds were appropriated for repairing the jail and for restoring the old corps de garde which would serve as a temporary parish church. The Cabildo members held sessions in the Government House, a French institution built prior to the Spanish regime. The building at Decatur and Toulouse Streets later served as the Louisiana capitol until it burned in 1828.

Don Almonester, The Great Benefactor

Soon after the fire of 1788, Don Andres Almonester y Roxas, the wealthy real estate developer, had agreed to rebuild the St. Louis church and its presbytere at his own expense. Since there were no funds in the city treausry in 1795 following the second fire in 1794, Don Almonester, a member of the Cabildo himself, assumed the financing and construction of the new Cabildo, too.

His architect, Don Gilberto Guillemard, with the former projects under construction, drew the plans for the latter as well. Guillemard used the same plan for both Cabildo and Presbytere, although the design of the new Cabildo was greatly influenced by the ruined walls of the original corps de garde.

Almonester died in 1798 prior to the completion of the Cabildo in May of 1799. His estate was repaid for the financing of the new seat of government. Before his death, in partial payment, he took title to the lots on two sides of the Plaza de Armas on which his daughter, Micaela, the Baroness Pontalba, would build her own monument in 1850.

The completed city hall had a guard house, jail, and notary offices on the first floor and an elaborate chamber and offices for the council on the upper story.

Background on the Great Purchase

The Cabildo was now appropriately impressive for one of the most bizarre flip-flops in sovereignty on the world scene, and one of the most far reaching ceremonies in American history.

Spanish rule ended by a secret treaty in 1800 as the Louisiana territory was retroceded to France at the insistence of First Consul, Napoleon Bonaparte. Since the United States was already using the port of New Orleans to ship almost 38 percent of all its marketable produce, President Thomas Jefferson feared the French occupation. He directed his minister, Robert Livingston, to negotiate the sale of New Orleans and the Floridas from France, but Napoleon had other ideas. His fleet was organized and prepared to sail across the Atlantic to rebuild French influence in North America. Only an unusual ice-locked North Sea and Channel ports prevented the French from sailing. When spring arrived so had the enemy, British warships. With England controlling the seas the Louisiana territory could not be defended in the forthcoming war, so Napoleon had a quick change of heart toward the American envoy. Since the territory would be lost anyway, why not sell it to the Americans. Livingston was shocked when the French Minister Talleyrand offered him not only New Orleans, but the entire Louisiana territory.

Secretary of State James Monroe arrived in France with authorization to spend $2 million to secure New Orleans. After three days of negotiations, the Americans agreed to pay $11.25 million for Louisiana and to assume $3.75 million of claims by American citizens against France. The treaty was signed on May 2, 1803. Word reached New Orleans on August 7th.

The Louisiana Purchase

The French colonial prefect who had been sent to Louisiana by Napoleon to take over the colony from Spain found himself as the middle man in a colossal real estate transaction. Within 20-days Pierre Clement de Laussat was to sign for the transfer of Louisiana from Spain to France (November 30th), and then give it over to the Americans on December 20th. Each occasion was an elaborate exchange of documents in the sala capitular on the second floor of the Cabildo. Each time the citizenry was released from their allegiance to the outgoing country. Each time the principals went onto the balconies which signaled the lowering of one flag, and the raising of a new one. Each time the Frenchman Laussat hosted a grand party with dancing, gambling, and toasts to the roar of saluting cannon. In 20 days the residents of New Orleans had been the citizens of three countries.

The territory involved in the Louisiana Purchase would later become 15 states. In 1803 barely 50,000 persons, not counting native Indians, occupied the land. Most were in the present state of Louisiana. The population of New Orleans at the time of the transfer was about 8,000. In addition to the Frenchmen, Spaniards, Germans, Americans, and Indians, the Negroes made up more than half of the city's population.

Regular U.S. troops were stationed on the lower floor of the Cabildo until 1805 when it reverted to the police. The Mayor, city council, and superior court also had offices there. When Charity Hospital burned in 1809 the Cabildo's upper gallery became an emergency hospital for 30 patients. The Louisiana Legion used the same space as a banquet hall to celebrate the anniversary of the Battle of New Orleans during the 1830's. The building has also housed several libraries.

Lafayette Slept Here

President Thomas Jefferson offered him the governorship of Louisiana (after first offering it to James Monroe, the man who negotiated the Louisiana Purchase). He was an honorary American citizen, and the hero of the Revolutionary War, but General Lafayette would accept nothing for his personally financed service to American independence. The French Revolution, however, drove Lafayette out of his own country at the loss of his family fortune.

In 1794 Congress paid the General over $24,000 in back pay which he had previously refused. His debts soon exhausted it. At the time Revolutionary War veterans were being given homesteads in the West, but the dignity and popularity of the French-American patriot demanded more. Jefferson had offered the governorship, and in his courteous and noncommittal way Lafayette had declined. The Congress, however, came through with a special bill giving Lafayette about 1,000 choice acres in New Orleans. Some of the property in the grant was contested, but a settlement was made in an 1807 law. Lafayette became the owner of real estate on both sides of present day Canal Street plus cotton lands around Pointe Coupee. His agent promptly sold part of the grant to free the General from debt. Other tracts were offered for development over the years, and some of the speculations were to embarrass him. The last of the property was sold by his son in 1841.

Lafayette was 68-years old when he came to New Orleans in 1825. The heroic deeds of his twenties (he was 24 when the war ended at Yorktown) were more than half a century in the past, but he could not have been more honored in the city if he had come fresh from the victory. The city council appropriated $15,000 to decorate the Cabildo as a residence for his six day visit. The city government moved out into a rented house.

The General and his party arrived at the Chalmette battlefield on the steamboat Natchez and were welcomed by the Louisiana Governor. A long procession of horse drawn carriages proceeded on the muddy road to town during the rainy day. A tremendous crowd waited at the Place d'Armes and Lafayette reviewed a military parade from the Cabildo balcony. His schedule was full. He received prominent visitors by day, and attended dinners, balls, operas, and theater performances in his honor every night. A second parade was held at mid-week. Lafayette's personal secretary later wrote that the New Orleans visit had equaled "everything" they had seen on their American tour.

The Mansard Roof

The flat roof of the Cabildo was a cause for severe leaking until 1847 when a new third story was created by the construction of a mansard roof and dormers. The plans of Mandam Pontalba for the city square dictated the structural changes for both the Cabildo and the Presbytere. The construction of a two-story facade for her buildings facing the square was designed to give the square a character similar to that of the public gardens of the Palais Royal in Paris.

With the official changing of its name from Place d'Armes, and the dedication of the new St. Louis Cathedral, Jackson Square assumed the symmetry in 1851 that is seen today. Two years later, a consolidated city government moved out of the Cabildo into a glittering new building that had been designed as a municipal hall for the city's second district. The new City Hall (now Gallier Hall) demonstrated that political influence had crossed Canal Street into the territory of the Anglos.

The Calaboose

The Cabildo is built around a central court with stairs running from gallery to gallery. Cells with grated doors and windows on each level served as the infamous Calaboose, or city jail. Runaway slaves, errant merchant seamen, and criminals of all sorts spread the legend of this horrible residence.

Pierre Lafitte, brother to fellow pirate Jean, escaped from the Calaboose just prior to the Battle of New Orleans. Despite the $1,000 reward placed on his head by Governor Claiborne, both of the Lafitte brothers chose the American side against the British. The so-called Lafitte cell cannot be authenticated.

The Cabildo exhibit includes stocks and a pillory where persons were publically punished for minor offenses until 1847. Slave owners could bring unruly slaves to the Calaboose warden for whipping. In 1830 the fee was 25 cents to register and 25 cents for each slave whipped.

The exterior of the Calaboose cells were restored in 1968-69.

Napoleon's Death Mask

When former Emperor Napoleon Bonaparte died on St. Helena, one of his attending physicians, Dr. Francisco Antommarchi, came into possession of a death mask of his famous patient. Some years later, four bronze casts were made from the mold.

In 1834 Dr. Antommarchi came to New Orleans. Because of his association with Napoleon he was given a rousing reception by French and Creole admirers. The Doctor was moved to part with one of his bronze death masks, and formally presented it to the city. The importance of the death mask was overlooked in the remodeling of the City Hall in 1866, and it was thrown out in the trash. An alert passerby picked up the bronze and it passed through several private hands until it was returned to the State Museum in 1909. The death mask is now on display along with other Napoleon memorabilia on the second floor of the Cabildo.

Inside the Cabildo

The Centennial celebration of the Louisiana Purchase in 1903, and the Louisiana Purchase Exposition of 1904 in St. Louis generated a collection of artifacts that was to become the genesis of the Louisiana State Museum. By 1914, the Cabildo and the Presbytere were filled with documents, books, paintings, furniture, war relics, natural history specimens, and costumes acquired or donated to the Museum.

The restoration of the Cabildo (1966-1969) uncovered the original brick floor of the corps de garde, and the large room was restored to its 1751 appearance. The Louisiana Transfer room, or Sala Capitular, on the second floor, the gallery, and the mayor's offices were also restored as historic rooms. The third floor restoration left the large beams and trusses exposed to reveal the construction methods of the mansard roof and dormers. The Mississippi River Gallery occupies this space today. Amid the paintings, models, and articles from the salons of great steamboats there is an exceptional photographic view from a dormer window overlooking Jackson Square where the passing of the steamboat Natchez on the river might give you a memorable photo.

THE PRESBYTERE

The Presbytere is the twin of the Cabildo. It was begun in 1794 as a residence for the Cathedral priests, and although it was never used for that purpose, the tradition minded New Orleanians kept the original appellation. When the building was finally completed in 1813, the city government took the Presbytere for use as a courthouse. It has been a museum since 1910.

The exhibits here include the elaborate costumes of former Mardi Gras Kings and Queens, 150 years of fashions, antique toys, firefighting equipment and more. Outside the entrance is the **Pioneer**, the first iron submarine, built by the Confederate Navy in 1861 at New Orleans.

The Museum Gift Shop has an excellent collection of books on New Orleans, plus tasteful gifts. Reproductions of mechanical coin banks dating from 1891, and antique map reproductions are popular gifts. Docents of the museum conduct walking tours of the French Quarter at 9:30 and 1:30 Tuesday through Saturday. The 2-hour experience ($5) is a great value.

The Presbytere and the Cabildo are part of the Louisiana State Museum. Each is open 9-5, Tuesday through Sunday. Each has a separate admission. Adults $1, children over 12, 50 cents.

THE PONTALBA BUILDINGS

The history of Jackson Square and the five buildings which border it is synonymous with the family narrative of Don Andres Almonester y Roxas and his dynamic daughter, Micaela, who through marriage became the Baroness Pontalba. Their initials "AP" are entwined in the tendril pattern of the cast-iron work along the spacious galleries of the Pontalba Buildings which flank the square. The Baroness herself designed the monogram.

The "A" recognizes the contributions of Don Almonester whose real estate fortune financed and built the Cabildo, the St. Louis Cathedral, and the Presbytere. The "P" is for the Baroness Pontalba whose vision for the Place d'Armes was modeled on the proportion and symmetry of the Public Garden of the French Palais Royal. It was her plan and drive which raised the mansard roofs on the Cabildo and Presbytere to complement the two-story facade and arcades of her new buildings. The Baroness, in fact, changed the center of old New Orleans into what we enjoy today.

The architecture, however, is only part of her legacy. The stormy conduct of her passionate life is one of the city's favorite legends, and the retelling of it is required melodrama if you are to walk these streets.

Micaela's Early Life

Micaela Leonarda Almonester was born in 1795 when her father, Don Almonester, was 70-years old. The only other child of this May-December second marriage died at age four. Micaela was only three when her father died and left the widow and child a large fortune. The widow married six years later and became Madame Castillon, and then was widowed again in five years.

The widow Castillon built a mansion for herself and her 15 year old daughter at the corner of St. Peter and Decatur, and soon arranged a marriage for Micaela with Joseph Xavier Celestin Delfan de Pontalba, a 20-year old cousin from a wealthy and aristocratic French family. The elder Pontalba had been born in Louisiana, and his family fortune had been made in Louisiana real estate before they returned to France.

The bride and groom of the arranged marriage had never met prior to Celestin's arrival from France for the wedding. Their honeymoon was shared with both mothers-in-law en route to Europe. The widow Castillon never returned to New Orleans.

Micaela was educated by the Ursulines in their New Orleans convent. She was not a pretty girl, but intelligent. As an only child, raised fatherless in an atmosphere of wealth and social superiority, Micaela was both willful and self-indulgent.

Her husband, in contrast, seemed emasculated by the domination of his father, Joseph Xavier Delfan. Although he had a brief career in the French Army, he was perceived as an ineffectual personality.

A Marriage In Trouble

Trouble began when the groom's mother agreed to a large wedding settlement without the consent of her husband, the baron, who remained in France. Although Baron Pontalba could not disclaim the wedding contract, he secretly got his weak son to sign a disclaiming document. Unfortunately, Micaela discovered the paper in her husband's desk. When Mme. Castillon, Micaela's mother died, she added fuel to the controversy by denying her son-in-law participation in her daughter's large inheritance.

Living in France, the couple had a disjointed domestic life. Micaela prefered the society of Paris to the quiet life of the country Chateau. After being twice estranged, Micaela sailed for Louisiana in 1831, and wrote Celestin that she wanted a divorce. Their further communication was usually via bankers. Micaela took charge of her business and properties in New Orleans and then returned to France via Havana, New York, Quebec, and Saratoga. Back in France, the Pontalbas separated, and she took custody of the three sons by the marriage.

The Baron Attempts Murder

When the old Baron learned that his 17-year old grandson had run away from military academy to join his mother in Paris, he cut all of Micaela's children out of his will. The stage was set for the tragic events of October 19, 1834. When their eldest son proved to be unmanageable, Micaela went to the Chateau Mon l'Eveque to ask her husband's family to supervise the wreckless youth. She was not received with courtesy, and after seeing her husband, with nothing resolved, she was preparing to return to Paris when her father-in-law entered her room, locked the door behind him, and confronted her with two double-barreled pistols. With bitterness and animosity at their height, the old Baron advised Micaela to commend herself to God as she was about to die. She replied, "You will never dare to fire on me," and he shot her in the chest. He fired two more shots at point-blank range, and then aimed a fourth shot at her temple, but the gun misfired twice. The Baron then got busy priming his weapon for the coup de grace. Somehow the badly bleeding woman managed to crawl to the door, unlock it, and fall into the arms of members of the household.

Assuming that he had killed his daughter-in-law, the Baron locked himself in his private study and fired two pistol shots into his own heart, and died. Convalesing in Paris from four chest wounds and a mutilated left hand (she lost the first finger of the hand warding off one of the shots), Micaela became the Baroness de Pontalba by virtue of her husband's ascendancy to the title on the suicide of his father. The news of the Pontalba scandal shocked both Paris and New Orleans.

The Pontalba Plan for the Square

In 1838, following a bitterly contested divorce suit, Micaela was free. Her mansion in the Rue du Faubourg Saint-Honore in Paris (now the residence of the United States Ambassador to France) was already under construction. She was 43.

During this period the Baroness evolved her plan for her New Orleans properties on the Place d'Armes, and she asked the City Council to reliquish the sidewalks to her for the purpose of erecting colonades to match the Cabildo and Presbytere. Her father and mother had both contributed to the holdings fronting the public square. The two-story arcaded facade would stand in front of existing buildings on the two streets which she owned, and give the square a symmetry rivaled only in the major capitals of the world.

The French Revolution of 1848 drove the Baroness out of France and eventually back to New Orleans. The old square by this time was in decay and in dire need of a facelift. Madame Pontalba assumed direct control over the redevelopment project and exasperated several architects (including the revered James Gallier) before construction plans were finalized. The proposed arcades became galleries and the buildings rose to three stories in the new plan. Architect Henry Howard made the final plans, and then withdrew from the project. The Baroness had informed him that she could teach him something about architecture, "having done a great deal of building in France."

The proposed facade became in fact new construction when the old buildings on the square proved too dilapidated to repair. Builder Samuel Stewart began erecting 16 houses fronting on the square along St. Peter Street in 1849. Madame Pontalba put on pantaloons and climbed ladders to examine the construction work. She was often seen leaning over the shoulders of draftsmen to make suggestions on detailed drawings. She became by her own force of will the on-site supervising architect.

She haggled over material prices, and was considered obstinate, if not interminable, in making decisions. The Upper Pontalba Building fronting St. Peter Street was completed in the fall of 1850. The Baroness and her two youngest sons moved into Number 5 (now 508).

The 1850 House

The street level of the new building was reserved for shops, while the upper levels provided apartments. Each "house" had a separate entrance on the street which led by a flagged passageway to the main staircase, a courtyard, and service area. The ground floor store was entirely separate from the house and could be rented to a different tenant.

The salon on the second floor had full-length windows opening to the gallery overlooking the square. The dining room was behind the larger room, and a kitchen and service rooms were located in a wing that extended above the courtyard. The third floor was designed for bedrooms, with the attic reserved for servants and storage.

The 1850 House at 525 St. Ann Street is one of these restored apartments in the Lower Pontalba. It shows the life style of the merchant class during the period. The ground floor store displays many items that were sold in the shops along the square. Upstairs, the furnishings are eclectic in style, but authentic down to toys for the children, and cooking and serving utensils. This Louisiana State Museum tour is the only opportunity to see inside the Pontalba buildings above the ground level shops. The other "houses" are rented and there is a long waiting list to live in this historic location. Tour hours and admission prices are the same as the Cabildo and Presbytere.

The Baroness Departs

The completion of the Upper Pontalba Building and its elegant town houses coincided with the visit of the most celebrated singing voice of the age, Jenny Lind. Madame Pontalba could not have had a better opportunity to promote her rentals, and she saw to it that Miss Lind was installed regally in one of her apartments. So popular was Miss Lind, and so businesslike was the Baroness, that the entire furnishings of the apartment where she stayed for about a month were auctioned off to impetuous buyers.

Jenny Lind departed New Orleans on March 10, 1851, and soon after the second Pontalba Building was completed and settlements made with the contractors. The Baroness put her properties into the hands of agents, and on April 5th boarded a steamboat with her two sons, never to return to New Orleans. Back in Paris, she found her former husband ill and his financial interests in turmoil. To her credit, she arranged for his care, and managed his economic affairs. She died in France in 1874 at the age of 78.

The Legacy of the Pontalbas

The Pontalba Buildings suffered with the disruption of trade following the Civil War. (Read "War Between The States" if you are a Southerner.) The square, renamed Jackson Square after the General's visit in 1840, had declined as a social and business center, and the Baroness's buildings had been neglected by her heirs in France. The apartments became a haven for the poor immigrants who flooded into the port city. Chickens were kept in ground level tenements, and once health officers even discovered a full grown cow in one of the upper rooms. By 1911 the Lower Pontalba became the home for Father P.M. H. Wynhaven's St. Vincent's Hotel, a welfare haven for the neighborhood indigent.

A reawakening of interest in the city's architectural heritage occured in the 1920's. The 17 Pontalba heirs, after years of apathy, sold the Lower Pontalba in 1921 to William Irby, a pioneer preservationist, who willed the property to the State Museum. The Upper Pontalba was sold to an American group who in 1930 resold it to a Museum Association established to finance its purchase. The Works Progress Administration (WPA), a program born of the Great Depression of the 1930's, made the Pontalba Buildings restoration one of its projects, and the extensive repairs once again attracted desirable tenants.

The buildings stand today under the protection and management of the State Museum as a landmark of history, and a monument to a unique, strong-willed woman.

THE ANDREW JACKSON STATUE

In January of 1840 Andrew Jackson returned to New Orleans where 25-years earlier his victory over the British had propelled him to fame and ultimately to the Presidency. The white-haired ex-President arrived by steamboat and passed through a horde of well wishers on Canal Street. He was escorted by his old battle comrades, the Louisiana Legion and the Washington Battalion. A ceremony at St. Louis Cathedral was followed by a military review in the Place d'Armes.

After a week of continual entertainment on city raised funds, Jackson laid the cornerstone of the monument you can see in the center of the renamed square today. Old Hickory then boarded the steamboat Vicksburg as thousands lined the levee to bid him farewell.

Sculptor Clark Mills completed the 10-ton statue in 1856. There were three castings made. The remaining duplicates are located in Washington across from the White House, and in Nashville, Tennessee.

The inscription, 'The Union Must and Shall Be Preserved," on the base of the statue is a corrupted Jackson quote. It was placed there by Gen. Ben Butler during the occupation of the city during the Civil War. It was another reason for the citizens to loathe the Yankee General. Ironically, the General's brother was named Andrew Jackson Butler. His shady dealings in Louisiana made him infamous, too.

WASHINGTON ARTILLERY PARK

Here is a fine place to get close to the river and see the full perspective of Jackson Square. Cross Decatur Street and ascend the marble stairs of the raised park promenade. This spot is the most popular photographic platform in the city.

The park was constructed in 1976 as a Bicentennial project. The site was used since 1718 for redoubts forming the "Great Battery." Guns here, in coordination with the guns of Ft. St. Charles (Ft. San Carlos) at the foot of Esplande Avenue, and Ft. St. Louis (Ft. St. Luis) at the river end of Canal Street, were able to bring a withering cross-fire on any enemy attacking from the Mississippi.

One block downriver was an artillery park where cannoniers and bombardiers fired salutes of welcome to distinguished visitors. French, Spanish, and men of the famed Washington Artillery manned this strategic position during the course of history.

The Washington Artillery (141st Field Artillery) fought in the major battles of the Civil War and at Anzio and Normandy during World War Two. Its motto is "Try Us."

MOON WALK

Behind Washington Artillery Park, across railroad tracks and the levee, is a long wharf with lighting, park benches and landscaping. Moon Walk is a romantic place. You can see the curve of the river that gives the Crescent City its name, and witness the dynamics of large ships, barges, and tour steamers as they pass close to your riverside position. The unique over-water park is named for Mayor "Moon" Landrieu.

STREET ARTISTS

The artists doing quick portraits or offering their work in Jackson Square are licensed by the city. They pay an annual fee and store their rolling supply and display carts in a nearby building. No one has rights to any specific spot around the square. It's first come, first serve, so the artists are out early to get a preferred spot. If you have the time, treat yourself to a portrait. Watch the artists at work and select the one that pleases you. While you're sitting for your masterpiece, you have one of the best people watching seats in New Orleans.

STREET ENTERTAINERS

It's a white haired black man with his guitar on a bench near the Cabildo; a couple from Denmark who are touring, playing twin banjos; a sad faced girl accompanied by two friends on guitars who is singing the blues; another girl playing the flute; a man with a violin; two old jazz players with a rolling piano and saxophone; a lone trumpeter on the Moon Walk playing against the moonlit background of a passing ocean freighter. Their open music cases, or a hat invites your gratuities. Some of the younger singers, players, magicians, and jugglers play a circuit, following the sun and the tourists to spots that welcome street entertainers. Some of them make a living performing in the streets. Since there is no vaudeville, it is one way of getting an audience and polishing up your act. No city license is required to perform, but entertainers realize that they cannot block sidewalks with the crowds they gather, and that they can't stay in one spot for more than half an hour. Do a set, then pack up and move to another corner is the unwritten rule. The performers generally work it out among themselves.

HORSE AND CARRIAGE RIDES

There is much erroneous information on things historic in New Orleans, and the most obvious offenders are the carriage drivers. Although the buggy captains are licensed, colorful, and well meaning, their monologues are seldom factual. We have heard the Presbytere pointed out as the "Presbyterian center" and "Presbyterian hall." The myth that the Pontalba buildings were America's first apartment houses is another falsity perpetuated by the drivers. The ride, about 2.25 miles through the Quarter, is a romantic way, nevertheless, to see the sights. Look for the rigs at the foot of Jackson Square near the river, or on St. Louis St. across from the Royal Orleans Hotel. Allow about half an hour for the ride and $5 per person.

CAFE DU MONDE

Cafe au lait and beignets under the open portico of Cafe Du Monde is a New Orleans tradition. The repast of strong chicory coffee, poured together with hot milk, and the square French doughnuts, sprinkled with powdered sugar, gives one time to relax and watch the activity on the corner of Decatur and St. Ann.

The cafe is open 24-hours a day. After 2 a.m., the place is usually still busy with French Quarter entertainers, and party goers ending their night. New Orleanians enjoy this outdoor window on the world as much as visitors.

THE FRENCH MARKET

N. Peters St.   Map, pg. 237   522-5730

The area south of Jackson Square has been a trading center for over 250 years. German settlers from upriver sold produce and fish here, and Indians sat on the levees offering their game and crafts. The market has survived hurricanes, demolitions, and reconstruction to preserve its historic function.

The original building, built by the French in 1813 to replace the open Spanish market, was designed as a meat market. It now houses the Cafe du Monde, which has been in this location since the early 1860's. The seven structures which now constitute the French Market are a mixture of the old and new. The new look was the result of a $3.2 million project in 1975.

There is still a vegetable shed where local farmers back their trucks up to the loading dock and offer fresh produce. Restauranteurs come early to hand pick the best products for their tables in the tradition of the old Les Halles of Paris. You are welcome to browse and buy something to eat on the spot. The Indians and Germans have been replaced by the Flea Market traders who display their wares Saturdays and Sundays from about 7 a.m. to 7 p.m.

Specialty shops, restaurants, and craft stalls add to the color of this busy marketplace.

PHARMACY MUSEUM

514 Chartres Street   Map, pg. 159

This apothecary shop dates from 1823. The loyola College of Pharmacy was instrumental in having it established as "La Pharmacie Francaise," a city maintained museum, in 1950. Exhibits include cachets of medicines and medical instruments of the 1800's, a red and black Italian marble soda fountain, and rosewood fixtures circa 1870.

The hand-made mahogany and rosewood fixtures, crystal pharmacy jars, mortars, pestles, pill rolling machine, records, and old prescription books were donated to the Museum in 1953 by Irma Samson Barnett. Max Samson's Drugstore, a store familiar to New Orleanians for 87 years, was located at 117 Camp Street. The generosity of Samson's daughter made much of the Museum's collection possible.

This is an interesting stop for the medically oriented. Nominal admission. Open Tues.-Sat., 10-5.

ARCHBISHOP ANTOINE BLANC MEMORIAL

1112 Chartres Street   Map, pg. 237   529-3040

This square bounded by Chartres, Ursulines, Governor Nicholls and Decatur   Streets is often confused with the Ursuline Convent. The Ursuline nuns moved out in 1826 and established their convent on State Street at Claiborne Avenue. See the separate profile. The nuns made history on this site however when they arrived in 1745 to staff the Royal Military Hospital. The oldest building of record in the Mississippi Valley, and the only building remaining from the French Colonial period is at the heart of this six building complex.

Today the memorial is owned by the Catholic Archidocese of New Orleans. In addition to a Historic Archives, Our Lady of Victory Catholic Church has services on a limited schedule for tourists and French Quarter residents. Archbishop Blanc is remembered as the first archbishop of New Orleans, for the rebuilding of the St. Louis Cathedral, and for the establishment of some 47 church parishes.

Persons interested in seeing this rich historical site can join individually guided tours at 1, 2, and 3:00 p.m. on Fridays. Adults $2.50, Children under 12, $1. The tour includes the church and its stained glass depicting the Battle of New Orleans, the worn wooden steps tread by the nuns, and exhibits of drawings and documents relating to its history.

BEAUREGARD-KEYES HOUSE

1113 Chartres St.   Map, pg. 237   523-7257

A few weeks after the surrender that ended the War Between the States, the "hero of Sumter," veteran of Manassas, and Shiloh, General Pierre Gustave Toutant Beauregard returned to his native New Orleans and became a lodger in the slave quarters of the mansion at 1113 Chartres. The raised cottage house was built in 1826, and by 1925 it was in such poor condition that it was only saved by a group of citizens who formed the Beauregard Memorial Association.

Restoration on the house, however, did not begin until it was purchased by socialite-novelist Frances Parkinson Keyes in 1944. Mrs. Keyes had written two books about New Orleans before she made the house her winter residence. The interior reflects her own tastes and interests in addition to the furniture and portraits contributed by Beauregard decendants. Mrs. Keyes worked on her novels, and nonfiction books in a slave quarters study lined with her published works, some 51 titles at the time of her death in 1970 at age 84. Her best seller, **Dinner At Antoine's,** published in 1948 sold 20 million copies. Among her ten books set in or around New Orleans, **The Chess Players** (1960), the life of chess prodigy

FRENCH QUARTER I

△ ATTRACTIONS
1. US Customs House, pg. 87
2. Tourist & Visitors Center, pg. 72
3. LA Wildlife Museum, pg. 72
4. Musee Conti Museum of Wax, pg. 77
5. Hermann-Grima House, pg. 79
6. D.H. Holmes Store, pg. 321
7. Maison Blanche (closed)
8. New Orleans School of Cooking, pg. 77

☐ ACCOMMODATIONS
1. New Orleans Marriott, pg. 191
2. De La Poste, pg. 156
3. Holiday Inn French Quarter, pg. 157
4. The Monteleone, pg. 163
5. Bienville House
6. St. Louis, pg. 168
7. Royal Sonesta, pg. 167
8. Saint Ann, pg. 167
9. Prince Conti, pg. 165
10. Chateau Le Moyne, pg. 155
11. Dauphine Orleans, pg. 157

◯ RESTAURANTS
1. Messina's, pg. 240
2. K-Paul's, pg. 235
3. Parker's, pg. 241
4. El Liborio, pg. 230
5. Acme Oyster Bar, pg. 223
6. Mr. B's Bistro, pg. 241
7. La Louisiane, pg. 235
8. Anything Goes, pg. 224
9. Felix's, pg. 231
10. Andrew Jackson, pg. 223
11. Tony's, pg. 246
12. Pastore's, pg. 244
13. Begue's, pg. 226; Desire Oyster Bar, pg. 230
14. Gin's, pg. 233
15. Brennan's, pgs. 72, 225
16. Tortorici's, pg. 246
17. Benihana's, pg. 226
18. Galatoire's, pg. 232
19. Ralph & Kacoo's, pg. 243
20. Vieux Carre, pg. 247
21. Arnaud's, pg. 225
22. Maison Pierre's, pg. 239
23. Broussard's, pg. 227
24. Steaks Unlimited, pg. 244
25. Castillo's, pg. 228

🍸 NIGHT SPOTS
1. Lobby Bar, pg. 313
2. Duke's Place, pg. 312
3. Mystic Den, pg. 315
4. Old Absinthe Bar, pg. 316
5. New Blue Angel, pg. 315
6. Paddock Bar, pg. 316
7. Famous Door, pg. 313

26. Houlihan's, pg.233

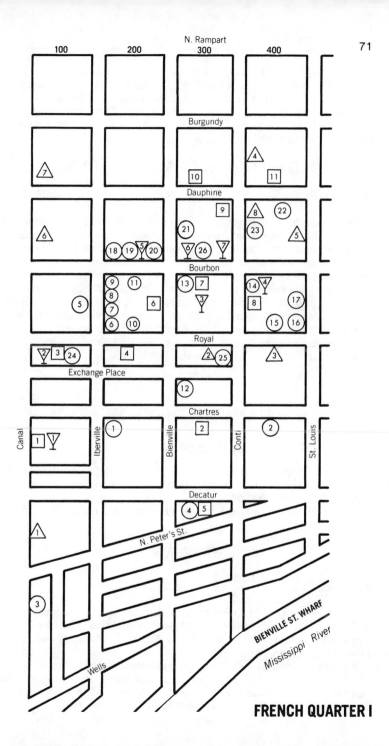

FRENCH QUARTER I

Paul Morphy, and **Madame Castel's Lodger** (1961), a story about Beauregard, use the house as a setting. The house today is operated by a foundation which preserves the rooms, the garden, the collection of dolls, and fans, and porcelain veilleuses much as Mrs. Keyes (pronounced to rhyme with highs) left them. Open 10-4, Mond.-Sat. Closed Sun. Last tour 3:30. Adults $2.50, children 75 cents.

THE VISITOR INFORMATION CENTER

334 Royal St.   Map, pg. 71   522-8772

The venerable building which now houses the Visitor Information Center of the Greater New Orleans Tourist and Convention Commission has been an important landmark for over 150 years. The structure began its history as the Bank of Louisiana in 1826. Bankrupt in 1868, it was briefly the state capitol in 1869, then an auctioneers exchange, and then a concert beer hall known as Flynn's Varieties. In 1874, the city acquired and remodeled it for the superior criminal court. Since that time it has endured fire, use as a junvenile court, and designation as an American Legion hall.

Today it's a convenient stop for the current events calendar, directions, or an encouraging word from the helpful people behind the counter. A water fountain and rest rooms are also convenient.

LOUISIANA WILDLIFE MUSEUM

400 Royal St.   Map, pg. 71

The Spanish-style town houses in this block were demolished in 1907 to make way for this courts building. The bottom floor houses the Louisiana Wildlife Museum. The galleries are full of stuffed snakes, birds, and animals native to the state. Admission is free. Open 8:30-4, Mon.-Fri.

BRENNAN'S

417 Royal Street   Map, pg. 71

This house, now a landmark restaurant, dates from 1801 when it was built for the maternal grandfather of French Impressionist painter, Edgar Degas. His painting of the New Orleans Cotton Exchange is now in the Louvre Museum in Paris.

The "BL" initials in the balcony railings date from the period when the building was used as the Banque de la Louisiana. Paul Morphy, the legendary chess champion lived and died here. The house was a fashionable private residence through the city's golden era.

THE HISTORIC NEW ORLEANS COLLECTION

MERIEULT HOUSE &
THE WILLIAMS RESIDENCE

533 Royal St.   Map, pg. 159   523-7146

The Merieult House was built in Spanish colonial times and was one of the few survivors of the 1794 fire. Through a public trust established in 1966, the rooms now display prints, paintings, documents, maps, rare books, and everyday articles that portray the social and cultural history of New Orleans. There are eleven galleries in all, and a serious research library with a professional staff to assist searchers of primary resource materials.

Beyond the main courtyard of Merieult House, and opposite its ballroom is the Williams Residence, one of the hidden houses of the Quarter. General Williams lived with taste and elegance, and his home was a focal point for New Orleans society for many years in this century. The beautiful rooms have been restored, sensitive even to the detail of fresh cut flowers. The house dates from 1888, and includes a touch-tour for the blind.

Open 10-5, Tues.-Sat. First floor exhibition room free. Guided tour upstairs and the residence, adults $1, children (upstairs only) 50 cents.

COURTYARDS

There are many private courtyards which can be glimpsed through decorative iron gates guarding the entrances to carriage portals and narrow passageways. The greenery of trees and lush semi-tropical plantings peek around the edges of walls. This is where French Quarter residents live outdoors away from the noise and dirt of the streets. You can get an idea of these walled environments by seeing some of the courtyards and patios which are accessible to the public.

The Brulatour Court is the home of WDSU-TV. You are welcome to view the courtyard at 520 Roayl during normal business hours. The Court of the Two Sisters dates from 1832. The restaurant serves meals and drinks around a wishing well. The courtyard is one of the largest in the Quarter, and it is much photographed. La Marquise Pastry Shop at 625 Chartres not only has the city's best croissants and beautiful French pasteries, but it has a narrow passageway leading to a cool courtyard where you can take your coffee and goodies.

Many French Quarter hotels and motor inns have landscaped swimming pools in their courtyards. There is usually bar service to the pool, and it's a lovely atmosphere for relaxing. Don't neglect to visit some of these beautiful spots during your walking tour. You will also be checking out hotel options for your return to New Orleans.

ANTIQUE FURNITURE OF NEW ORLEANS

In the 1830's there were more than 100 furniture manufacturers, dealers, cabinet makers, and upholsterers on or near Royal Street. The hot humid climate dictated large rooms with high ceilings, and they created the massive furniture to fill them. The most popular woods were mahogany and rosewood. Veneers were seldom used because of the dampness.

Simeon Seignouret was the first great New Orleans furniture maker. His bedroom and dining room pieces are characterized by scroll and curves, and the use of delicate rippled beading.

P. Mallard was trained in France, and arrived in New Orleans in 1838 to become Seignouret's successor in the making of distinctive furniture. Mallard used many of Seignouret's designs. He was famous for his four poster beds which had large canopies lined with silk or satin. The egg and dart carved detail is characteristic of Mallard pieces.

Look for Furniture by Seignouret and Mallard during tours of French Quarter, Garden District, and Plantation antebellum homes.

ART GALLERIES

There are more than twenty art galleries in the French Quarter representing original prints, paintings, and sculpture by local, regional, national, and international artists. Some galleries also show posters, pottery, crafts, and photography. New Orleans is a major U.S. art market, and many of the Quarter gallery owners cater to the serious, knowledgeable collector. One man and group shows are common.

Royal Street, with a dozen galleries, is the major art thoroughfare. Second would be Chartres Street. There are other shops in the Quarter, some off remote carriage ways where the artist works and offers his wares in the same space.

Another concentration of galleries is along Magazine Street, uptown. The serious gallery goer should pick up a copy of the Friday edition of the **Times-Picayune/States Item.** A tabloid section called **Lagniappe,** contains **The Calendar,** a weekly update on entertainment opportunities in the city, plus a schedule of gallery showings.

THE LABRANCHE BALCONIES

Royal and Peters St.   Map, pg. 159

The double tiered balconies connect 11 separate three-story Greek Revival brick row houses, and wrap around one of the most traveled corners in the Quarter. The cast iron has the popular oak leaf and acorn design and is painted white. It is one of the most photographed balconies in New Orleans.

Jean Babtiste Labranche built the houses in 1840. Labranche's German ancestors came to the city as Zweig, meaning "twig," but changed their name, as many immigrants did, to the French equivalent.

GALLIER HOUSE

1118-32 Royal St.   Map, pg. 237   523-6722

Perhaps no other residence in the French Quarter has been so thoroughly researched and accurately restored as the 1857 home of James Gallier, Jr., the noted architect. Archaeologist scraped the walls to uncover the original paint colors, and dug the garden and trash pits to discover the lifestyle of the family. The historic restoration includes fine examples of furniture, decorative plaster cornices, ornamental iron work, and crystal as well as other beautiful artifacts from the city's Golden Age.

The tour of the house and garden that Gallier, an Irishman, shared with a beautiful Creole wife and four daughters, recreates the ambiance of a lively family group. The amenities of hot and cold running water, and a patent water closet were advance features for their time, as was Gallier's design for walk-in closets. The decor and decorations of the house are changed to reflect the seasons much as the family, itself, would have done.

Tour hours are 10-4:30, Mon.-Sat. Last tour leaves at 3:45. Allow about 45-minutes to see the house and the adjacent museum building; more time if you want to see the films on the restorative arts. Adults $2, children $2, family rate $5. Complimentary coffee and desserts are served on the gallery overlooking Royal Street following the tour.

THE BOURBON STREET HONKY-TONKS

Middle-aged ladies who would never darken these illicit doors can stand in the street among the crowd and titter at the exposed, almost-nude girl (or guy) on stage when the street barker teases passersby by holding open the door for a few seconds. The state of the art of burlesque is reduced to an assortment of young women and men and a bevy of female impersonators who take their clothes off with uneven erotic style. Some of their movements pass for dancing but mostly it's the standard bumps and grinds. If voyeurism is a vice, naked fantasies come true on Bourbon Street for the price of two drinks.

The attraction of Bourbon Street is that it mixes the tawdry with the sublime. A striptease bar is a few doors from a great restaurant. Cajun country music exists on the same block as traditional Dixieland jazz. A garden green courtyard in an elegant hotel is only steps away from the staccato of a trumpet and the moaning blues of an alto saxophone.

The street is blocked to vehicular traffic at night and so it becomes the midway of a constant urban carnival. Everyday and all night, the crowds, the colors, the smells, and the sounds of music have been a lure to millions of people from around the world.

VOODOO MUSEUM

739 Bourbon Street   Map, pg. 159   523-2906

The cult of Marie Laveau, the Voodoo Queen, still lives in this, her descendants' former home. The term "museum" is perhaps stretched a bit for this combination shop and backroom display area. There are voodoo gris-gris, candles, and potions for sale as well as occult items. Psychic readings and voodoo tours and entertainment are also available. Open 10:00 a.m. to midnight.

LAFITTE'S BLACKSMITH SHOP

941 Bourbon   Map, pg. 159

Oral Legend says that this structure dating from 1772 was more than just a blacksmith shop. It was a clandestine meeting place where buyers could arrange to purchase the smuggled goods and slaves of the Lafitte brothers of Barataria.

The architecture is of an early colonial style with bricks between the posts construction. This was necessary because the locally made bricks were too soft to support themselves. In recent years the building has housed a neighborhood bar.

GARDETTE - LE PRETRE HOUSE

716 Dauphine Street   Map, pg. 159

This large house, now subdivided into apartments, at the corner of Dauphine and Orleans dates from 1836. In June 1861, General Beauregard sent part of the captured flagstaff from his victory at Ft. Sumter to this house where it was ceremoniously presented to the Orleans Guards.

In 1792, a wealthy Turk occupied the house and gave lavish parties for New Orleans society. There was a rumor that his wealth, and his five beautiful "family members," were liberated from his brother, a sultan. After hearing screams in the night, neighbors found the Turk and his five beauties murdered. The Turkish servants had disappeared, and the riches were missing.

CABRINI DOLL MUSEUM

1218 Burgundy   Map, pg. 237   586-5204

The doll "museum" is a collection of about 500 dolls that were gathered by the Haspel family from their world-wide travels. Unfortunately, the valuable collection is not shown well, and the visitor questions the stewardship shown by the city in attempting to maintain the dolls in such an unfavorable environment.

Beyond the small structure that houses the collection is a patio and a slave quarters where a free art school for children is conducted under the amazing leadership of artist Gothlyn Reck. Be sure to see the children's art work if you visit. Hours 1:30-6:00, Mon.-Fri; 9:30-5:00 on Sat.

THE NEW ORLEANS SCHOOL OF COOKING

835 Conti   Map, pg. 71   525-3034

There is a kitchen in the French Quarter where you can learn to prepare such New Orleans treats as Jambalaya, Shrimp Creole, File Gumbo, Bread Pudding, Pecan Pralines, Bananas Foster, Cafe Brulot and more. Weekday demonstration classes run from 10:00 a.m. to 12:30; Saturdays 1:00 p.m. to 3:30 p.m. The cook-instructors are Joe Cahn and Al Malus, men with a love for food and a talent for sharing their cooking skills. The $15 session includes a slide presentation of food sources, recipes, and a sampling of the cuisine.

The school does convention demonstrations and offers special evening classes where guest chefs from local restaurants demonstrate specialties.

MUSEE CONTI MUSEUM OF WAX

917 Conti St.   Map, pg. 71   525-2605

The history of New Orleans is recreated in 31 life sized tableaux that are remarkable for their authenticity and craftsmanship. There are 144 costumed wax figures in detailed period settings that trace the events and legends of New Orleans in chronological order. The Battle of New Orleans, and the Haunted House of Madame Lalaurie are in the single level gallery that winds past Napoleon, Jean Lafitte, Mark Twain, and other historical figures.

The wax museum opened in 1964. Programs are available in French and Spanish. Open 9:30-9, June 1st thru Labor Day; 10-5:30 weekdays, and until 9 p.m. weekends during the rest of the year. Adults $3, children (6-12) $1, juniors (13-17) $1.25.

As an added attraction, The Haunted Dungeon, brings to wax 23 monsters of note in 10 neck biting, wolf howling settings. Real fun for Frankenstein lovers at no extra cost.

HERMANN-GRIMA HOUSE

820 St. Louis St.   **Map, pg. 71**   525-5661

This house was built by a German immigrant who became a wealthy merchant, and enjoyed social distinction during the city's "Golden Age." Samuel Hermann's tastes in 1831 reveal the "American" influence on New Orleans architecture. Hermann lost his fortune in the cotton crash of 1837-38, and sold the house in 1844 to Judge Felix Grima whose family lived here for five generations.

The Christian Women's Exchange purchased the house in 1924 and began an extensive, well researched restoration in 1965. The house, grounds, garconniere and open-hearth kitchen now interpret an elegant lifestyle circa 1830 to 1860. The petticoat mirrors, heavy red drapes, baseboards painted to resemble marble, fire screens, the hand carved Malliard bedroom sets, the portraits, and even the candy and fruit on the sideboards are in place as if a family were still in residence.

The courtyard is one of the largest in the Vieux Carre and is planted as an early 19th century garden. Adjoining the courtyard is a three-story brick building which served as servants quarters, washroom, wine-cellar, and kitchen. A 6,000 gallon castiron cistern dated 1831 can be seen at the rear of the lot. The kitchen is especially well done and period cooking demonstrations are regularly scheduled.

The property next to the main residence was Judge Grima's stable in 1850. It now is the Exchange Shop. This shop offers ham glaze, jams, crab apple jelly, jewlery, and hand made crafts, and clothing amid the old stalls and hay racks. It is a clue to a tradition of service that was 100 years old in 1980. The Christian Woman's Exchange was established as an outlet to enable needy women to help themselves and to provide a source of revenue for impoverished widows of Confederate soldiers. The Exchange Shop continues to sell goods on consignment, and there are often old china, glass, silverware and antiques on sale.

A pleasant guided tour of the house and gardens lasts about 45-minutes. Open weekdays and Saturday 10-4, Sundays 1-5, closed Wednesdays. Adults $2, students $1.

ONE MO' TIME

615 Toulouse   **Map, pg. 159**   522-7852

This 1920's jazz musical has received well deserved rave reviews. The Lyric Theatre comes alive as Big Bertha Williams and her touring company present their nightclub show. The set allows you to be part of their audience, and to also witness their sordid backstage problems. The recreation of these black entertainers is a unique musical comedy experience. Showtime is 8:30 p.m. Friday, Saturday, Sunday, and Monday.

After the show, the Toulouse Theatre becomes the Original Jazz Cafe offering live jazz music, and full bar service. Stars of the show often do extra bits for the people who stay late.

CASA HOVÉ

723 Toulouse St.   Map, pg. 159   525-7827

After having seen how the wealthy, like James Gallier, Jr. lived, you may wish to see the more humble, but tasteful abode of the merchant class. Casa Hové was once the shop and residence of a gunsmith. The house itself appears on a map dating from the 1720's and reflects a Spanish influence, especially in the design of an open air porch.

The downstairs shop is now a third generation parfumeur dating from 1931. Honeysuckle, Bayou D'Amour and Mantrap are among the 50 parfumes made on the premises, and offered for sale. With a descriptive flyer in hand, the tour passing through the carriage way, and up the stairs to the living spaces is unescorted. Pieces by Mallard and Seignouret are mixed with Chinese Chippendale and Duncan Phyfe. The original ceiling beams and hand hewn cypress floors seem to contrast with framed Carnival Ball invitations, and a small portrait of singer Jenny Lind. The eclectic collection of furniture and personal collectables is probably the way many residents of the Quarter lived.

Casa Hové and the Hové Parfumeur keep the same hours, generally 10-4:30. Closed Sundays and holidays. Adults $1, children under 12, 50 cents

PONTALBA HISTORICAL PUPPETORIUM

514 St. Peter Street   Map, pg. 159   522-0344

The Puppetorium is a series of tableaux in which media-automated marionettes portray the life of Jean Lafitte and the events leading to the Battle of New Orleans. It is strictly for kids. Admission is charged.

The front of the Jackson Square shop offers a large selection of puppets, dolls, and marionettes for purchase.

THE ARSENAL AND JACKSON HOUSE

615 St. Peter St.   Map, pg. 159

The arsenal dates from the days following the Louisiana Purchase. The new state of Louisiana built the arsenal for the Louisiana Legion, a military unit comprised of sons from the best Creole and American families. During the years of Spanish dominance, the site had been used for the prison, or calabozo. When Andrew Jackson arrived in the city in 1814 to prepare to defend the city from the British, this was his headquarters.

General Ben Butler, the Union officer who occupied New Orleans from 1862 to 1871 also made this his headquarters.

Today the Spanish Arsenal, as it is called locally, is part of the Louisiana State Museum. The three floors of the Arsenal and the Jackson House (Jackson used the house, but never owned it.) have been interconnected to showcase an eclectic collection of 19th century artifacts. Folk arts, silhouettes from the 1830's, mourning portraits, a hand pumper fire engine, an 1851 horse drawn cab, and a cigar store squaw are a sampling of the displays.

Hours and admission fees follow those of the Cabildo and Presbytere.

LE PETIT THEATRE DU VIEUX CARRE

616 St. Peter St.   Map, pg. 159   522-2081

This theatre is one of the oldest and most productive community theatres in America. It has showcased plays for over 65 years. Subscribers occupy most of the 460 seats, but visitor tickets are usually available. The curtain is usually 8:30 p.m., and it opens on popular plays and musicals presented by talented casts. Call for information on the current playbill and ticket availability. The theatre also has an award winning children's theatre schedule that is worth investigating.

SPRING FIESTA ASSOCIATION HOUSE

826 St. Ann Street   Map, pg. 159   581-1367

This small, elegant house was donated to the Spring Fiesta Association (see Annual Events) in 1977 by a former member, the late Mrs. Edna Tate Halbedel. The grandfather clock in the hall is dated 1840, about the same year the house was built. The furnishings include fine antique pieces from the mid-19th century. A spiral staircase with a velvet-wrapped rail ascends from a marble-floored entrance hall. The Victorian furniture and objects d'art demonstrate a style of gracious living from the city's golden age. Open 11-3, Mon. & Thurs. Donation $2.

VIEUX CARRE BUS LINE ROUTE

OFF PEAK ROUTE

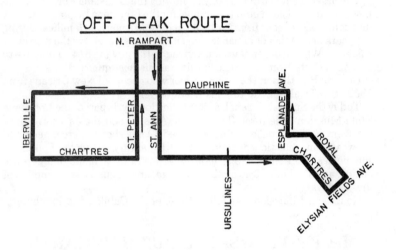

PEAK HOURS ROUTE

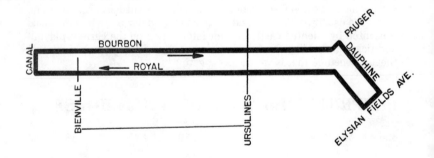

Photo courtesy of The Historic New Orleans Collection.

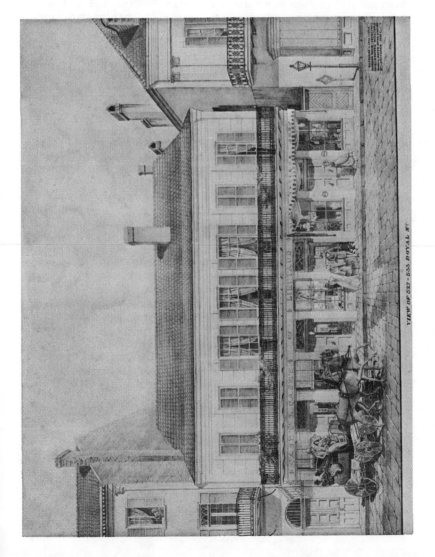

MADAME JOHN'S LEGACY

626 Dumaine St.   Map, pg. 159

Madame John was a quadroon character created in a short story by fiction writer George W. Cable. Ever since the story, **Tite Poulette**, this building, which may be the oldest structure on the Mississippi River, has been called by this romantic name. The original design of the 1726 house was followed when it was rebuilt after the fire of 1778. The house is a raised cottage typical of those in the West Indies. There are no hallways. Each room opens into the next. The furniture is simple. There are no drapes, or carpets, which is representative of early New Orleans. The property is now part of the Louisiana State Museum. The above ground basement, built of brick to protect against floodwaters, is now used as a display area. The house was restored in 1972-73 to capture the city's colonial period. Open Tues.-Sun. 9-5. Adults $1, student 50 cents.

OLD U.S. MINT

400 Esplanade   Map, pg. 237   568-6968

In 1838, this branch of the U.S. Mint began minting gold and silver coins. The massive Greek Revival structure is constructed of fire brick, granite, and iron and is considered fireproof. The mint is on the site of Fort San Carlos, one of the Spanish fortifications dating from 1792.

The mint was abandoned and looted at the outbreak of the Civil War, and later used to coin Confederate money. It has also served as a Coast Guard headquarters and a Federal jail.

The Old Mint has recently been renovated to house the Jazz Collection, Mardi Gras Collection, library, and archives of the Louisiana State Museum. It's public hours are 9-5, Tuesday - Sunday. Admission is charged.

GAUCHE HOUSE

704 Esplanade   Map, pg. 237   Map, pg.

This private residence at the corner of Royal and Esplanade is perhaps the richest house in the French Quarter. It was built in 1856 by John Gauche. The peach colored Italian Villa has elaborate cast-iron balconies on three sides of the building.

THE INTERNATIONAL SHRINE OF SAINT JUDE

411 N. Rampart St.   Map, pg. 309   525-1551

Pere Antoine (see St. Louis Cathedral) broke ground himself for the Mortuary Chapel in 1826. The numerous victims of yellow fever and cholera required a separate place for their funerals convenient to the St. Louis cemeteries. During its long history, Civil War veterans, Italian immigrants, and Spanish speaking people adopted the small church which now carries the name of Our Lady of Guadalupe.

The Shrine of Sant Jude, the saint of the hopeless, consists of statues, murals, fountains, and candlelit grotto adjacent to the church. Small stone and metal plaques engraved with the word "thanks" in three languages give testimony to answered prayers. The primary shrine is located in an alcove to the left of the main altar. To the right of the altar is Our Lady Guardian of Police and Firemen. The church provides chaplains to both city departments.

BEAUREGARD SQUARE

The location of the park, is both historic and ironic. The area had first been called **Congo Square** where black slaves held secret voodoo ceremonies. City officials, hoping to pacify the slaves' need for self expression through music and wild, sensual dancing allowed the blacks to gather on Sunday afternoons until the 9 p.m. curfew cannon boomed. The Congo Square spectacle attracted as many as 2,000 spectators. The rhythms of the drums and the spontaneity of the musicians influenced the creation of jazz. Following the Civil War, Congo Square was renamed for the man who ordered the first shot of the conflict at Fort Sumter, Gen. P.G.T. Beauregard, a native New Orleans hero.

Today the square is a pleasant tree-shaded public space fronting the N. Rampart Street side of the Municipal Auditorium. A multi-gyser fountain adds to the relaxing impact of this place.

MUNICIPAL AUDITORIUM
Map, pg. 309

This multi-purpose, large (12,000 seat) facility is now part of the Cultural Center complex which includes the Theatre of the Performing Arts, and the attractions of Louis Armstrong Park. The building dates from the 1930's and was a WPA project. It was built in the area of a canal that once linked the city and Lake Pontchartrain in 1796. The auditorium has been the traditional site of major Mardi Gras balls. Major entrances are on the Basin St. side.

LOUIS ARMSTRONG PARK

Map, pg. 309

The 31-acre Louis Armstrong Park was dedicated on April 15, 1980 when a 12-foot-tall statue of the beloved jazz trumpet musician by Elizabeth Catlett was unveiled by his widow. More than one thousand contributors from 26 countries financed this monument. The who's who of jazz music participated in the opening ceremonies and the many memorial concerts that followed.

Enter the park from the French Quarter on St. Ann Street. As you near Rampart St., you will see an arcade of white lights spelling out "Armstrong." Raised walkways and bridges meander over a lagoon. Period lamp posts form a semi-circle around a unique overhead fountain, spray pool, and outdoor concert performing area. The rolling contours of the pathways, the open spaces, and seating areas make the park an interesting visual experience.

PERSEVERANCE HALL & JAZZ MUSEUM

Map, pg. 309

Armstrong Park contains a small square bordered by four buildings which contain Perseverance Hall, a Jazz Museum, and food and beverage concessions. The three-hour film, "A Tribute to Louis Armstrong," filmed during the Newport Jazz Festival and incorporating footage of interviews with "Satchmo" is shown as well as photographs and memorabilia from the musician's life. Louis Armstrong, 1900-1971, jazz originator, "scat" singer, and American music ambassador to the world is remembered with great fondness in his native city.

ST. LOUIS NO. 1 CEMETERY

400 Basin Street   Map, pg. 309

This cemetery was established in the 1740's to serve the parish of the St. Louis Church. It is now a walled-in city of tombs with only one entrance. A large palm, and a large magnolia tree stand out among the graves. Burials are still conducted here, and many of the tombs are cared for by the church. Others, however, are in disrepair and are actually crumbling apart to reveal the red brick construction. Wild vegetation grows out of the unattended tombs.

To the left of the entrance, five tombs along the wall and then right is the alleged tomb of Marie Laveau, the famous voodoo queen. Her tomb is marked with the name of her second husband, Glapion. Plastic flowers, the remains of candles, and the red X-marks from brick dust attest that there are still believers who covet her magic.

Dominique You, Lafitte's lieutenant and expert gunner who helped to turn back the British at Chalmette, is also burried here. For personal security reasons, it is not recommended that you visit this cemetery without a tour group.

U.S. CUSTOMS HOUSE

423 Canal Street   **Map, pg. 309**

The main point of interest here is a huge marble vaulted hall, with a 3-story high ceiling supported by 14 massive columns. It is one of the most outstanding Late Greek Revival rooms in America. The marble floor and counters contrast with the dark wooden counter windows that process documents for the Customs service. Two large waist-high working tables for sorting paper work stand under the chandeliers. The sides are angled for the convenience of the clerks. Customs transactions have been conducted at this location since 1792. It is the oldest Federal building in the South. The present building was begun in 1848, but was not completed until 1880.

The Custom House was used by the Army of the Confederacy for the manufacture of gun carriages and cannon shot, and later by the Union Army as a headquarters and a prison. Then Major P.G.T. Beauregard was the construction superintendent. Enter Room 200 at the center of the building after climbing the twin staircase from the Canal Street entrance.

The battleline at Chalmette National Historical Park.

CHALMETTE

THE BATTLE OF NEW ORLEANS

One date in the history of New Orleans unites all its ethnic voices and raises them in common glory and valor. On this day, January 8, 1815, Creoles and Kaintock frontiersmen, sailors and pirates, Indians and Free Men of Color united 4,000 strong to defeat the pride of the British Army and thus preserve America's claim to the Louisiana Territory and the West.

The battle, fought before a peace treaty between the combating countries could be ratified, was the last in a war that began in 1812. At that time Great Britain and France were near the end of a waring period that lasted 22-years. Both European countries had violated American neutrality, but the British stopped American ships at sea and "impressed" American sailors into the Royal Navy. Frontier America was suffering from a depressed economy, and westerners blamed the British. They lobbied for war.

At first Great Britain did little offensively, but the defeat of Napoleon in 1814 released British troops for a triple thrust against the United States. Their Lake Champlain fleet was repulsed, and after burning the White House and the Capitol, the second thrust was halted at Baltimore's Fort McHenry. The third invasion was targeted for New Orleans.

The Opposing Generals

The commander of the British invasion was Sir Edward Pakenham, brother-in-law of the Duke of Wellington, and at 36, a vigorous combat veteran of the European campaigns. His troops included veterans of the wars against Napoleon.

His opposition General was an Indian fighter of the American frontier, 47 years of age, and in poor health. He was recovering from a pistol shot that he had received in a Nashville street brawl the year before, and the effects of wilderness campaigns against the Indians. Andrew Jackson was the son of Scotch-Irish immigrants who had served as an armed messenger at age 13 in the American Revolution. He lost both brothers and his mother in that war and hated the British.

Jackson had served in the Congress from Tennessee, but he was better known as a militia leader against frontier Indians. He earned the affectionate nickname of "Old Hickory" from his men while enduring the wilderness hardships of their campaigns. Following a victory over the Creeks in 1814, Jackson became a Major General in the Regular Army with command of all forces in Tennessee, Mississippi Territory, and Louisiana. Louisiana had just become a state in 1812.

Lafitte Joins the Defense

While Jackson was assuming his command, British officers were in Barataria soliciting smuggler-pirate-slave trader Jean Lafitte as an ally. They offered him land, protection, cash, and the rank of captain in the Royal Navy. Lafitte stalled for time, and although he was an outlaw, and his brother Pierre a prisoner in the Cabildo Calaboose, he advised Louisiana Governor Claiborne of the proposition and offered his services to America in exchange for a pardon for himself and his men. Claiborne refused the offer, Pierre Lafitte mysteriously escaped from prison, and Lafitte's Barataria hideout was destroyed by U.S. Navy forces before the Americans and the Baratarians were to unite.

Andrew Jackson arrived in New Orleans in early December, established headquarters at 106 Royal Street, and began to organize his defense. The British fleet arrived and won control of Lake Borgne and began to seek an attack route via the bayous to the river.

New Orleans was panic stricken, and the backbone of its salvation was so ill that he issued orders from a reclining position on a sofa in his headquarters. When Jean Lafitte secretly visited the General, Jackson, who had stubbornly refused to ally himself with the pirate, changed his stance, and accepted the help of the Baratarians. The artillery detachments formed under expert gunners Dominique You and Renato Beluche proved significant to the outcome of the eventual battles.

The British Advance

The British probed the bayou approaches to the city and found an almost unguarded access to the river within nine miles of the city. Jackson made the most important decision of the campaign and attacked the weary British troops before they were reinforced. Without Jackson's offensive the reinforced enemy might have entered the city easily.

With 2,000 men assembling where the De La Ronde Oaks stand today, Jackson attacked at night from two wings following an effective shelling by his 15-gun sloop-of-war **Carolina** positioned on the river. The British were clearly surprised, but in the darkness troops on both sides became disoriented and the action broke up into many small fights. Christmas Eve dawned and the American army withdrew to the De La Rone mansion. Its losses were 24 killed, 115 wounded and 74 missing. The British loseses were 46, 167, and 64.

The Line Is Drawn

Jackson chose the Rodriquez Canal which formed the boundary between the Chalmette and Macarty plantations for his defensive line. The canal was from 10 to 20 feet wide and from four to eight feet deep, and it ran from the river to the swamp. It crossed a narrow strip of dry land that was directly across the route of the British advance. It was two miles from the scene of the night battle and only six miles from the center of New Orleans. The ground was too wet for trenches so the men ransacked the vicinity for tools and materials to erect a mud rampart. Fence rails were driven into the soil and the men worked in unceasing shifts to ready the field fortification.

The Carolina continued to harrass the Redcoats from the river until the British gunners secured howitzers from their fleet and destroyed the sloop with red-hot cannon balls. General Pakenham realized that he must break through the American line, or seek another route to the prized city. He committed to attack the line.

The Battle Intensifies

On the 28th Pakenham probed the American line in force, but was repelled by accurate artillery fire from the American land batteries, and the sloop Louisiana firing from the river. Losses on each side were slight.

During the next days the Americans harrassed the enemy with bombardments from the Louisiana. At night, Tennessee Indian fighters ambushed enemy sentinels. Both sides increased their firepower with the arrival of cannon and more men.

A serious artillery duel on New Year's morning stopped the band and the parade that was forming behind Jackson's line. Dominique You distinguished himself with accurrate fire that silenced the British batteries, but not before 11 were killed and 23 wounded. The enemy losses were 32 killed, 44 wounded.

More reinforcements arrived for Jackson. The Kentucky Militia contributed 2,250 men, but only 550 of these were armed. On the day of the major battle Jackson had about 4,000 men on the line against an attacking force of about 5,400.

The Great Victory

The British veterans began the attack through the morning fog. The defenders stood three and four deep behind the mud wall, each taking his turn to fire and then stepping back to reload. Small arms fire from 1,500 pieces and the deadly artillery broke the columns of British in 25-minutes. They counterattacked. Pakenham, and his senior officer both fell and died. In two hours the British lost more than 2,000 men. The American losses were seven killed, six wounded. It was an astounding victory over first-rate soldiers.

Across the river, the British were also attacking and met little resistance. If American defenders had not spiked their cannon before retreating, the British might have raked the rear of Jackson's line and undone its victory. But the British victory across the river was of little use since the main force had been so terribly defeated. The enemy withdrew, and the open door to New Orleans was forever shut to their ambitions.

After the War

There were a few small actions before the Ghent Treaty ending the war was recognized, but the incredible victory gave the nation a significant spiritual lift. Following the jubilation in New Orleans, Jackson imposed martial law and kept his troops assembled until March over the objections of the Governor and the legislature. Nevertheless, Jackson was an immediate national hero. He lost the

CHALMETTE NATIONAL PARK

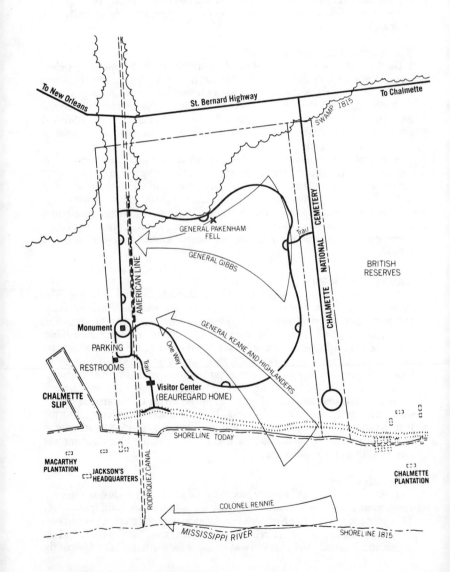

Presidency in 1824 in the Electoral College after a four man race, but won the next election in 1828 and served two terms.

President Madison pardoned the Baratarians. Captain Dominique You stayed in New Orleans, entered local politics, and died in poverty. Renato Beluche made admiral in the Venezuelan Navy. The most enigmatic character of all, Jean Lafitte, who had provided the powder and flints for Jackson's cannon and the men who so skillfully used them, sailed away into the realm of legend beyond the sight of history.

CHALMETTE NATIONAL HISTORICAL PARK

Map, pg. 170

The site of the Battle of New Orleans on the Chalmette plantation is preserved today as a National Historical Park. The 100-foot marble monument was begun by the State of Louisiana in 1855, and completed by the Federal Government in 1907. The park covers 141 acres which includes the Chalmette National Cemetery.

The Rene Beauregard House, circa 1830, has been restored and serves as a park visitor center. Models, pictures, uniforms, weapons, and a "talking map" give insights to the battle. A wharf on the river behind the house allows tour boats to dock.

The Rodriquez Canal is only a depression in the plain that once grew sugar cane. Since 1815 the Mississippi River has claimed some 800 feet of land. Lost under the river are the remains of the canal, Jackson's headquarters, and the battery sites at this end of the battle line. You may walk along the reconstructed line however and view sections of the mud rampart, and the positions of the American units and batteries. Cannons point toward the British battleground.

To drive to the Park from Canal Street follow the main thoroughfare that begins at Rampart Street and merges into St. Claude Avenue, then into St. Bernard Highway. The highway passes the De La Ronde ruins and oaks, and the Park itself.

THE DE LA RONDE OAKS

Map, pg. 170

The great live oaks lead from the river to the ruins of the De La Ronde mansion. Some say the oaks were planted as early as 1762; others that Peter De La Ronde planted them on his 21st birthday in 1793.

General Jackson rallied his troops on the site for the night battle of December 23, 1814. The British General Pakenham camped among the young trees, and there is also a legend that he died under their branches after being mortally wounded on the battlefield at Chalmette. Some accounts mistakenly refer to the stand of oaks as Pakenham Oaks or Versailles Oaks.

The huge trees are located on private property near the Chalmette site, and are easily seen from St. Bernard Highway, LA Rt. 39.

FAUBOURG MARIGNY

Marigny is a respected Creole family name. In 1800 when Peter Marigny died, his 15 year old son was perhaps the richest boy in America. Young Bernard went to Europe, learned a dice game, taught it to his friends in New Orleans, and lost $1 million by the time he was 20. The game became known as "craps."

Bernard was then forced to subdivide part of his plantation nearest the city into lots. The property, separated from the city by crumbling fortifications and the commons beyond them became the Faubourg Marigny. Bernard's names for the streets reveals something about his personality. There was his Champs Elysees, Rue des Grande Homme, Rue d'Amour, Hope, Duels, Genius, Poets, and of course, a Rue Craps. A city ordinance in 1850 erased the colorful street names. Congregations of three large churches on Rue Craps petitioned the City Council for the change.

Today the Faubourg Marigny bordered by Esplanade, St. Claude, Franklin Avenue, and the River is regarded as a Historic District, and preservation efforts are being made to save its rich architectural resources. Many of the Creole Cottages and Shotgun Houses were built of flatboat timber. Don't be deceived by the decay of this neighborhood. Some of the simple facades conceal 30-room houses with lavish gardens which were once enjoyed by the best of Creole society.

Few restored homes in Marigny are open to the public, and those only by appointment. Your interest will be rewarded, however, by meeting individuals whose knowledge and enthusiasm for the Creole story is unavailable in any other part of the city.

SUN OAK:
THE FAUBOURG MARIGNY COLLECTION

2020 Burgundy St.   **Map, pg. 170**   945-0322

Two private homes, in a master plan that will include a third, are now open for tour by appointment in the Marigny National Register Area.

The first is a restored Greek Revival galleried Creole cottage triplex built in 1836 by merchant Asher Nathan. Three residential units, each five rooms deep, share common walls under one roof. The painted masonry simulates a rusticated brick facade. The emphasis on furnishings is Louisiana originals, and the garden is extensive, including some large, fruit bearing banana trees. The property gets its name from an ancient oak tree whose spreading branches dominate the patios of both houses.

The second house is another Creole Cottage in the Victorian style. French, Creole, and Acadian antiques and decorative arts are shown to amplify 19th century lifestyles in Louisiana.

The personality behind the Marigny Collection is architect Eugene Cizek, who will personally show the houses and share the Creole legacy.

The houses are also available for private receptions and catered dinners. Call for appointment.

JACKSON BARRACKS

6400 St. Claude Ave.   Map, pg. 170

In the days when New Orleans was protected by forts on the river, Jackson Barracks was the depot for troops stationed there. The headquarters was constructed like a fort itself. Its main buildings that have a plantation look date from 1834. It is said that Andrew Jackson, wary of Creole plots against American rule, designed the barracks in case he should ever have to defend himself from New Orleans!

Jackson Barracks is now the headquarters of the Louisiana National Guard. There is a small military museum in the old powder magazine which traces the history of the barracks. Open Tues.-Sun., 9-4. Adults $1.50, children 50 cents.

STEAMBOAT HOUSES

400 and 503 Egania St.   Map, pg. 170

River pilot Captain Milton Doullot built the octagon-shaped three-tiered house nearest the river in 1905 to memorialize the passing era of steamboats. In 1913, his son built its twin across the street.

The ground floor is white tile brick. The second level, or deck, is reached by a pair of exterior staircases. The shipboard motif is carried out by narrow interior halls, squared corners, and a pilothouse on top. The distinctive gingerbread accent to the deck level gallery is achieved by large wooded beads, graduated in size and strung between the posts on steel wires.

The houses are private residences, and like many New Orleans homes which are interesting to view, the privacy of the families should be respected.

Walter Johnson: On Developing An Estate

"You've started your climb to the top. People already accept you as a coming leader in your profession and business. Your income is growing. You're just beginning to tap your potential.

We know, from experience, that you have your own goals. And your own "in" needs—investments and insurance. But they have to be specially designed for you. That's why we don't try to fit you into a computerized pigeon hole. We don't bring you preconceived ideas on your needs.

Instead, we'd like to talk to you about your objectives and goals. We'll review the tax implications and opportunities of your current investment programs. And when you're ready, we will talk to you about:

- Corporate risk free tax shelters
- Tax sheltered trusts

- Personal estate analysis
- Business preservation programs
- Personal life and disability income insurance
- Tax deferred annuities

We'll talk to you about developing an estate, not just protecting one.

We can assist you in designing a richer future, by capitalizing on today's opportunities. Give us a call."

 Walter Johnson
Senior Associate

- **Roland Hymel & Associates, Inc.**
- **Roland Hymel Agency**

Suite 100, Financial Planning Center, 2475 Canal St.,
New Orleans, La. 70119 (504) 827-2900

State Mutual Life Assurance Company of America
Worcester, Massachusetts 01605

CENTRAL BUSINESS DISTRICT

Map, pg. 105

THE RIVERGATE

The Rivergate, completed in 1968, is one of the major exhibition and convention facilities in the city. It's enormous concrete canopy, 500-feet long and more than two-stories high at the foot of Canal St. is opposite the Trade Mart and the Canal St. Ferry.

The Main Hall is a clear-span, column free meeting space that can seat 17,500 for a speech, or 9,000 for an elegantly catered dinner. The entire Bacchus Mardi Gras parade enters the Rivergate for the krewe's annual ball. The facility has many options for meetings and events for all sizes.

The cafeteria and lounge in the Rivergate is open to the public and offers a convenient, often uncrowded, refuge from a sudden shower or a 90-degree day.

CANAL STREET FERRY

Here's your free ride on the Mississippi. The ferry leaves from the foot of Canal St. and makes the round trip to Algiers on the West Bank in about 25-minutes. The new ferry carries both auto and foot passengers.

Algiers Point is the sharpest turn and the deepest point of the entire river, some 200-feet deep. At night, ships negotiating the turn seem to go broadside and disappear into the land.

INTERNATIONAL TRADE MART

The 33-story ITM Trade Center houses 185 private enterprises and government agencies generally associated with the maritime industry. The tennants include 24 foreign consulates and trade offices, and there is a Visitors International Program Center on the 29th floor providing multi-lingual services to foreign visitors. There is much to see here, however, for any visitor.

OBSERVATION DECK

An outside, observation elevator takes you to the 31st floor where you can look directly up Canal St., watch the river traffic, or get a bird's eye view of the Vieux Carre. The views run 360 degrees, and the floor has seats, air conditioning, and restrooms for the weary. Access to the observation deck via the special elevator is $1.50 for adults, 50 cents for children. Open daily 8 a.m. to 10 p.m.

LOUISIANA MARITIME MUSEUM

For an additional small admission (50 cents), visit this small, interesting museum on the observation deck level. The displays include ship models, rare documents, antique nautical instruments, weapons, and furniture from the elegant steamboat era. A ship's radio allows you to hear the captains and pilots negotiating Algiers Point below. Open 9 a.m. to 4 p.m. except Sundays and holidays.

TOP OF THE MART LOUNGE

There is no cover or admission to this high rise watering hole on the 33rd floor. The lounge is circular, and terraced so that its patrons can see the city below as it revolves 360 degrees every 90-minutes. Lots of frozen drink specialties, and a combo entertaining nightly. Open 10-2 weekdays, 11-3 Saturday, 4-12 Sunday. A plush and romantic rendezvous that is very popular with the convention crowd.

THE FOUR FOREIGN PLAZAS

There are 44 governments with representation in New Orleans, and the major influences on the city are recalled by the Place de France, the Plaza de Espana, the Piazza d'Italia, and British Place.

The Place de France is the square between the Rivergate and the Trade Mart. President de Gaulle, who was much impressed by New Orleans during his visit in 1960, dedicated the statue of Jeanne d'Arc which stands here.

The Plaza de Espana is directly behind the Trade Mart on the river. The Spanish government donated the tile and granite while the city financed the large fountain which sprays water as high as 50-feet. Spanish city coats-of-arms can be seen worked in color tiles around a circular wall which showcases the fountain. There are places to sit, but no shade is available on this vast expanse of stone.

The Piazza d'Italia is about four blocks from the Trade Mart on Poydras St. and Tchoupitoulas. Every Columbus Day (2nd Monday in October) it becomes an Italian marketplace as New Orleanians celebrate their Italian heritage with parades, music, crafts, and foods. The plan for the public park and fountains is striking.

Bristish Place is the landscaped circular area at the entrance of the New Orleans Hilton Hotel near the Trade Mart. The nine-foot bronze statue is the familiar Sir Winston Churchill.

LOUISIANA 1984 WORLD EXPOSITION

339 ITM Building   Map, pg. 105   (504) 566-1984

The 85-acre site of the May 12th to November 11th, 1984 event lies along the river between the Hilton Hotel and the Mississippi River Bridge. A great deal of waterfront redevelopment, and the construction of the New Orleans Convention and Exhibition Center at South Front and Julia Streets, will transform this wharf area into a world class attraction.

The theme of the Exposition, which is not unlike a World's Fair in scope, is "The World of Rivers—Fresh Water As A Source of Life." Exhibitors are expected from many foreign countries. The Louisiana World Exposition will not only showcase the products and potentials of Louisiana as a whole, but will also launch New Orleans as a site for the largest international conventions and exhibitions.

NEW ORLEANS CONVENTION AND EXHIBITION CENTER

South Front and Julia Streets   Map, pg. 105

The 14-acre site of the new Convention and Exhibition Center, up river from the Hilton Hotel, will be at the heart of the 1984 Louisiana World Exposition. The bi-level facility will have 351,000 sq. ft. of contiguous ground level space divisible into four halls, and additional meeting rooms on the second level.

The addition of this extensive meeting facility is the final jewel in a crown which makes New Orleans royally appropriate for the largest of international exhibitions and conventions. The construction of new Sheraton, Intercontinental, and Holiday Inn hotels by 1984 will give the city a total of 18,000 hotel rooms. The Convention and Exhibition Center will be used to showcase Louisiana World Exposition exhibits and activities during the May to November event, and then will be available for convention groups in 1985.

LOUISIANA WORLD EXPOSITION
NEW ORLEANS, MAY 12-NOV. 11, 1984

SECURITY CENTER

147 Carondelet Street   Map, pg. 105   522-1254

The Security Center Building was once a Federal Reserve Bank. It was constructed like a fortress with two narrow entrances and walls six-foot thick. The building is now privately owned and offers personal and corporate storage of valuables to the public.

Documents, furs, jewels, art objects, and other articles may be placed into the Center's vaults with access 24-hours a day. The surprisingly reasonable fees are based on weekly, monthly, or annual usage. Guards and sophisticated electronic surveillance add to the Center's security.

On the first floor of the Security Center is the Vincent Moun Gallery which specializes in Impressionist painters.

THE PORT OF NEW ORLEANS

New Orleans is one of the most important ports in the world. Nearly 5,000 vessels arrive annually, and move cargos in foreign trade valued at $12 billion. Ships from Japan, United Kingdom, Germany, Netherlands, Brazil, Russia, and China enter the Mississippi River passes from the Gulf of Mexico and make the 100 mile passage to one of over 100 berths in the New Orleans port. They bring crude petroleum, coffee, iron and steel products, machinery, sugar, crude rubber, and take away grain, oils and fats, animal feeds, organic chemicals and the products of American industry.

From Tulsa, St. Louis, Nashville, Memphis, Louisville, Kansas City, Cincinnati, Chicago, Birmingham, and even Minneapolis (1717 river miles away), the products of a country's heartland come by barge to the historic port. The spirit of Mark Twain still lives on the river as captains of 5,000-horsepower tugboats maneuver 1000-foot tows of barges through Cat Island Bend, Horseshoe Cut-off, Fort Adams Reach, Bayou Goula Bend, and Gypsy Light.

To see the Port of New Orleans, and to appreciate its 15 miles of docks, its shipbuilding and repair industry, and its concentration of 900 manufacturing plants encompassing some 200 standard industrial classifications, you must take to the river. See the section on river cruises for full details.

LOUISIANA SUPERDOME

1500 Poydras St.   Map, pg. 105   587-3645

If you have watched the Super Bowl or the Sugar Bowl on television, you already know something about this architectural wonder of the world. Begun in the summer of 1971, it took four years, and a lot of political controversy to complete the Louisiana Superdome. Price tag? Think in terms of $200 million.

The Superdome catalyzed a New Orleans building boom in the seventies that equipped the city to compete for the largest national and international conventions.

The huge white dome covering 9.7 acres, and its gleaming concave metallic circular wall makes the Superdome appear like an other world space vehicle. The "room" inside is the largest in the world. It will seat 72,675 for a football game, and 95,427 when arranged as an auditorium. Some of the unique features include six giant (22x26-feet) TV screens which hang from a 75-ton gondola, and portions of the stands that move on rails to create configurations for the various professional and collegiate sports played inside.

The Superdome has three major levels designed with large meeting rooms, catering facilities, and ultra modern utilities to provide services for conventions and trade shows. For the economic elite there are 64 plush box suites, and the Stadium Club with a gourmet restaurant. Both have waiting lists.

If you don't have time to attend an event in the Superdome, you can take a guided tour whenever the main facility is not in use. Enter Gate A on Poydras St., and look for metered parking for short term visitors. Allow at least 45-minutes for the tour. The ticket desk and waiting lounge is on the Plaza level. Tours leave on the half hour daily between 9:30 and 3:30. Adults $3, children (5 to 12) $1.50.

INTERNATIONAL HOUSE

607 Gravier Street   Map, pg. 105   522-3591

International House is a trade association of international businessmen enjoying reciprocal privileges with other World Trade Centers on five continents. Since 1943, its club facilities have been an international hospitality center. Services include telex, printing, interpreters, communications and projection equipment, a library, language study labs, trade publications, and research facilities.

With 45 foreign governments represented in New Orleans, International House and its sister-organization, The International Trade Mart, are the focal points for a great deal of economic and social discourse. IH has 2,500 members.

SAENGER PERFORMING ARTS CENTER

143 N. Rampart Street   Map, pg. 105   524-0876

When the Saenger opened in 1927 at a cost of $2.5 million, it was one of the most remarkable theatres in America. The auditorium was out of the Italian Renaissance, "an acre of seats in a garden of Florentine splendor."

Detailed marble facades with columns, arches, and heroic statuary dominated the side walls of the theatre. Stars twinkled in the ceiling, the glow of an evening sun set in the West, and mechanical clouds passed overhead.

Everyday, 100 uniformed "palace" ushers formed up for inspection in the long narrow marble foyer. They guarded elaborate chandeliers hanging from decorative ceiling rosettes, replicas of Michelangelo and Verrocchio statuary, plush carpeting, and the Robert-Morton "Wonder Organ," a 40-ton pipe organ which had the capability to immitate any instrument in the orchestra.

After 50 years of use, the great theater was in decay, filled with tons of trash and water from a flood. E.B. Breazeale purchased the Saenger in 1978 with a dream to restore the theatre to its original grandeur. His achievement can be seen today as the 3,400 seat facility hosts Broadway touring companies, concerts, and other stage entertainments. The cost was $2 million, and the restoration earned the Saenger the designation as a national landmark. See a production or concert here if you can.

△ ATTRACTIONS

1. Lee Circle & Monument, pg. 116
2. Confederate Museum, pg. 116
3. Lafayette Square, pg. 116
4. Gallier Hall, pg. 117
5. Union Station, pg. 19
6. LA Superdome, pg. 101
7. Tulane Medical School
8. Charity Hospital
   LSU Medical School
9. The Rivergate, pg. 97
10. Canal Street Ferry, pg. 97
11. International Trade Mart, pg. 97
    Observation Deck, pg. 97
    LA Maritime Museum, pg. 98
12. Convention and Exhibition Center, pg. 99
13. LA 1984 World Exposition, pg. 99
14. Security Center, pg. 101
15. International House, pg. 102
16. Saenger Performing Arts Center, pg. 102
17. River Cruises, pg. 25
18. The Four Foreign Plazas, pg. 98

Y NIGHT SPOTS

1. Blue Room, pg. 311
2. Le Club, pg. 189
   Pagoda Bar, pg. 317
3. Woody Herman's, pg. 319
4. Pete Fountain's, pg. 317
   The Rainforest, pg. 188

☐ ACCOMMODATIONS

1. International Center YMCA, pg. 190
2. Sheraton New Orleans, pg. 195
3. Le Pavillon, pg. 195
4. Fairmont, pg. 187
5. Howard Johnson's, pg. 187
6. Hyatt Regency, pg. 189
7. The Warwick, pg. 197
8. Hilton & Towers, pg. 188
9. International, pg. 190
10. Marriott, pg. 191

◯ RESTAURANTS

1. Hummingbird, pg. 250
2. Bon Ton Cafe, pg. 250
3. St. Charles, pg. 254
4. Kolb's, pg. 253
5. Maylie's, pg. 253
6. Bailey's, pg. 249
   Sazerac, pg. 254
7. Jonah's, pg. 251
   Georgie Porgie's, pg. 249
   Imperial Regency Palace, pg. 251
8. Saxony, pg. 279
9. Winston's, pg. 255

CENTRAL BUSINESS DISTRICT

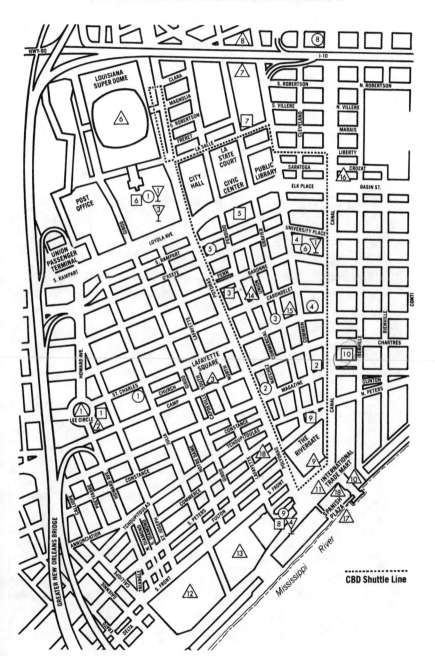

CBD Shuttle Line

The main building of the Dixie Brewery dates from 1907.

MID CITY

METAIRIE CEMETERY HERITAGE TRAIL

Metairie Rd. at I-10 Service Rd.   **Map, pg. 170**   486-6331

Metairie Cemetery was once the site of a famous racetrack and Jockey Club which was a primary New Orleans attraction until the Civil War. The oldest parts of the cemetery conform to the oval of the old track. In 1854, former President Millard Fillmore and a crowd of 20,000 people witnessed the great race between the Kentucky-bred Lexington and the champion of Louisiana, Lecomte. Lexington won both four mile heats and the skeleton of the famous thoroughbred is now in the Smithsonian.

In 1872, when the track fell on the hard times of the Reconstruction, Jockey Club members formed an association and developed the cemetery. Metairie Cemetery became the final resting place for many of the military and political leaders of the Confederacy. The monuments and statuary are significant to Southern heritage.

The Heritage Trail is a suggested route that covers most of the Civil War memorials, plus other tombs of historic or design interest. You are welcome to view by foot or vehicle any part of the cemetery.

The Washington Artillery cenotaph honors a fabled fighting unit whose history began with the Battle of New Orleans. Its gallantry at Manassas (Bull Run), and the major campaigns in Virginia, Maryland, and Pennsylvania is well documented from the Civil War. A lone artilleryman stands atop the monument which was erected in 1880. The names of its battles, and patriots are inscribed on the base.

The Army of Northern Virginia is honored by a towering memorial capped by a statue of Lee's trusted officer General Thomas "Stonewall" Jackson. Jefferson Davis was first entombed here, before his remains were removed to Richmond. His tomb here was sealed forever and his signature carved into the slab with a memorable epitaph. A Louisiana Division was part of Lee's Army of Northern Virginia.

The Army of Tennessee memorial is in some ways the most dramatic of the Confederate shrines. A large mound visible from the highway, I-10, covers the large tomb and supports a staute of Gen. Albert Sidney Johnson on horseback. Another sculpture by Alexander Doyle at the base of the mound depicts a Confederate soldier calling the roll. In the mausoleum lies the remains of New Orleans hero Gen. P.T.G. Beauregard, and others, including the first Southern officer to die in the war.

William C. C. Claiborne was first buried elsewhere, and removed later to this modest family tomb. A Virginian by birth, he represented Tennessee in the Congress, and after casting the deciding vote that put Thomas Jefferson into the White House, he became the Governor of the

METAIRIE CEMETERY

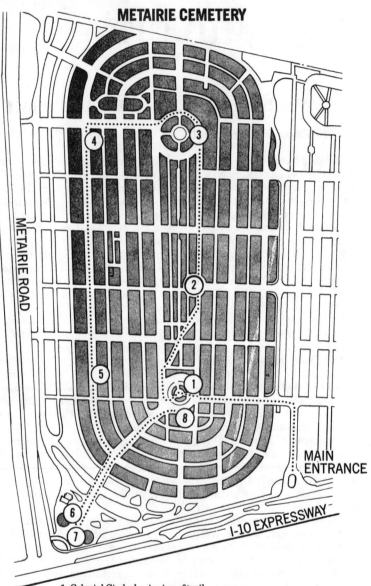

1. Colonial Circle: beginning of trail
2. The Washington Artillery Memorial
3. Army of Northern Virginia Memorial and Tomb
4. From this position, the race track configuration can be seen.
5. Tomb of Gov. W.C. Claiborne and Claiborne family
6. The Moriarty Monument
7. Army of Tennessee Memorial and Tomb
8. Classic tomb of W.S. Pike, early banker.

Mississippi Territory. After the Louisiana Purchase, he was at first the territorial governor, and then the elected first Governor of Louisiana. He died at age 42.

The Moriarty granite tower, 50-feet high, dominates the Metairie Rd. and I-10 corner of the cemetery. A memorial to Mary Farrell Moriarty by her husband Daniel, the structure is one of the most elaborate in the South. The four statues represent Faith, Hope, Charity and Memory.

Josie Arlington's tomb is pink marble. The life sized statue of a young woman is posed on the steps and appears to be rapping at the closed doors. Josie Arlington was a Storyville madam, and legend has it that the figure either symbolizes the fact that she was turned away from home as a teenager, or that she had an iron-clad rule against employing virgins. When a traffic light adjacent to the cemetery cast a reddish glow on her tomb, the irony of the situation renewed her legend. Due to changed traffic patterns, and the closing of an old entrance to the cemetery, the disquieting light is gone, but the curiosity remains.

David C. Hennessy was the city's popular Irish police superintendent in 1890 when he was gunned down by alleged Mafia assassins. When it appeared that justice might not be done to the suspects, citizens met in Lafayette Square, marched to Parish Prison, then stormed to the jailhouse, and lynched 11 men of Italian descent. A diplomatic incident ensued with Italy, and the U.S. settled by paying an indemnity. In response to the unpopular decision, "his countrymen" erected a marble shaft to the slain officer, complete with the chief's crescent, star badge, and a policeman's night stick.

CITY PARK

Esplanade Ave. & Wisner Dr.　　　　Map, pg. 170　　　　482-4888

The huge 1500-acre New Orleans City Park is bordered by historic Bayou St. John. French explorers were shown this portage used by the Choctaw Indians between Lake Pontchartrain and the Mississippi, and an 18-year-old Frenchman named Bienville, following the Bayou St. John to the river set his mind on establishing a settlement there. He was 37 before his dream could be realized.

Reminders of the city's history begin with the equestrian monument of General P. G. T. Beauregard, unveiled by his granddaughter in 1915 at a grand ceremony that attracted elderly veterans, bands, and a 17-gun salute by the Washington Artillery. Esplanade Ave. crosses Bayou St. John at this point, and leads to the entrance of the park and the Museum of Art. The Duelling Oaks are to the right of the Beauregard statue as you cross the bayou.

City Park is a public recreation mecca with four 18-hole golf courses, a large tennis center, horseback riding, ball diamonds, fishing lagoons, picnic shelters, gardens, carnival rides, and even bocci courts. There are two ways to see America's largest city park that will appeal to the short term visitor: the 2½-mile miniature train ride, and the boat rentals.

The train runs daily May to September, 10 to 5, and in winter Sat.,-Sun.

only. The depot across from the Casino concessions building is near the Museum. The ride takes about 15-minutes and you may exit at the carnival ride area and reboard on the same 75 cent ticket. Canoe and skiff rentals are available at the Casino. Open all year, Wed.-Sun. 9 to 5. $2.50 per hour to find your way among the lagoons, past the giant moss covered oaks, gliding with the swans in a lush semi-tropical environment. Obviously popular with the romantics.

DUELLING OAKS

The colossal live oaks were standing in 1700 when explorers under Iberville passed along the Bayou St. John. The oldest tree, named after John McDonogh who donated the land for City Park, is probably 600 years old. Its branches spread some 142-feet.

In the duelling era, the Metairie Oaks at sunrise was a rendezvous for the settlement of affairs of honor. The area was rural in those days, and provided relative privacy for the contests of killing skill and nerve. Duelling has always been against the law. Louis XIV outlawed it, and in 1847 every state in the Union prohibited it.

DUELLING, THE CODE DUELLO

Duelling, or the Code Duello, was a social institution in New Orleans from 1805 until the last duel was fought in 1889. Only officers and gentlemen fought duels. Combatants and their seconds were required to be equal in rank and social position. A gentleman avenged or defended his honor by a duel on the "field of honor." In New Orleans, the field was often under the Metairie Oaks. The site is now to the left of the entrance of the New Orleans Museum of Art in City Park.

The code of duelling was brought to New Orleans by immigrants from San Domingo, and later by officers from Bonaparte's army. From 1830 to 1870 fencing academies flourished in the French Quarter and duelling became firmly established by its masters and practitioners. Early duels were fought with rapiers, swords, or sabers. These were romantic weapons true to the spirit of the code. Drawing blood was often enough to give satisfaction, and there were few deaths. But when the Americans arrived and enthusiastically adopted duelling, the weapons changed to knives, pistols, rifles and shotguns, and duels nearly always ended with one or both duellists seriously wounded or killed.

Governor Claiborne fought a duel in 1807. There were duels on horseback, a duel with harpoons at 20 paces, and bloody affairs with knives. Many duels were fought for trivial reasons. The record does not support the popular belief that most duels were fought over women. One Neapolitan nobleman fought 14 duels to prove that Dante was a greater poet than Aristo, and then admitted on his death bed that he had never read the works of either.

The height of duelling in New Orleans occurred between 1820 to 1840. A common scene under the Oaks was the combatants, each with two seconds and a personal surgeon. There would be a toss of coin for position, and the principals would agree on the words and the person who would say them. The words might be: "Gentlemen, are you ready? Fire, one, two, three." The agreement would stipulate that each man must fire after the word "fire," and before the word "three."

Although some accounts of duelling say that there was duelling under the Oaks everyday during its heyday, these are probably exaggerated. The New Orleans Public Library has card indexed only 32 newspaper accounts of duels. One might argue, however, that duels were so common during the period that few of them were deemed newsworthy.

NEW ORLEANS MUSEUM OF ART

City Park   **Map, pg. 170**   488-2631

Until 1971, this was the Delgado Museum, named after the sugar planter who financed its primary construction in 1911. With three new wings, the museum has expanded to exhibit its large collection of Latin Colonial paintings and sculptures, and Pre-Columbian Indian artifacts. Donations of special collections of 13th through 18th century Italian paintings, 19th century French art, Chinese jades, and portrait miniatures, plus others, are making this museum more important each year.

It was no small artworld coup to be selected as one of the few museums to present the 1977-78 U.S. tour of the Treasures of Tutankhamun. The New Orleans Museum of Art continues to be the showcase for major international exhibitions in the Southeast.

Look for the large painting of Estelle Musson which was painted by her cousin, Edgar Degas, during his visit to her Explanade Ave. home in 1872. The artist, famous for his ballet dancers, is represented by seven pieces in the second floor Impressionists gallery.

The museum is open Tues.-Sun. 10-5, Thurs. 1-9. Adults $1, children 50 cents. Free on Thurs. Light luncheon fare available from noon.

LONGUEVUE HOUSE AND GARDENS

7 Bamboo Rd. off Metairie R.   **Map, pg. 170**   488-5488

Longue Vue is an 8-acre city estate built by Edith and Edgar Stern in 1942. It is one of the great examples of what wealth and good taste can accomplish in the pursuit of lifestyle in the 20th century.

The gardens of the house have been on display since 1968, but the house was only opened to the public in 1980. The Greek Revival, stucco over brick, house projects the raised cottage effect seen in Louisiana architecture. An alley of live oaks, pruned into a cathedral arch, leads to the front door. The seven cloistered patio gardens frame The Spanish Court, the dominant showcase that was redesigned in 1966 to be reminiscent of the Generalife Gardens in Granada, Spain. Fountains and sculptures enchance the enjoyment of manicured boxwood and fragrant seasonal flowers.

Inside the large two-story mansion, English and French antiques in the dining room and drawing room share billing with Art Deco in Mr. Stern's dressing room, and Kandinsky, Vasarely, and Picasso art works. The rare collection of Queen's Ware, and Leeds Pottery stems from an eclectic acquisitiveness that also includes 17 animation cells from eight early Walt Disney productions.

Longue Vue Center for Decorative Arts is open Tues.-Fri. 10-4:30; Sat.-Sund. 1-5. Closed Mon. and national holidays. Adults $5 for Center, $2 for Gardens. Children under 12, $3 and $1. Ask about the three 30-minute color films on Louisiana gardens and plantations that are scheduled in the Playhouse.

Longue Vue is near Metairie Cemetery and might be incorporated in a visit there. Allow at least an hour at Longue Vue.

PITOT HOUSE

1440 Moss St.   **Map, pg. 170**   482-0312

James Pitot (1761-1831) came to Spanish colonial New Orleans in 1796. He was a French native, but had begun his career as a commission merchant in Saint-Dominque where he married a Creole.

In the colonial city he became a member of the Cabildo (City Council), and after the Louisiana Purchase he became the first democratically elected mayor. Governor Claiborne appointed him the first judge of the Parish Court of New Orleans where he had a distinguished career.

Pitot bought his house and 30-acre plantation on the Bayou St. John in 1810. It is typical of the West Indies style mansions that lined each side of the bayou in those days. The house was rescued from demolition, moved to a neighboring lot, and carefully restored by the Louisiana Landmarks Society.

Costumed docents escort visitors on a tour of this unique restoration every Thursday, 11-4, Admission to the house and gardens is $1.50.

FAIR GROUNDS RACING

1751 Gentilly Blvd.   **Map, pg. 170**   944-5515

Thoroughbred racing has been a tradition at the Fair Grounds since 1872. The season runs generally from late November through the month of March. There is usually no racing on Mondays and Tuesdays. The $200,000 added New Orleans Handicap and $200,000 added Louisiana Derby, both run in March, attract the best 3 year olds in the country. A turf course was added in 1981.

The new computerized A.B.C. Mutuels makes every mutuel window an all betting and all cashing position.

The Clubhouse opens at 11:00 a.m. for lunch on one of three levels seating 2,000 race fans. Corned beef is the house specialty. Seat reservations are taken for the Turf Club. Both the Clubhouse and the Grandstand are glass enclosed. It is truly one of the finest racetracks in the country. The giant oaks of the Fair Grounds' infield and the Bugle Boy are part of the color of this, the third-oldest track in America. The first race post time is 12:45 p.m.

The huge parking lot accommodates 3,000 cars. F ee $2. General admission is $2; Clubhouse $4. Discounts and catering are available to groups of 25 or more.

The track is convenient (10 minutes) to French Quarter hotels via Esplanade to Bayou Road which becomes Gentilly Blvd.

THE GARDEN DISTRICT

Map, pg. 269

In the lush antebellum decades, Louisiana beyond New Orleans was almost completely rural. The wealth of the state was controlled by less than three percent of the population. Aristocratic Creoles showed less passion for the accumulation of wealth than the Americans and immigrants who poured into the city following the Louisiana Purchase. The population doubled within ten years of statehood. The steamboat appeared in 1811, and with it the rise of the great plantations. By 1833 the sugar and cotton exports were valued at $20 million. New Orleans became one of the great export ports in the world. Steamboats lined the levee unloading cargos from the heartland of America, and reloading with every conceivable type of goods for the return trip.

In the 1840's this trade produced great wealth, and the great plantation homes, and mansions in the Garden District were built. Plantation families had two homes, and two seasons. New Orleans was not only their economic capital, it was their social and cultural center as well. The rich Americans, snubbed by Vieux Carre Creole society, created their own municipalities, and developed home sites along the route of the New Orleans & Carrollton Railroad. The railroad track is precisely the same right-of-way now used by the St. Charles streetcar. Then, as now, it provides convenient transportation to Canal Street and the financial district.

The rural area which was transformed by palatial mansions on spacious landscaped grounds came to be known as the Garden District. Its boundaries are Jackson Avenue to Louisiana Avenue, about 13-blocks, and St. Charles Avenue to Magazine Street toward the river, a distance of 5-blocks. Washington Avenue is the mid-point of the district, and it is a good place to leave the St. Charles Avenue streetcar if you are exploring by foot.

As you explore the residential streets shaded by live oak, magnolias, and palm trees, and see the Victorian turrets, cupolas and gingerbread rising from wide lawns, you will appreciate how the district earned its name. Please remember that the homes in the Garden District are private, and except for Spring Fiesta, and other special occasions when some of the residences are open for tour, no trespassing is the rule.

LEE CIRCLE

When the monument to the South's most beloved warrior was dedicated in February 1884, 15,000 people, including the late general's daughters attended the ceremonies. General Beauregard himself had been the major fundraiser for the R.E. Lee Monumental Association.

The 16-foot bronze likeness of Robert E. Lee shows the general in full uniform, his arms folded as if surveying his troops. The statue, atop a 96-foot granite shaft, faces north. The monument was torn down and reconstructed in 1953-54 when problems were discovered in its foundation. Today the imposing monument separates the busy traffic at Howard and St. Charles Avenues.

CONFEDERATE MEMORIAL HALL

929 Camp St.   Map, pg. 105

This is a "must see" for Civil War buffs. Several Confederate Veteran organizations desired a common place of deposit for their historical material and were accommodated by philanthropist Frank T. Howard. Out of this effort came the Louisiana Historical Association in 1889, and the construction of the brown pressed brick museum and meeting hall dedicated in 1891.

The large hall-like exhibition room with exposed oak beams in the ceiling was the place where Jefferson Davis, president of the Confederacy, lay in state after his death in New Orleans in 1893. Bloodstained flags, sections of tree trunks mutilated with shot of all sizes, and a Washington Artillery cannon, which 13 men died to defend, attest to the cruelty of that long ago war.

In addition to the uniforms and arms, a set of medical instruments, and part of Robert E. Lee's camp silver service is displayed. Open 10-4, Mon.-Sat. Adults $1, students 50 cents, children under 12, 25 cents. The Hall is only about a block from Lee Circle.

LAFAYETTE SQUARE

All the streets in New Orleans originated by the common law of dedication. When land was subdivided, and streets created, the land owner donated the streets to the public. John Gravier not only conveyed the streets, but a public square when he developed his property along what is now St. Charles Avenue. He later changed his mind, and wanted the square back, but the courts refused him. The square got its name in 1824 following the visit of the French hero of the American Revolution.

Lafayette Square is the second oldest square in the city, and was an important gathering place when Gallier Hall was a city hall. The statues of John McDonogh, a 19th century philanthropist, Henry Clay, the Kentucky statesman and orator who was popular in the city, and Benjamin Franklin adorn the green oasis. In 1852, the square was the scene of an elaborate memorial funeral for Clay, Daniel Webster and John C. Calhoun, and in 1874 it was the rallying point for the White League prior to their battle with "the carpet-bag government."

GALLIER HALL

545 St. Charles   **Map, pg. 105**   Map, pg.

When New Orleans was operating as three separate municipalities, the American sector, the Second Municipality, built a glittering Greek Revival city hall designed by architect James Gallier, Sr. Gallier Hall was built between 1845 and 1850, and in 1853, when the city was united under one administration, it replaced the Cabildo as a city hall.

Rex, the King of Carnival, pauses to toast dignitaries at the old city hall when his Mardi Gras parade reaches this point each year.

In 1957, the opening of a new civic center relocated the seat of city government, and the venerable building on St. Charles was renamed to honor its architect. The building today accommodates wedding receptions, and other private parties on a rental basis.

WOMEN'S GUILD HOME

2504 Prytania St.   **Map, pg. 269**   899-1945

This is the only house in the Garden District open to the public on a regular basis. Its restoration and maintenance is the work of the Women's Guild of the New Orleans Opera Association. The house was built in 1858, and is a hybrid of the traditional galleried Greek Revival style associated with the Garden District, and the Italianate style. The interior mahogany balusters, intricate cornice work, and ceiling medallion reflect the Italianate style. Many artifacts reflect the elegant tastes of New Orleans' golden age.

The Guild Home is open from one to four p.m. Monday through Friday for tours. Closed in August.

"JEFFERSON DAVIS" HOUSE

1134 First St.   **Map, pg. 269**

This house is often refered to as the Jefferson Davis house because he died in one of its ground floor rooms in 1889, but the Confederate President was

ST. CHARLES AVENUE STREET CAR ROUTE

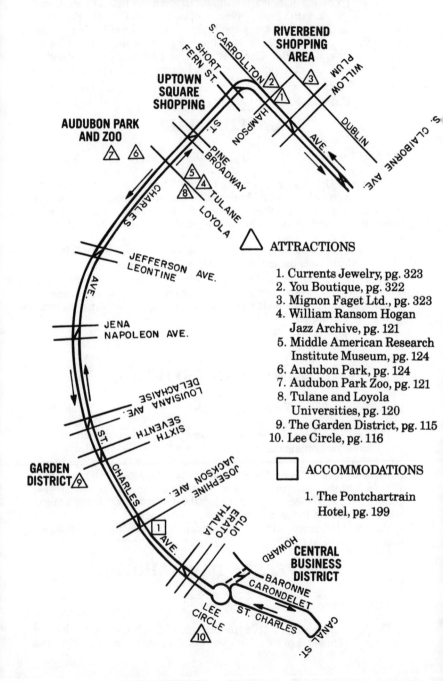

△ ATTRACTIONS

1. Currents Jewelry, pg. 323
2. You Boutique, pg. 322
3. Mignon Faget Ltd., pg. 323
4. William Ransom Hogan Jazz Archive, pg. 121
5. Middle American Research Institute Museum, pg. 124
6. Audubon Park, pg. 124
7. Audubon Park Zoo, pg. 121
8. Tulane and Loyola Universities, pg. 120
9. The Garden District, pg. 115
10. Lee Circle, pg. 116

☐ ACCOMMODATIONS

1. The Pontchartrain Hotel, pg. 199

only a frequent guest of his friend Judge Charles Fenner. After the Civil War Davis enjoyed the hospitality of this beautiful 1850's house and gardens. He wrote **The Rise and Fall of the Confederate Government** here, and introduced his daughter to New Orleans society from its portals. When he became ill at Beauvoir, his plantation home in Biloxi on the Mississippi Gulf Coast, Davis was brought to Judge Fenner's home for care. The home remained in the hands of Fenner's descendants until 1935.

LAFAYETTE CEMETERY NO. 1

Washington & Prytania   **Map, pg. 269**   Map, pg.

This cemetery was planned for the city of Lafayette, as the Garden District was called then, in 1833. By 1852 the victims of yellow fever had almost filled it. Burial here, as in all New Orleans cemeteries, is above ground. A city of individual tombs is walled in by rows of burial ovens.(See Legends, Cemetery for details on burial practices.) Note the group tombs, and the many foreign names of immigrants who did not survive the Bronze John season.

THE ORNAMENTAL IRONWORK OF NEW ORLEANS

The cast-iron industry in New Orleans dates from the establishment of the Leeds Iron Foundry in 1825, and reached its peak just prior to the Civil War. Ornamental cast iron was most popular during the 1850's. New Orleans then enjoyed a decade of astounding prosperity, and hundreds of ironworkers were listed in the city directory.

Most of the decorative iron work that you see in the streets of the French Quarter and the Garden District is cast iron as differentiated from wrought iron. The difference in the product is the variance of its carbon content and thus its workability. Wrought iron has less carbon and is a malleable substance which can be shaped by hammering, stretching, or rolling. Craftsmen work with heated bars, rods, and plates and shape them into decorative forms on an anvil. The product is strong, dense, and very resistant to rust.

Cast iron contains much more carbon, and is a brittle substance which can fracture on impact. The material, available in pigs, is melted in a furnace of 2,000 to 3,000 degrees, and the molten metal is poured into a mould prepared from a laboriously carved pattern. The pattern is generally pressed into fine sand which accepts the impression of the detailed pattern. The finished product has a rough surface on the interior parts, and should be painted for protection against rust.

Some early fences combine wrought iron members with small decorative cast iron castings. Generally, cast iron products replaced the earlier wrought iron decorations.

The Golden Age of Cast Iron

During the golden age of cast iron, iron products were advertised as "cheaper than wood." In 1859, Wood Miltenberger & Co. offered 200 varieties of gallery railings, and 50 patterns for verandas. Styles included Gothic, Classical, geometric patterns and naturalistic ones. Naturalistic was the most popular in New Orleans. Look for roses, fuchsias, morning glories, acorns, oak leaves, fruit, and trailing vines imitated in iron along your walking tour.

Cast iron was also used for window lintels, or mouldings. Often they were painted to appear like stone. Cast iron replaced carved wood for Ionic and Doric fluted columns, Corinthian capitals and bases, tie-ends, stairs, rosettes, cornices, ventilators, and downspout boots. Ceiling centerpieces, fireplace fronts, and mantels were also popular. Cast iron fences were often used to surround tombs, and sometimes the tomb itself was cast in iron. Cast iron garden furniture, fountains, and other ornaments were also manufactured.

Classic Examples of Cast Iron Today

The full cast iron verandahs with the "AP" monogram on the Pontalba Buildings flanking Jackson Square are probably the earliest in the city. They date from 1849. The wood pattern for the monogram was carved in New Orleans to the Baroness Pontalba's design. The iron work was cast in New York, and it was originally painted a bronze color.

The home of architect James Gallier at 1132 Royal Street is a rare surviving example of a verandah cast in the popular rose and tendril pattern. The five supporting columns and the elaborate door grill are also cast iron. The work is circa 1860.

The Garden District home at the corner of Fourth and Prytania Streets is surrounded by a distinctive cast iron fence resembling cornstalks and morning glory vines. The fence is now green, but when it was erected in 1859 it was probably hand painted in naturalistic colors. A local foundry, Wood, Miltenberger & Co. cast the fence as well as the rose and geometric patterned verandah. Another "cornstalk fence" can be seen in the French Quarter at 915 Royal Street.

New Orleans is a treasury of ornamental iron work. Keen observers will be rewarded by the fascinating variety and detail of the iron workers craft as they walk the streets of the older parts of the city.

TULANE AND LOYOLA UNIVERSITIES

6300-6400 St. Charles

Tulane University began as the Medical College of Louisiana in 1834, and later merged with the University of Louisiana. A $1 million bequest by Paul Tulane in 1883 united the two institutions under one name. The medical school is now located on Tulane Avenue near Charity Hospital, but most other departments, including the law school, are on this campus. The Napoleonic

Code is still taught and used in Louisiana as a system of law. Sophie Newcomb Memorial College for Women is now an undergraduate college for Tulane. Sugar Bowl Stadium was once located behind the academic buildings. The stadium is gone, but the tradition continues at the Superdome.

Loyola University is the largest Catholic university in the South. It was established by the Jesuits in 1911. The church on the Loyola campus is Holy Name of Jesus Church which dates from 1911. Its spire can be seen over the oak trees from Audubon Park.

Audubon Place is one of the last privately owned streets in the city. The gatehouse protects the so-called "millionaire's row." The white house near the gate is the home of the Tulane University president.

THE WILLIAM RANSOM HOGAN JAZZ ARCHIVE

Tulane University Library   865-6634

The Jazz Archive was originally conceived as a depository for the collection of oral history related to the development of New Orleans jazz. Its holdings now include 1,500 oral history tapes of personalities associated with jazz, recordings of jazz music, sheet music, photographs, scrapbooks, documents memorabilia, and some 13,000 books and 12,000 issues of serials.

This is not a museum. There is limited exhibit area, and access to the collection must be arranged by appointment. For use of the reading and listening rooms, call or write the Director of the Archive.

AUDUBON PARK ZOO

6500 Magazine Street   861-2537

This attraction deserves special mention because it is developing into a world-class zoological garden. Only a few years ago the zoo itself seemed endangered. Then a spirited revitalization took place which attracted citizen, government, and corporate support. The results are still in development, but already the Audubon Park Zoo is outstanding. Its 58 acres are lush in tropical vegetation, waterfalls, lagoons, and century-old oak trees. More than 1,000 animals, many in natural habitat, can be seen among its major exhibits.

The Zoo's largest exhibit is Grasslands of the World where animals and birds from the African Savannah, the South American pampas, and the North American Grasslands roam freely together. The Mombasa Safari Railroad ride is a convenient way to see this 20-acre exhibit. The informative guided tour ride has a separate admission; however the animals may also be seen on foot.

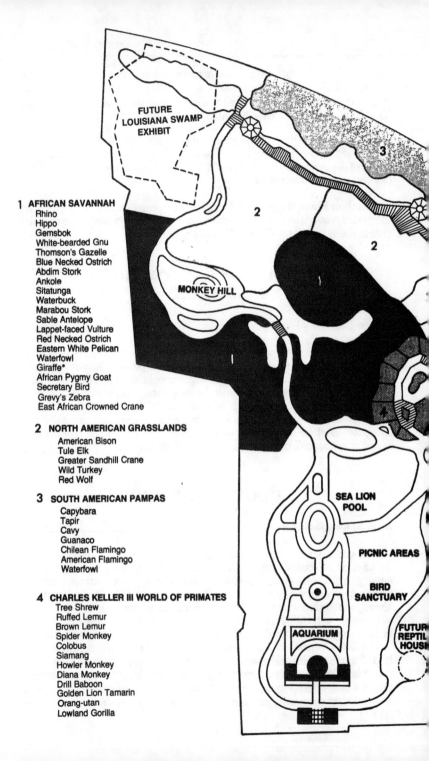

FUTURE LOUISIANA SWAMP EXHIBIT

3

2

2

MONKEY HILL

1 AFRICAN SAVANNAH
Rhino
Hippo
Gemsbok
White-bearded Gnu
Thomson's Gazelle
Blue Necked Ostrich
Abdim Stork
Ankole
Sitatunga
Waterbuck
Marabou Stork
Sable Antelope
Lappet-faced Vulture
Red Necked Ostrich
Eastern White Pelican
Waterfowl
Giraffe*
African Pygmy Goat
Secretary Bird
Grevy's Zebra
East African Crowned Crane

2 NORTH AMERICAN GRASSLANDS
American Bison
Tule Elk
Greater Sandhill Crane
Wild Turkey
Red Wolf

3 SOUTH AMERICAN PAMPAS
Capybara
Tapir
Cavy
Guanaco
Chilean Flamingo
American Flamingo
Waterfowl

4 CHARLES KELLER III WORLD OF PRIMATES
Tree Shrew
Ruffed Lemur
Brown Lemur
Spider Monkey
Colobus
Siamang
Howler Monkey
Diana Monkey
Drill Baboon
Golden Lion Tamarin
Orang-utan
Lowland Gorilla

SEA LION POOL

PICNIC AREAS

BIRD SANCTUARY

AQUARIUM

FUTURE REPTILE HOUSE

ZOO GUIDE

5 WISNER CHILDREN'S ZOO

6 ASIAN DOMAIN
Malayan Sun Bear
Striped Hyaena
Bengal Tiger
Axis Deer
Ruddy Shelduck
Nilgai
Blackbuck
Sarus Crane
Mandarin Duck
Asian Lion
Asian Elephant
Muntjac
Barasingha
Asian Leopard
Clouded Leopard

RESTROOMS

GIFTS

7 FOOD AND BEVERAGE

8 SAFARI TRAM STATION

ANIMAL HOLDING AREA

FUTURE AUSTRALIAN EXHIBIT

ELEPHANT RIDES

Giraffe

5

5

7

8

REFLECTION PLAZA

6

6

HOSPITAL

ED. BLDG.

ADMIN. BLDG.

BIRD HOUSE

DIXIE BEER GARDEN

7

Flight Cage

FUTURE RESTAURANT

ENTRANCE

Natatorium Drive

TENNIS COURTS

PARKING

The Wisner Children's Village is an activity center for children where they can pet friendly sheep and goats, and observe baby animals. A Nocturnal House reverses the day-night cycle for skunks, owls, and bats so that they can be seen in their active state.

The World of Primates and the Asian Domain include the popular monkeys, orangutans, and gorilla, and the big cats: lions, leopards, and tigers. There are elephants, of course, and even an opportunity to ride on the back of a huge pachyderm.

True to its namesake, the Audubon Park Zoo shows birds especially well. The Audubon Flight Exhibit, and the Tropical Bird House and Rainforest should not be missed on a visit to the zoo. The Sea Lion Pool at feeding time, and the Aquarium area also attract excited viewers.

There is a small hill just off the trail that passes through Grasslands of the World which is the subject of a local legend. It is said that Monkey Hill was built so that the children of New Orleans, living in a flat, marshy environment, could see it and thus understand the concept of hills. Aside from the raised wooden walkways that carry visitors over many of the habitat exhibits, Monkey Hill is the highest elevation in the park.

The Zoo is open 9:30 to 4:30 weekdays, and until 5:30 on weekends and holidays during daylight savings time. Admission is $2.50, adults; and $1.50, children (3-15). The Mombasa Train Ride is $1. Parking is free. Wheelchair and stroller rentals available. Food services and a gift shop are also located within the Zoo.

AUDUBON PARK

St. Charles Avenue   Map, pg.

The statue of John James Audubon is posed in a grove of trees as if the naturalist were still making notes for his bird studies. The alleys of live oak in the park date from the days when Etienne de Bore first granulated sugar here on his plantation in 1794. The 340-acre public park begins with an 18-hole golf course on the St. Charles Avenue side, and then spreads in a large rectangle down to the river. The golf course area was once the site of the World's Industrial and Cotton Centennial Exposition in 1884-85. The Exposition was a financial disaster, and there is no trace of its main exhibition hall which was once the largest building in the world.

The major entrances to the park are at St. Charles Avenue, and at Magazine St. where public bus service goes to Canal St. near the French Quarter. The Magazine St. entrance is convenient to the Zoo, swimming pool, and tennis courts. There are many shaded pathways for walking or bike riding. Bike rentals are available. Picnic areas, gazebos, shelters, and playgrounds are scattered throughout the park.

MIDDLE AMERICAN RESEARCH INSTITUTE MUSEUM

6823 St. Charles Avenue   865-4511

The Museum is reached by stairs to the right of the main entrance of Dinwiddie Hall, one of the three original stone Gothic structures of Tulane University. On the fourth floor there is a large single gallery displaying artifacts from all ages of Middle American culture.

The collection has been growing since 1924, and includes finds from pre-Columbian sites, and casts and models of the Mayan period.

Hours are 9-4 Mond.-Thurs., and 9-12 Fri. No admission.

URSULINE MUSEUM

2635 State Street   866-1472

The 12 acre site of the Ursuline Convent and Academy is the fourth home of the Sisters of Saint Ursula since their arrival in New Orleans in 1727. The museum is on the second floor of the Tudor-Gothic styled main building. Three rooms of exhibits contain antique items for the Mass, personal items of the Sisters, and documents relating to their historic role in New Orleans.

The Old Ursuline Convent dating from 1750 is on Chartres Street in the French Quarter. The State Street convent dates from 1915.

The museum is open 10-1 on Tues. & thurs. Adults $1.50, children 75 cents.

LEE BARNES COOKING SCHOOL

8400 Oak   866-0246

Lee Barnes is a well known and respected name in the art of cooking. The new Riverbend location of her cooking school also houses a complete gourmet kitchen shop. It contains "everything from toothpicks to copper pots."

Visitors to New Orleans will be interested in the Lee Barnes Wednesday afternoon Creole Cooking classes. The single session course begins at 2 p.m., and lasts about 2½ hours. The fee is $15, and reservations should be made two days prior to the class.

On Saturdays at 2 p.m. there is always a free cooking demonstration at Lee Barnes. At other times, there are single session and multiple session courses (usually four weekly 2½ hour sessions) in ethnic and specialty cooking. In addition to Creole, Classic French, Chinese, and Italian courses, as well as seasonal specialties such as candy making, are offered. About once a month a famous visiting chef will appear at the school for a special demonstration.

The Lee Barnes school has held classes since 1976. A major New Orleans hotel even offers a visitor package which includes courses at this established institution.

OTHER BOOKS IN THE INSIDERS' GUIDE SERIES

If you enjoyed **The Insiders Guide to New Orleans** you will want to have other books in the Insiders' Guide series.

THE INSIDERS GUIDE TO SOUTHEASTERN VIRGINIA is the complete guidebook to Colonial Williamsburg, Jamestown, Yorktown, Virginia Beach, Norfolk, Hampton, Newport News and the adjacent area. Added attractions include Kings Dominion (with detailed map), The James River Plantations, and Dismal Swamp. Here is what reviewers have said about this book: "The best and most informative guide to Tidewater Virginia that you can get." **Richmond Times-Dispatch.** "If you expect to explore that portion of Historic America this year, Insiders' Guide should be your constant companion." **Seattle Post.** 392 pgs., Illustrated, Indexed, ISBN 0-932338-00-3.

THE INSIDERS GUIDE TO THE OUTER BANKS OF NORTH CAROLINA is the comprehensive guide to Kill Devil Hills, Roanoke Island, Kitty Hawk, Nags Head, Hatteras, and Ocracoke. It is full of fascinating legend and lore, and has a complete fishing guide chapter. Here is what critics have said: "We'd paraphrase the television commercial to say of their book, 'Don't leave home without it.' " **The West Virginia Hillbilly.** "It answers geological, historical and practical questions, and it doesn't give the subject an impersonal all-is-rosy brochure treatment. The book is as much for reading as for guiding." **Charlotte News.** 280 pgs., Illustrated, Indexed, ISBN 0-932338-01-1.

THE INSIDERS GUIDE TO OCEAN CITY MARYLAND has been called "without a doubt the most informative, comprehensive, and interesting publication ever seen regarding Ocean City." Over 70 restaurants, and 60 hotels and motels are profiled including prices. Special chapters on fishing, marinas, attractions, recreations, and shopping make this book the ultimate travel reference to Ocean City and the Delmarva Peninsula. Coverage includes Assateague Island, the Chesapeake Bay Islands, Crisfield, Easton, St. Michaels, the Lower Delaware Coast and Dover. 336 pgs., Illustrated, Indexed, ISBN 0-932338-02-X.

HOW TO ORDER
To order by mail, send $4.95 plus 65 cents postage for each book with your name and mailing address to:

Insider Guides
2475 Canal St./Suite 108
New Orleans, LA 70119

Insiders Guides are also available at Waldens, B. Daltons, and other leading booksellers.

LAKE FRONT

LAKESHORE DRIVE

Map, pg. 170

This scenic 5 1//2-mile boulevard follows the lakefront from near the New Orleans Lake Front Airport to the old lighthouse at the West End. The airport is a general aviation facility for private and charter aircraft. Sightseeing flights in small planes are available here. Lakeshore Drive passes the University of New Orleans campus, Pontchartrain Beach, and miles of public areas adjacent to the terraced seawall.

During the hot weather months Lakeshore Drive is bumper to bumper on weekends as New Orleanians look for a picnic spot, or a place to lie in the sun. The shallow water shore is not suitable for swimming, but the people, the lake breeze, and the movement of sailboats on the expanse of water are an attraction.

The large fountain in Lakeshore Park is the Mardi Gras Fountain. Plaques around its base recognize the Mardi Gras krewes, and when it is operational, lights play on the water in the Mardi Gras colors, purple, green, and gold.

PONTCHARTRAIN BEACH
AMUSEMENT PARK

Elysian Fields Ave. & Lakeshore Dr.   **Map, pg. 170**   288-7511

From the Sky Lift on the shores of Lake Pontchartrain you can see the skyline of downtown New Orleans on the Mississippi River. Looking toward the 23-mile wide lake, sailboats, and a few ocean-sized freighters come into view. For the more adventurous, a ride on the Ragin' Cajun, a roller coaster with a 360-degree loop and upside-down curve, can be next. There are about 100 rides, games and live entertainments going on in this clean, well run, family amusement center. It has elements of the old style boardwalk parks like Ocean City, MD, and the more modern theme parks like Kings Dominion or Disneyworld.

The amusement park is open from late March through Labor Day; 5 to midnight on weekdays, and 12 to 12 on weekends. There are limited and full ticket plans in the range of $4-$7. Parking is free.

WEST END LAKESHORE PARK

Lake Avenue   Map, pg. 170

The West End is the pleasure boating center of New Orleans. The small island-like park is surrounded by marinas, yacht clubs, and boats of every description. Adjacent to the park is the group of lakeside restaurants which has lured downtowners to the West End for decades.

The Southern Yacht Club here dates from the 1840's and is the second oldest in the country. Some of its yachtsmen have earned the Olympic Gold Medal.

Beginning in the 1870's a railroad carried city dwellers to the lakefront where one of the attractions might be a lake showboat docked at the West End.

LAKE PONTCHARTRAIN

Iberville named this large lake for the Minister of Marine in France. The Choctaw Indians had called it Okwata, or wide water. And wide it is: 25 miles wide and 40 miles long. The toll causeway which crosses it is the longest bridge in the world at 23 and 3/4-miles.

The lake has been an important waterway since Indian days. Through bayous, and Lake Borgne, the lake has access to the Mississippi Sound and the Gulf of Mexico. Ships from the lake enter the Port of New Orleans via the Inner Harbor Navigation Canal (or Industrial Canal) which connects with the Mississippi River below the French Quarter.

Lake Pontchartrain has been the training waters for many world class sailors. Its sudden storms, and variable shallows make it a formidable testing ground.

FAT CITY

Map, pg. 170

For Suburbanites in Jefferson Parish who wanted a piece of the French Quarter a little closer to home, Fat City was created. The area bordered by North Causeway Blvd., Veterans Blvd., Division Street and West Esplanade, offers a concentration of nightclubs, restaurants, bars, cafes, and specialty shops. The emphasis in entertainment is disco and country-western music for dancing. More than ten Mardi Gras Krewes celebrate Carnival with parades on the standardized six mile Veterans Blvd. - Fat City route. From the Central Business District take I10 West and exit at the Causeway Blvd. North exit.

JEFFERSON DOWNS

Kenner Off I-10   Map, pg. 193   466-8521

The thoroughbred racing season here runs from early April through the end of October. Post time is 7:15 p.m. Wednesday through Saturday. (Check the current dates for Tuesday racing and holiday matinees.) The track is about 20-minutes from downtown. Special buses run from five major hotels. Make reservations through Southern Tours. Public express bus transportation leaves from South Liberty and Canal Streets starting at 5:30, and runs every 15-minutes until 6:30 p.m.

If you drive, we recommend the valet parking ($3). Admission to the huge, air-conditioned Clubhouse is $2.00. A full dinner menu is available beginning at 5:30, and there is drink service to your Clubhouse box. Grandstand admission is $1 for theater type seats on three levels. The lounge areas offer close circuit, color-TV coverage of the races. The track attracts a crowd of more than 5,000 fans on the weekends. Minors, 12 and older, may attend races with parents, but cannot bet. Winning tickets can be claimed for 120 days. (You can bet the Exactas, leave the track before the end of the 9-race program, and still collect.)

Special arrangements can be made for parties or groups. Races can even be named in honor of a business or group, and its representatives can make the presentation in the Winner's Circle, and have their photos taken with the horse and jockey.

RIVER ROAD PLANTATIONS

There had been plantations along the Mississippi before the steamboat appeared in 1812, but commerce by flatboats when compared to the steam powered packets was like a dirt country road being turned into a super highway. The steamboat seemed to be the final puzzle piece that turned large scale farming into the greatest enterprise of the century. The other key pieces were a method for the granulation of sugar from sugarcane syrup, and the abundance of slave labor. Sugar, especially on the plantations near New Orleans, generated great wealth in the decades between 1820 and 1860. Ironically, the dependence on slave labor that made the boom possible was also the instrument for its collapse as the nation divided and went to war with itself.

But in those antebellum years the romantic planters reveled in their good fortunes over the providences of nature, and set themselves to reap its fullness without fear or concern of the future. New Orleans was truly "the city that care forgot." The port city, overflowing with the products of the Mississippi, and bound in trade with the rest of the cultured world, became the most socially and culturally exciting city money could buy. Its style and decadence now traveled upriver by steamboat and transformed working farms into estates worthy of grand mansions.

A plantation was a working farm that was self-sufficient. In many respects, large plantations with their own sugar mills resembled small factory towns. In addition to the cash crops, garden produce and animals were cultivated to feed the owner's family and the workers. The family in the great house managed the farming enterprise with the aid of an overseer. It was no small occupation, and the first families who cleared the land and won it from the river were indeed hardy pioneers.

They built their homes to face the river and planted new rows of oaks to form a shaded canopy under which their guests could arrive. There were frequent house guests, and the visits were long. Large families and frequent entertaining required a large house, and the climate dictated design. From the clay at the river they made bricks. From the cypress swamps they cut beams and flooring to withstand the dampness. The roofs must be slanted to carry off the frequent rains, and the house must be built off the ground to escape the river's floods. A garconniere would be built to give the young men of the family and their sometimes rowdy guests privacy. The kitchen would be away from the main house to avoid the danger of fire. An overseer's office would have to be nearby, and perhaps some pigeon

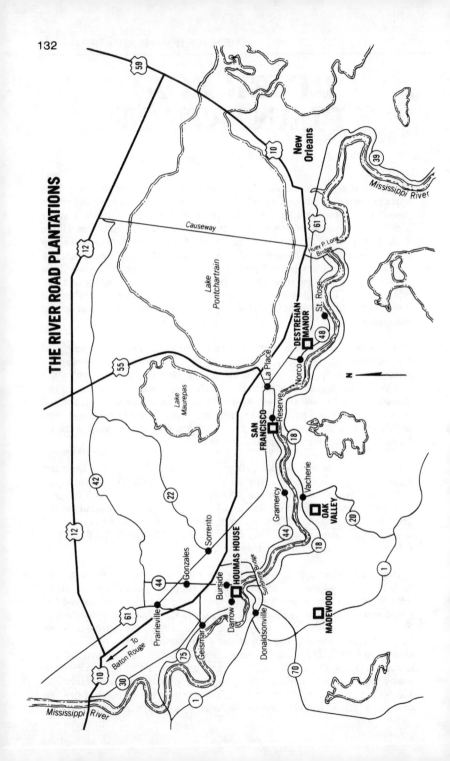

THE RIVER ROAD PLANTATIONS

houses. The stables, the mill, and the slave quarters would be constructed near the fields and out of sight of the house.

If you examine old maps of the mid 19th century you can see that hundreds of plantations fronted along the Mississippi River and the major bayous that afforded access to it. After 1865, the system that created the plantation economy crumbled, and in time so did its symbols, the mansions. Fire, disuse, industrial appropriation of the land, and natural disasters like floods and hurricanes have eradicated most of the evidence of the period. A few properties remain, and none of these are the legacies of the original owners. River Road, the highway that runs nearest to the Mississippi on both sides, is the main pathway to the proud edifices which have endured to link us to their era.

Tour buses are perhaps the easiest way to see the restored plantation houses for visitors to New Orleans. The Gray Line, Southern Tours, and Dixieland Tours offer all-day (6 1/2 hour) excursions to the plantation country for under $25 per person. Each tour includes a commentary as you travel along the River Road, a stop-over at two of the five plantations in the area offering tours, and a luncheon break at a colorful restaurant usually serving Cajun specialties. Lunch cost is not included. (See the Tour section for more detailed information.)

HOUMAS HOUSE

La. Rt. 942   522-2262

Houmas House is one of the most photographed plantation homes in America. **National Georgraphic, House Beautiful, Holiday** and other national publications have focused attention on its grandeur, and it has been used as a set by movie companies. The Bette Davis film "Hush, Hush, Sweet Charlotte" was shot here.

The house itself was built in 1840 by the daughter of Revolutionary War General Wade Hampton. She and her husband wisely preserved the original four-room dwelling at the rear of the mansion. It dates from Spanish colonial days and is connected to the main house by an arched carriage way. In 1857, the house and its 10,000 acres were purchased by Irishman John Burnside for about $2 million. Burnside expanded the property to 20,000 acres, and built four mills to process the vast fields of sugar cane. It made Burnside the largest sugar producer in America. Houmas House was saved from the Civil War disasters that befell other properties when Burnside prevented Union General Ben Butler from occupying his plantation. He declared immunity as a British subject.

Even after Burnside died in 1881, and the plantation passed to another family, it produced 20 million pounds of sugar a year. The plantation stayed active until 1899.

Credit for the authentic restoration of Houmas House, which derived its name from the Indians who once occupied these lands, goes to Dr. George B. Crozat of New Orleans. He purchased the house and the remaining grounds in 1940 and spent the last 25 years of his life restoring it to its former elegance.

The live oaks, magnolias, lawns, and formal gardens frame the fabled 2 1/2-story house. The dormered roof, supported by 14 white columns on three sides, overhangs a wide second floor gallery. The style is Greek Revival. Adjacent to the mansion are two hexagonal brick garconnieres, or bachelor residences. The colonial kitchen is completely restored with a collection of copper and brass utensils. Inside the main house, the three story spiral staircase is an artful engineering masterpiece. The low door knobs, and the scale of the beds and fine antique furniture attest that people were smaller in the 19th century than they are today. The standing mirrors near the floor, however, were for ladies to check their petticoats.

Houmas house is open daily 10-4. Adults $3.50. The property goes down to the levee. Riverboats still dock occasionally at the plantation's wharf.

OAK ALLEY

La. Rt. 18   523-4351

Some 300 years ago an unknown settler carefully planted 28 live oak trees exactly 80 feet apart so as to form an alley to the Mississippi River. Perhaps a humble frontier cabin stood at the head of the two rows of small trees. By 1832, when Jacques Roman came to build his 70-feet square Greek Revival mansion on the site, the quarter-mile avenue of live oaks was already an impressive 100-years old. Roman set his home at the head of the oaks and surrounded his structure with 28 fluted Doric columns to match the number of trees. Although Roman named his estate Bon Sejour. people seeing the pink plaster-over-brick house between the great oaks called it instinctively Oak Alley. The name stuck.

After its period of grandeur Oak Alley was abandoned until 1914. In 1926 Mr. and Mrs. Andrew Stewart acquired the house and restored it to the point that it was designated a National Historic Landmark. The restoration is incomplete, and the furnishings reflect the tastes of the now deceased Stewarts rather than an authentic period collection. Former staff members show the house to visitors.

The magic of Oak Alley is the view from the broad second-story gallery as you look up the alley of oaks toward the river, and the walk under the canopy of oaks to look back at the house from nearer the river. These two views have attracted many commerical photography crews. Oak Alley is open daily 9-5:30. Admission is $3.50.

SAN FRANCISCO

La. Rt. 44   535-2341

In 1849 Edmond Bozonier Marmillion envisioned a house that would capture the feeling of a grand steamboat. Its broad gallery would be like a ship's deck. Its twin front stairs would be like those leading to a steamboat's grand salon. The house, like the pleasure palaces which floated on the river, would teem with scroll work, fluted pillars, and rococo grillwork. Marmillion poured money into his dream house, his "san frusquin" (one's all), until he was "sans fruscin" (broke). He died, and his son, Valsin, finally completed the house in 1854. Perhaps the headlines of the San Francisco gold rush of 1849 aided in the corruption of "san frusquin" to San Francisco House.

The house, and others which mix the raised cottage look with Victorian gingerbread, and Gothic facades have been forever designated "Steamboat Gothic" from a 1952 novel of the same name by Frances Parkinson Keyes. The action of the novel takes place on the San Francisco plantation.

When you see the interior of San Francisco you will understand why Marmillion gave his all. The walls and ceilings are alive with the delicately colored frescos of Dominique Canova, and each room has its measure of hand carved woodwork. These and other remarkable features of the house were faithfully restored in 1954. 18th century French and English furniture, paintings, and china help to make the restoration complete. The Marathon Oil Company is to be congratulated for preserving this landmark.

Open daily except for major holidays. Admission $4.25 for adults; $3.00 (ages 12-17), $2.00 (ages 6-11).

MADEWOOD

La. Rt. 308   524-1988

Colonel Thomas Pugh was the youngest of three brothers, and he set out to build a house that would be grander than his elder brother's mansion. For four years he supervised the cutting of cypress timbers and the making of bricks. Madewood refers to the fact that the wood was cut and trimmed on the plantation itself. He spent another four years in construction, making a Greek Revival structure of 20 rooms, with 25-foot ceilings. Details included a carved, winding walnut staircase, a huge ballroom, and the "modern" convenience of built-in closets. Pride, in this case, certainly came before a fall. Pugh died in 1848, a yellow fever victim, just before the house was ready to be occupied.

The Harold K. Marshall family restored Madewood in 1964. The two-storied white Ionic columns gleam, the old kitchen is restored with antiques, and the rest of the house has been elegantly furnished in period furniture. The plantation on the Bayou Lafourche once covered 3,000 acres. Its mansion is one of the best-preserved antebellum homes in the South.

Open for tours daily 10-5. Admission $3.

DESTREHAN MANOR

La. Rt. 48   Map, pg.

This manor house may be the oldest plantation mansion left intact on the Mississippi. It was built between 1787 and 1790 when New Orleans was a Spanish colony. The style reflects the influence of the West Indies. Double galleries supported by Doric columns are shaded by a hipped roof. The two wings are additions to the original building which has undergone remodeling over the years.

The American Oil Company deeded the unrestored Destrehan property to the River Road Historical Society which has undertaken the task of saving this important example of early plantation architecture. The exterior has been repainted, and the interior decorated with pieces typical of the early plantation period. Exhibits include insights into the methods of constructing the house itself. The grounds include some of the oldest live oaks in Louisiana.

Open 10-4 Admission $3.

NOTTOWAY

La. Route 405 River Road   504-545-2730

Nottoway, the South's largest plantation home is magnificently restored and reflects the absolute height of plantation opulence and grandeur. Listed on the National Register, this palatial mansion was designed by the famous New Orleans architect, Henry Howard for Mr. and Mrs. John Hampden Randolph and his family of eleven children. The mansion was ten years in the planning to its completion in 1859, when riverboat passengers exclaimed as Nottoway came into view that surely this was "The White Castle of Louisiana."

This American castle has 64 rooms with over 53,000 square feet under roof. One of few southern mansions providing breath taking views of the Mississippi River, this castle also features a magnificent white ballroom adorned with hand carved corinthian colums.

Nottoway featured many unusual amenities for the time period including gas lighting, indoor plumbing with bath rooms, 26 original closets, six interior staircases, 200 windows and 165 doors. This magnificent mansion has never been left vacant, thus it retains its original splendor and it has always remained a private home.

Internationally acclaimed as an American castle, the mansion offers Louisiana cusine served daily in the home between 11 a.m. and 3 p.m. and overnight accommodations in the mansion with advance reservations

Open for tours daily from 9 to 5. Admission $4.00.

AN INVITATION FROM MONTY

Over the years I have discovered that all my friends have something in common: they all want me to bring them a great bargain from my next trip. With inflation high, and the cost of travel so dear, having an experienced shopper on your side is a real advantage.

Since part of my reporting job is to seek out unusual shops and items of exceptional value, I often meet artisans and manufacturers. In recent years I have learned about importing items of exceptional value and craftsmanship, and have passed the benefits along to my friends. Their enthusiasm has encouraged me to consider buying larger and larger quantities whenever I can find something really exciting.

Generally I can recommend only one or two items on a trip. Sometimes, for a variety of reasons, I come home empty handed. Nevertheless, if you would like to see the results of my latest trip, please send me a self addressed stamped envelope and I will send you a description of the items and their cost. If you want the item, send me a check. When you receive the item and you are disappointed for any reason, return it and I will give you a complete refund.

My policy is to honor all requests on a first come, first served basis. When the item is sold out, regretfully I'll have to return your check.

I appreciate the fact that you have purchased my book, and thus allow me to continue to travel and write about what interests you. I hope that in the next year I can find an exceptional bargain on a virgin wool sweater, a hand made ornamental lacquered box, or some silver jewelry by a skilled craftsman. In 1981, I discovered an American custom clock maker, for example, who has made some beautiful fine wood wall clocks for my friends.

If you'd like to share in my next travel shopping discovery, send the self addressed stamped envelope to me, Monty Joynes, Insiders Guides, 2475 Canal St./Suite 108, New Orleans, LA 70119.

THE MARDI GRAS

Mardi Gras is French for Fat Tuesday, that feasting day before Ash Wednesday when the penitential season of Lent calls for 40-days of lean abstinence prior to Easter. Mardi Gras is the culmination of the Carnival season which begins on the Epiphany or Twelfth Night (January 6th) and ends on Shrove Tuesday. Carnival translates "farewell to flesh," and for centuries Christians have made it a time of uninhibited reveling.

The idea of Mardi Gras was deeply rooted in the heart of French people. It is perhaps the fullest and most accurate expression of the New Orleans spirit for New Orleanians have always loved a procession. Their history is full of parades, delirious street demonstrations, and outdoor pageantry. The Carnival season in New Orleans is not a manufactured tourist attraction with parades and balls scheduled almost every night for more than a month. It is rather a celebration for and by the people of New Orleans which happens to attract a multitude of onlookers.

The History of Mardi Gras

In 1699, the French explorer Iberville made his first camp on the Mississippi River. The date was March 3rd, and even in the wilderness it was a special day. Iberville named the point of land on the first great bend in the river Point Mardi Gras. Other than the adopted Indian names, it is the oldest place name on the entire Mississippi.

In French colonial times, the rich in New Orleans celebrated Mardi Gras at private masked balls while streets and taverns were left to the more rowdy public. With so much international intrigue and flag changing in Louisiana, it is little wonder that the Spanish and the new American governments prohibited the wearing of masks and the street celebrations of Mardi Gras. Finally however, French Quarter Creoles got permission for masquerade balls in 1823, and the wearing of masks in the streets in 1827.

In 1837 there was even a report of street parading, but most Mardi Gras reveling was still disorganized and growing increasingly violent and disreputable. By the 1850's Carnival behavior was so unsavory that there was a popular movement, supported by the press, to end the annual celebration.

Comus Saves Mardi Gras

On January 10, 1857, in the second floor club room of the Gem Bar at 127 Royal Street, 19 sensible men sat down to discuss how the Carnival could be saved and redirected toward order and dignity. The group formed a secret society and called it the Mistick Krewe of Comus. In doing so they coined the word "krewe," started the tradition of mythological namesakes, held the first organized street parade, used the first theme floats and costumes, and staged the first tableau ball. The Comus society not only saved Mardi Gras from its critics, but it also established the social traditions and pageantry which came to excite the entire city. In 1981, Comus celebrated the 125th anniversary of its first parade.

The City may have been going Anglo-American in the mid 19th century, but like so many other French and Spanish customs, the Protestants adopted Mardi Gras. They were catching the Latin joie de vie; "we prefer a merry nothing to a melancholy anything." The krewes of Twelfth Night Revelers (1870), Rex and Momus (1872) were formed, and then Proteus in 1882. New Orleans was on its way to a new tradition of Mardi Gras that could only be halted by war and natural disaster. When yellow fever canceled most of Carnival in 1879, the men of Comus used their parade and ball treasury as a relief fund for fever victims. No parades were held during the war years of 1918-1919, 1942-1945, and 1951 when Mars replaced Rex. Prohibition in 1920, the Great Depression in 1933, Hurricane Betsy in 1965, and the city police strike of 1979 also limited the magnitude of Mardi Gras for their own reasons.

Famous Parades

In the Reconstruction years of the 1870's, Mardi Gras krewes vented their pent-up feelings towards the Republican administration. In 1873, the theme of the Comus parade was "Missing Links to Darwin's Origin of Species." The mask of the Tobacco Grub bore a striking resemblance to the face of President Grant. A Hyena carrying a stolen silver spoon looked uncommonly like General Ben Butler. Each link seemed to have the face of a prominent national Republican. In 1877, Momus picked up on the moveable roast with a parade titled "Hades, a Dream of Momus." This time the ridicule was painful enough to reach Washington, and Louisiana Governor Nicholls was embarrassed enough to issue a formal apology. Nicholls, a carpetbagger himself, was among the politicians maligned in the parade.

The Mardi Gras Song and Colors

Alex Alexandrovitch, the Grand Duke of Russia, came to New Orleans during Carnival of 1872 in the romantic pursuit of a musical comedy star who was appearing in the city. True to its nature, New Orleans gave him a royal welcome, and when it was discovered that his favorite song was the lady's solo, "If Ever I Cease to Love You," every band in the Rex parade tried to play it. The royal duke and his lady moved on, but the song, trite and syrupy by today's standards, remained to be played year after year as the Mardi Gras anthem.

The royal colors and the Carnival flag were shown for the first time in the same parade honoring the Russian Grand Duke. But it was not until the Rex parade entitled "Symbolism of Colors" in 1892 that the public was informed that the purple, green, and gold represented justice, faith and power.

Carnival Traditions

The courts of Comus and Rex have been meeting as the climax to Carnival since 1882. The King of Rex is the King of Carnival, and it has always been a high honor to wear this crown. The Queen of Comus is the Queen of the Carnival, and she is selected from among the season's debutantes. The respective krewes parade on Mardi Gras day and keep a midnight rendezvous at the Municipal Auditorium, the site of their tableau balls.

The 100-year old tradition of krewe kings pausing on their parade route to toast assembled dignitaries at Gallier Hall, the old City Hall on St. Charles at Lafayette Square, was altered in 1958 when the route was changed to pass the new Civic Center. Tradition, however, won out, and by 1963 the Gallier Hall toasts were reinstated.

A 117-year old tradition ended in 1973 when the city issued a ban on parading through the French Quarter. The danger of fire was judged to be too great for the antique buildings, and the presence of massed floats could prevent fire fighting equipment from getting to the scene of the fire.

The flambeaux are kerosene torches carried traditionally by blacks dressed in white smocks and hoods. They dance wildly as they accompany various parades picking up tips thrown by an appreciative crowd. Being one of the flambeaux is exhausting and sometimes dangerous work. Momus, Comus, Proteus, and Babylon are famous for their flambeaux accompanied parades.

Parade "throws" have been dispersed along Carnival parade routes for a hundred years. In 1884, Rex threw coin-like medallions commemorating the World's Cotton Exposition, but it was not until 1960 with the issue of Rex's first doubloon that the aluminum coin craze began. Often the same krewe will issue doubloons in several colors showing the organization's coat of arms and founding date on one side and the parade theme and the year on the other. Bacchus threw one million, and Endymion two million doubloons in 1981. Some krewes also produce a limited edition (about 25,000) doubloon of anodized gold, or one of special design and weight to be thrown only by their captain. These throws become more valuable to collectors.

Throws in recent years have included millions of doubloons, the red Rameses necklace of Nefertari, krewe emblem drinking cups, key chains, minature footballs from the Gladiators, a sports-minded krewe, coasters, medallion beads, frisbees with krewe monograms, back scratchers, and coconut shaped beads thrown by Zulu. The monogramed Throw Cup is the new trend in throws.

Bacchus: The New Tradition

In the 1960's Carnival in New Orleans was dying from a variety of maladies. The old order of krewes was growing stale, and began to reuse previously decorated floats. There had been no new parade organizations formed in years. The hippie generation flocked into the city for the free annual show, and the crime in the Quarter had acquired a reputation that also drove tourists away.

Into this void, a new organization composed of businessmen without society credentials broke with the staid traditions of the past and infused Carnival with vitality.

Calling themselves Bacchus, they created super-sized floats, crowned Hollywood celebrities as their king, drove their floats into the Rivergate, and staged an elaborate dinner-dance for their members and guests. This infusion of spirit prompted the establishment of other krewes.

Prior to 1969, the only celebrity king to appear in a Carnival parade was Louis Armstrong, who reigned as Zulu in 1949. But Scatchmo was a native, the city's own, so that didn't count. It was Bacchus which broke with tradition in its first parade and made Danny Kaye its King. Bacchus also opened its ball to non-members, and paved the way for a new generation of krewe organizations that were not so tied to the noblesse oblige. Soon celebrities were riding in the lead float of many parades. Bob Hope, and other entertainment personalities from films and television, and sports stars have appeared.

The Krewes Parade

In recent years over 50 Krewes have paraded. Beginning in mid-February through Mardi Gras week, the parades are usually on weekends. During Mardi Gras week, they go daily, night and day. The parading is not confined to the St. Charles Avenue and Canal Street route; there are major street parades in ten locations within Orleans, Jefferson, and St. Bernard Parishes.

Krewes are formed and disbanded. Some have balls but do not parade, and vice versa. Parade routes and starting times change for a few parades each year. Carnival has no single overlord, or coordinating body. Anyone is free to form his own krewe, and organize a parade if he can get a city permit. In addition to the motorized, animated, thousand-plus member parades, there are also "Walkings Club" who make annual treks on routes especially selected for their abundance of bars. Pete Fountain's Half-Fast Walking Club is one of the more famous of these. The "Walking Clubs" do their "walking" early on Mardi Gras morning.

The bands that you see in the Carnival parades are from all over the nation. In order to attract them, several krewes sponsor marching band contests, and give trophies or cash awards. Alla, the 6th oldest parading organization, sponsors a contest, as do Pegasus, Selena, Mid-City, and Argus.

Carnival krewes are no longer made up of just secret, male only societies. There are business and civic organization krewes, women's club krewes, and even kiddie krewes. The largest krewe in recent years has been Endymion, with 800 members, 40 floats, two million doubloon throws, and a party for 9,000 at the Rivergate featuring entertainment by a host of star entertainers. The 1981 budget was over $1 million. For sheer length, the

Elks Orleanians produce a parade of 150 decorated flat bed trucks with 6,000 masked riders. It falls in behind the 25 float Rex parade, which has been preceded by the Zulu parade, which is culminated by the 6:30 p.m. starting of the Comus parade. From a position at Lafayette Square, or along St. Charles Avenue to Canal Street, one could see a constant parade from 8:30 in the morning until 10:00 at night. The person who held his ground would probably come away with a shopping bag full of throws. There are an estimated 45,000 New Orleans citizens actively participating in Carnival krewes, walking clubs, and truck parades. The average cost of participation is about $1,000 per person which includes costumes, ball tickets, and parade expenses. That's $45 million dollars a year spent on an 11-day party. The city of New Orleans spent another $1 million-plus for the necessary clean up and police overtime.

How to See Carnival

Room reservations during Carnival, and especially for the Mardi Gras weekend must be booked long in advance. Expect to pay a seasonal premium for the accommodation, and to pay for a minimum stay (usually four-days). Many of the best rooms are reserved on an annual basis. A tour package from a travel agent may be a good idea if you decide late that you have to see Mardi Gras this year.

The Carnival Balls are essentially private affairs. A few lucky ladies who are outsiders might be issued a "call out" card. The card entitles the lady to view the ball tableau from a reserved section. When the dancing begins, she is "called out" by the sender of the card for a whirl around the floor. The gentleman will give the lady a krewe favor before returning her to her escort. Others receive invitations to view the ball pageantry and tableaux from balcony theater-type seating.

Practical Advice

Most Carnival parades never seem to start on time. A great place to be during the waiting period is at the point where the parade originates. Although the floats are not yet moving, the excited krewe members often begin to throw to onlookers.

Downtown parades are always crowded, and they can be uncomfortable for families because of the frenzy for throws. Canal Street is often the worst place to be because the crowds are 20 to 30 people deep and often very pushy.

For night parades, select a well lighted area for viewing, and do not venture down dark side streets. Be mindful of your personal security.

There are reserved bleacher seats at Lee Circle, and at Lafayette Square on St. Charles. People on package tours, the elderly, and other interested spectators occupy these seats. They are not especially desirable if you are interested in collecting throws.

144

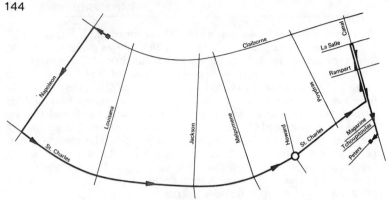

THE MARDI GRAS PARADE ROUTE OF REX

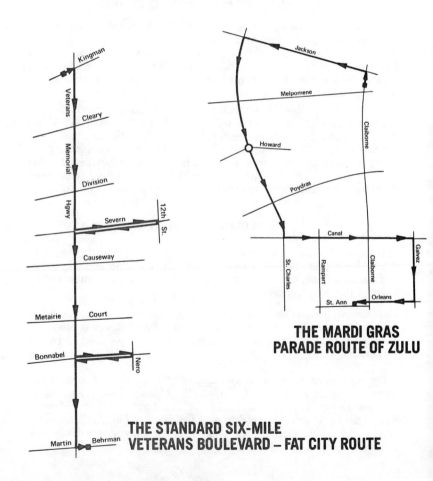

**THE MARDI GRAS
PARADE ROUTE OF ZULU**

**THE STANDARD SIX-MILE
VETERANS BOULEVARD – FAT CITY ROUTE**

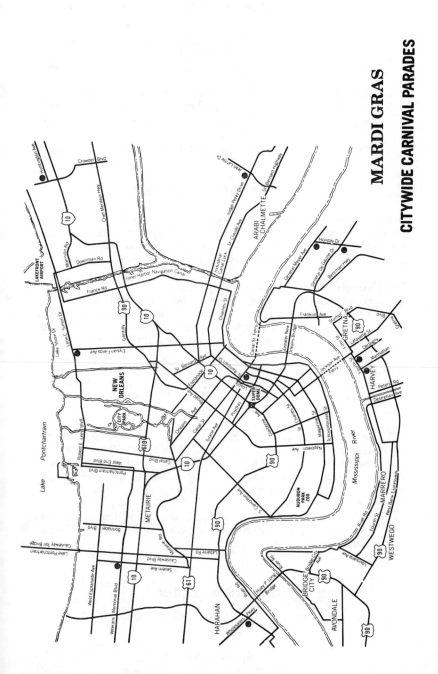

MARDI GRAS

CITYWIDE CARNIVAL PARADES

Parades Not To Miss

Bacchus	Celebrities and super-floats. Sunday night before Mardi Gras.
Endymion	The largest. Saturday night before Mardi Gras.
Mid-City	A children's parade with a battle of the bands. Midday Sunday before Mardi Gras.
Zulu	The famous black krewe. Mardi Gras early morning.
Rex	The King of Carnival. Mardi Gras mid-morning.

Other Things of Interest

Mardi Gras Indians There are blacks who spend a fortune on costuming themselves as Indians for Mardi Gras day. Their elaborate feathered costumes, war bonnets, and war paint can be seen as they dance along St. Charles and Canal Streets early on Fat Tuesday.

The French Quarter Parades may be banned from the quarter, but that does not mean that the streets are not overflowing with once-a-year sights. There are probably more costumes per block here than anywhere else in the city. The He-She people are especially evident, and they stage their own pageant on Bourbon Street during Mardi Gras day.

Costumes To join in the fun of Mardi Gras, wear a costume on Fat Tuesday. Many people unassociated with krewes, parades, or balls wear fantasy masks and clothing for the special day. It is traditional to unmask at midnight, ending the Carnival season.

The most practical guide to Carnival parades is issued annually by Arthur Hardy (P.O. Box 8058, New Orleans, La 70182). The booklet is called the **New Orleans Mardi Gras Guide**, and it has up-to-date information on the krewes and their parade routes. Mail order copies are available for $2.95, and the 80-page booklets are on the newsstands 30-days prior to Mardi Gras.

The Greater New Orleans Tourist and Convention Commission, 334 Royal St., New Orleans 70130 also provides updated Mardi Gras information on request.

Mardi Gras Dates

1982	February 23	1984	March 6
1983	February 15	1985	February 19

1986	February 11	1990	February 27
1987	March 3	1991	February 12
1988	February 16	1992	March 3
1989	February 7	1993	February 23

Mardi Gras is calculated to always fall 48 days before Easter.

ACCOMMODATIONS

New Orleans is perhaps the most unique city for hotel accommodations in the United States. There may be taller properties, and hotels with more rooms, and landmarks of curiosity in other cities, but no place in the country offers the depth and variety of public accommodations that are available in the Crescent City.

In a major convention city you expect to find Hilton, Hyatt Regency, Marriott, and Sheraton with huge meeting spaces, ballrooms, and a thousand-plus rooms. You are also not surprised to see a very large Fairmont and a Royal Sonesta; properties which enjoy good reputations in other cities. You even expect to find exceptional hotels like The Pontchartrain, The Royal Orleans, The Monteleone, Le Pavillon, and the International, all of which are New Orleans originals. The Holiday Inns, the Ramadas, the Best Westerns and other national chains are also in evidence and are to be expected.

What adds special dimension to the very competitive New Orleans hotel scene is the presence of so many high quality small and medium sized properties which are locally owned and operated. Primarily located within the French Quarter, these one-of-a-kind hotels utilize what is historic and native to the city's personality.

Taken all together, the New Orleans hotel community meets the needs and the pleasures of all guest categories. From strictly business to lovers on their honeymoon, there is a hotel in New Orleans with the class and the magic to meet the guest's greatest expectations.

Every profile in this section has been written after a personal inspection of the hotel property. The purpose of the profile is to guide you to a property that will suit the purpose and budget of your trip. A convention planner has one set of criteria; the head of a corporation another. A party on tour will have different objectives from a romantic couple. Vacationers with children and salesmen on the road obviously have different points of view about what they want in the way of hotel accommodations. The same person in New Orleans on a convention might desire a completely different type of hotel when he returns to the city on vacation. In profiling nearly 60 properties, the options in location, style, and price range are spelled out to aid you in your hotel selection. We have also included information on guest houses and campgrounds.

THE BASICS

Unless otherwise noted in the individual profile, the following policies, services and facilities can be expected:

Special Rates   Most hotels offer family plans, summer (off season) rates, and rates for military, government, commercial, and corporate guests. Special rates should be discussed and verified at the time of reservation.

Mardi Gras Rates Most hotels and motels demand their top rack (posted) rate, and a four-night, pre-paid reservation for this prime period. Choice rooms and suites are often reserved on an annual basis. Sugar Bowl and Super Bowl weekends also get top dollar with payment demanded prior to arrival.

Foreign Languages The international character of hotel staffing assures that French, Spanish, and German are spoken at most properties. Italian, Greek, Japanese, Chinese, Danish, Arabic, Hebrew, Turkish and Portuguese are also spoken at various locations.

Credit Cards American Express, Carte Blanche, Diners Club, Visa, and Master Charge are generally accepted.

Safe Deposit Boxes Boxes or sealed envelopes containing guest valuables can usually be kept in the hotel safe at no charge. It is a wise place to keep large amounts of cash rather than leaving it in your room or carrying it on your person.

Concierge Most front desk staff members are prepared to help guests with tour tickets, golf and tennis reservations, and rental cars. Some hotels provide specialized concierges who can obtain theatre tickets, charter fishing boats, and arrange more complex personalized services such as bilingual secretaries.

Color Television/Air Conditioning These amenities are now standard in all rooms.

Free Parking One space is allocated for each room, and parking validation is issued at the time of registration. Much of the parking in the French Quarter and the CBD is serviced by valets who appreciate gratuities. Hotel parking usually includes daily in-and-out privileges. Where there is a separate charge for parking, the daily rate is about $4. It is wise to discuss hotel parking at the time of reservation, prior to your arrival by car.

Free Local Telephone Calls Most hotels do not charge for local calls. If you plan to make many calls out of the hotel, i.e. you are a salesman, ask about the policy prior to making a reservation.

Valet Service/Babysitting These services are generally available at all hotels.

Check-Out/Check-In Times Check-outs run from 11 a.m. to 2 p.m. with noon being the average. Because Housekeeping needs time to prepare the rooms after check-outs, 3 p.m. should be considered an early check-in especially during the busy season. If you arrive early, and your room is not ready, let the hotel hold your luggage while you find a cozy cafe or bar to begin relaxing.

Swimming Pools This is also a standard hotel amenity. In New Orleans many pools are set in lush environments within a courtyard, or on a rooftop garden. Many pools are open for swimming at any hour, and most do not provide life guards. Children should be supervised. Many pools are heated for year round use. Beverage and light food service is available at most locations.

Pets Generally speaking, pets are NOT welcome in hotels due to local laws. Arrange through your hotel for kennel accommodations if you must travel with your pet.

Toll Free Numbers Most New Orleans hotels have toll free (800) numbers for obtaining reservation information. Use these numbers and save money. Don't forget to ask about special rates, seasonal packages, and room location options during the call.

Extra Persons In The Room Children under 12 years of age in the same room as their parents usually are free. Others pay a surcharge of $8 to $12 per night depending on the room rate.

Turn-Down Service This charming practice of European origin is now restricted to luxury accommodations. It is actually an evening maid service. While you are out, the maid will tidy the room, replace used towels, and "turn down" the bed. By tradition, she leaves a chocolate mint on your pillow to encourage sweet dreams.

RATE GUIDELINE

It is wise to make sure that you have a room in New Orleans by making an advance reservation. Most hotels will require that you guarantee the reservation by deposit or credit card. Very few hotels accept personal checks at check-out. Avoid embarrassment by pre-planning your method of payment.

Hotels and motels come in four basic flavors: Economy, Moderate, Deluxe, and Luxury. The terms are specific more to room rates than they are to definitive style and service. Hotels charging the same basic rates are not necessarily equal. There can be a great deal of qualitative difference between properties in each category. Factors such as location, age, and type of ownership come into play when you look beyond the numbers.

For your convenience, each hotel property has been placed within a rate category. The rate range is based on the double occupancy of a standard room with two double beds, or a king sized bed. Suite rates are based on the standard double plus another full room that serves as a parlor. Suite options are mentioned in the individual profiles.

Here are the definitions of the categories by rate:

CATEGORY	ROOM RATES:	SUITE RATES:
ECONOMY	$ 24 to $ 39	$ 45 to $ 64
MODERATE	$ 40 to $ 59	$ 65 to $ 99
DELUXE	$ 60 to $ 79	$100 to $174
LUXURY	$ 80 to $120	$175 to $350

These rates do **NOT** include the 10% Room Tax imposed in the City of

New Orleans. Consider this fact in estimating your total hotel bill. The tax raises a $100-a-day room to $110-a-day.

A new category of accommodation, Tower or Club rooms and suites, is geared for the person who requires exclusivity, privacy, security, and the pampered service generally reserved for V.I.P.'s. The premium for such rooms, double occupancy, is in the $135 to $150 per night range. Suites start around $200. Presidential Suites, and their counterparts in the various hotels, begin at $300 for one bedroom. Add at least $100 for each additional bedroom where the option is provided. The practical range for showcase suites is $350 to $800 per night. (Don't forget the tax, and the gratuity that should be extended to the housekeeping staff if you want your "class" to show.)

The spread in room rates not only represents properties within the category, but also individual rooms and suites within the same hotel. Size, location, and decor determine the price range of the same type of room within a property. If you want a room with access to the pool, or an inside room with a private balcony overlooking the courtyard, make your request when you make your reservation. Often you can get a choice room simply by asking and exploring the possibilities with your reservations clerk. Look for tips on the better rooms in each hotel profile.

The hotel profiles are arranged alphabetically by area. Each location is keyed to a detailed strip map which allows you to its position relative to nearby restaurants and attractions.

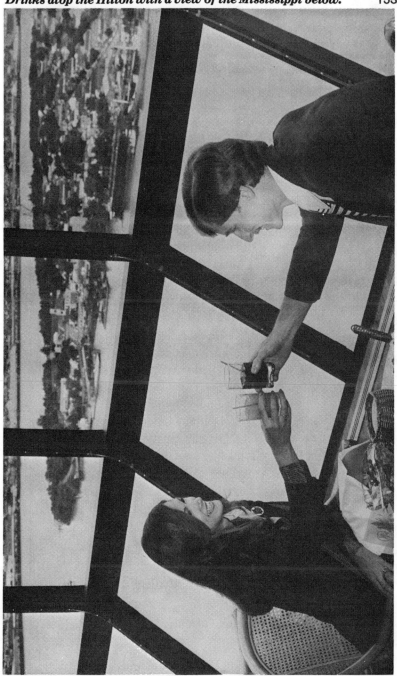

FRENCH QUARTER

BOURBON ORLEANS RAMADA

717 Orleans St.   Map, pg. 159   523-5251
Deluxe   800/228-2828

The massive front doors of the Bourbon Orleans are less than half a block away from St. Anthony's Garden at the rear of St. Louis Cathedral. In another age, the Orleans Ballroom and the Orleans Theater on this site were the scenes of the city's most lavish entertainments. Today, twin staircases in the hotel lobby lead to a restored ballroom which attempts to capture the feeling of the original. Ceiling murals and paintings depict the Five Bourbon Kings, The Battle of New Orleans, The Ball, and several allegorical subjects.

The 225 room hotel has balconied rooms on the Bourbon Street side, and 47 bi-level suites with a wet bar in the parlor, and spiral stair to the bedroom.

In past years the Bourbon Orleans was perhaps a luxury property. Its lower rate today, however, reflects its need for redecoration. The hotel has a large inner courtyard and pool, restaurant and cocktail lounge, and function rooms for small groups and parties in addition to its ballroom. Guests pay for parking. Kitchenettes available.

CHATEAU LE MOYNE

301 Dauphine St.   Map, pg. 71   581-1303
Luxury   800/238-5400

This is the showcase property of the Holiday Inn organization in the U.S. It incorporates the history, beauty, and style of the best in French Quarter hotels. Its name derives from Jean Baptiste Le Moyne, Sieur de Bienville, the founder of the city. Part of the hotel utilizes townhouses and their slave quarters dating from 1847 which were designed by famed ante-bellum architect James Gallier. The Slave Quarter, Garret, and Bienville Suites are among the most tastefully restored and decorated in the Quarter. The three floors of winding staircases that connect the Slave Quarters to the main house are architectural marvels which should be seen on their own merit.

The 170 room Chateau Le Moyne has a beautiful garden courtyard where food and beverages may be taken near the pool. Three function rooms host parties and meetings for up to 200 persons. The largest room (1,800 sq. ft.) opens onto a private patio, and is an elegant choice for receptions. The cozy piano lounge, and the full service restaurant featuring a champagne jazz brunch are well worth partronizing.

Rooms are large, harmoniously decorated, and accented with extra touches like fine linens, bubble bath and shampoo in the bathrooms, and cafe tables for enjoying a room service breakfast or writing postcards.

The hotel's location, and its free parking lot across the street, are especially convenient for guests who plan to use their cars, while it is still within easy walking distance to fine restaurants and attractions in the Quarter, and Canal Street shopping.

CHATEAU MOTOR HOTEL

1001 Chartres   Map, pg. 237   524-9636
Moderate

For travelers on a budget who want to stay in the French Quarter, the Chateau offers comfortable rooms and a slice of patio life around an awning covered cafe and adjacent pool.

There are slave quarter rooms on the patio, rooms with cathedral ceilings, and demi-suites with natural beamed ceilings. The cafe-bar serves breakfast and light lunch.

DE LA POSTE MOTOR HOTEL

316 Chartres St.   Map, pg. 71   581-1200
Deluxe

The De La Poste, like many French Quarter hotels, is a lot larger than it appears from its entrance. The street facade may look like a restoration, but the hotel actually dates from 1973. The 100 rooms are in three separate structures built around an extensive courtyard. A pool and sun deck occupy one end adjacent to the Bacchus Den Lounge while the other end rises to a second story veranda via a broad Italianesque staircase. In between, a bubbling fountain and groupings of cafe tables protected by umbrellas and small shade trees make for a relaxing setting.

Rooms here show contemporary decors, and are comfortably furnished. A slave quarter style building behind the main building has four demi-suites on two levels. The top level has courtyard balconies, and the ground level enjoys a private patio to its rear. In the five story mid-rise, second floor rooms have balconies, and other rooms and suites open on the veranda or courtyard.

The hotel has a full service restaurant, and a function room for parties of up to 65 persons.

DAUPHINE ORLEANS

| 415 Dauphine St. | Map, pg. 71 | 586-1800 |
| Deluxe | | 800/238-6040 |

The Dauphine Orleans offers a variety of rooms and suites. The main four story 18th century styled townhouse is designed as a motor hotel. Vehicles enter through a former carriageway and park in the enclosed, ground level lot. Most of the rooms have street front or pool patio view balconies. Rooms here are traditional in the decor of modern deluxe hotels.

Adjacent to the main building are two restored historic structures which were moved to their present site. The first is one of the cottages used by Audubon during his frequent residences in the French Quarter. The cottage is now converted into a function room for meetings and receptions, and also forms a part of the four Patio Suites. These suites are in single level cottages which open onto a private common courtyard.

The second historic building was once a famous Dauphine Street brothel. The Bagnio (sporting house) Lounge, and a few "hidden" suites occupy it now. Guests can see photos and Blue Book descriptions of some of the "ladies" in the lounge, and discover a reproduction copy of an 1857 license to be a Lewd and Abandoned Woman on their nightstand in the suite.

Across Dauphine are the hotel's Patio accommodations. The completely renovated site is new (1981), and is in the luxury category. Balconies open on a fountained courtyard with a large outdoor whirlpool in an alcove. Interior brick walls, exposed beams, and individually decorated rooms make this a charming, exclusive accommodation.

Hotel-wide extras include morning newspaper, evening turn down service, free coffee and donuts ($2500 worth a month) served in the Coffee Lounge, and in-room movies. Free valet parking.

HOLIDAY INN FRENCH QUARTER

| 124 Royal St. | Map, pg. 71 | 529-7211 |
| Deluxe | | 800/238-5400 |

The prime location of this 10-story high rise Holiday Inn keeps it busy all year. The 252 rooms are fresh, inviting, and have the standards you expect at a well run Inn. Many of the rooms have panoramic views of the French Quarter and the nearby river.

The Piper's Restaurant and lounge is on the the top floor. Its special buffets are popular with family groups. Laundry machines, children's menus, and an indoor pool are also welcomed by family travelers.

△ ATTRACTIONS
1. Steamboat Cruises, pg. 25
2. Moon Walk, pg. 66
3. Washington Artillery Park, pg. 66
4. Carriage Rides, pg. 67
5. Jackson Square, pg. 53
6. Napoleon House, pg. 43
7. Lower Pontalba, pg. 62
8. Upper Pontalba, pg. 62
9. 1850 House, pg. 64
10. Puppetorium, pg. 80
11. Central Grocery, pg. 212
12. Brulatour Courtyard, pg. 73
13. The Cabildo, pg. 57
14. St. Louis Cathedral, pg. 54
15. Presbytere, pg. 61
16. St. Anthony Garden, pg. 56
17. Street Entertainers, pg. 67
18. Street Artists, pg. 67
19. Preservation Hall, pg. 317
20. French Market, pg. 68
21. Pharmacy Museum, pg. 68
22. Petite Carre Little Theatre, pg. 81
23. Lafitte's Blacksmith Shop, pg. 76
24. Madame John's Legacy, pg. 84
25. La Branch Building, pg. 74
26. Historic New Orleans Collection, pg. 73
27. Voodoo Museum, pg. 76
28. Gardette-Le Pretre House, pg. 76
29. One Mo' Time, pg. 79
30. Casa Hove, pg. 80
31. The Arsenal & Jackson House, pg. 81
32. Spring Festival Association House, pg. 81

◯ RESTAURANTS
1. Cafe Maspero, pg. 227
2. Cafe du Monde, pg. 67
3. Moran's, pg. 240
4. Tujague's, pg. 246
5. Rib Room, pg. 243
6. Gumbo Shop, pg. 233
7. Chart House, pg. 229
8. Antoine's, pg. 224
9. Court of Two Sisters, pg. 229
10. Fatted Calf, pg. 231
11. Johnny White's, pg. 234
12. Embers, pg. 231
13. Louis XVI, pg. 238
14. Le Bon Creole, pg. 238
15. Jonathan's, pg. 243
16. Marti's, pg. 239

FRENCH QUARTER II

☐ ACCOMMODATIONS
1. Royal Orleans, pg. 165
2. Place D'Arms, pgs. 53, 164
3. Maison De Ville, pg. 160
4. Bourbon Ramada, pg. 155
5. Cornstalk House, pg. 182
6. Inn on Bourbon Street, pg. 160
7. Oliver House, pg. 164
8. Marie Antoinette, pg. 163
9. Maison Dupuy, pgs. 161, 238
10. St. Peter Guest House, pg. 183
11. Hansel & Gretel, pg. 182

🍸 NIGHT SPOTS
1. Steamboat Natchez, pg. 315
2. Toulouse Theatre Bar, pg. 318
3. Esplanade Lounge, pg. 312
4. Pat O'Brien's, pg. 319
5. Court Tavern, pg. 312
6. Crazy Shirley's, pg. 312
7. Chris Owen's Club, pg. 311
8. Al Hirt's Basin Street South, pg. 31
9. Maison Bourbon, pg. 315
10. Lucky Pierre's, pg. 313
11. Preservation Hall, pg. 317

FRENCH QUARTER II

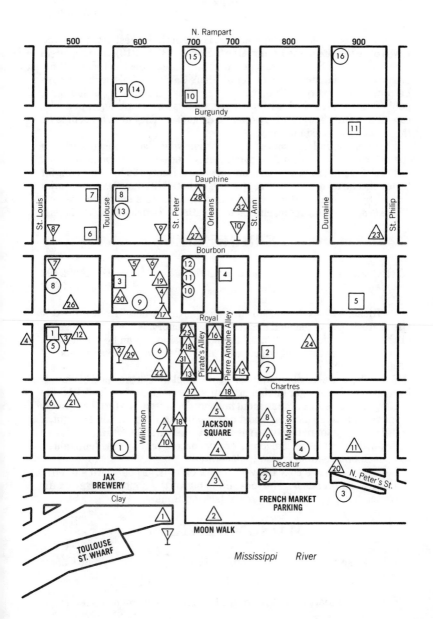

INN ON BOURBON STREET

| 541 Bourbon St. | Map, pg. 159 | 524-7611 |
| Deluxe | | 800/323-8818 |

The corner of Bourbon and Toulouse is one of the busiest in the Quarter. It was once the site of the French Opera House (1859-1919), the first opera house in the U.S. The present 86 room hotel, constructed in 1965, preserves the distinctive character of Vieux Carre. Half of the rooms have balconies opening onto Bourbon St., Toulouse St., or the garden patio pool. The second and third floor streetside balconies are equipped with cafe tables and chairs, and are open to all guests. They always seem to be the scene of a weekend party.

There are four large suites on Bourbon which get booked early for special events. The decors are comfortably modern with regional accents.

Three function rooms off the central patio can serve 30 to 70 persons for banquets and up to 150 for receptions. The hotel's 24-hour pancake parlor should be remembered by late nighters who desire a snack before bed. There is also a dining room, and a lounge with live Dixieland entertainment.

LE RICHELIEU

| 1234 Chartres | Map, pg. 237 | 529-2492 |
| Deluxe | | 800/535-9653 |

Le Richelieu was converted into an apartment-hotel from a historic Greek Revival row mansion and a macaroni factory. None of the elegance of the restoration was lost in its further transition to an 88 room hotel. Rooms are large,tastefully decorated, and reflect the pride and detail of local ownership.

Suites here are excellent values. Beatle Paul McCartney and his family lived in one of the larger kitchenette suites for two months. The VIP Suite is a large three bedroom apartment lavishly decorated by a former owner in a Spanish Castilian motif at a cost of $250,000 in 1964. At $300 a night, it is still a bargain for parties who wish to entertain in style. Other, less lavish suites with Chartres St. balconies or pool access rent as excellent values, too. Each has been individually decorated.

Le Richelieu has a cozy bar with a view of its large courtyard and pool. Parking is on premises. The location is out of the major Quarter traffic patterns, but only five blocks from Jackson Square.

MAISON DE VILLE

| 727 Toulouse St. | Map, pg. 159 | 561-5858 |
| Luxury | | |

Think of the Maison De Ville as a 21-room country inn just a few steps away from the crowds of Bourbon Street. Its primary accommodations are within a historic 18th century townhouse and its picturesque courtyard. The slave quarter rooms date from the 1840's, and the house itself was once owned by Peychaud, the pharmacist credited with inventing the cocktail. Tennessee Williams worked on his classic play, **A Streetcar Named Desire**, while staying in slave quarter room number nine.

The bedrooms of the hotel are furnished in authentic antiques, including four poster beds, and marble basins. The downstairs salon shows the French accent and is especially impressive. Sherry is served in the salon and in the courtyard for guests in the afternoon and evening.

Less than two blocks away, at 505 Dauphine, are the Audubon Cottages, hidden away in a secret courtyard with only one street entrance. John James Audubon, the celebrated naturalist, lived in Cottage number one around 1821. The six restored cottages retain their historic flavor. The private pool and pavillion with changing cabanas, and the unique character and privacy of this accommodation attracts star calibre guests. Cottage rates begin at about $200, a good value considering the space, privacy, and amenities.

Both the Maison De Ville and its annex, the Audubon Cottages, provide turn-down service, daily newspapers, mixers, soft drinks, ice, afternoon tea (sherry), and silver tray continental breakfast service as part of the tariff.

There is a charge for parking, and the hotel accepts no credit cards.

MAISON DUPUY

1001 Toulouse	Map, pg. 159	586-8000
Luxury		800/535-9177

This authentic architectural gem was constructed in 1974 using bricks from French Quarter sites more than 200 years old. The verdant courtyard is enhanced by the beautiful Fountain of the Arts. Many rooms, some including private balconies, open onto this quiet retreat or its adjacent pool and sundeck.

The decorating influence in the 195 rooms and public spaces is French Provincial. Rooms are individual in decor, and suites have a kitchenette and fully equipped dining area. The Van Gogh Suite, a richly furnished apartment with a formal dining room, is the most expensive in the Quarter at $600 a night. A total of three bedrooms can be added bringing the bill to $800, plus tax!

The Maison Dupuy (pronounced do-puee) has six function rooms to serve parties from 10 to 350 persons. The hotel restaurant, Le Bon Creole, features regional specialties in a formal French dining room. The popular Cabaret Lautrec has nightly entertainment amid life size murals depicting the lifestyle of French Impressionist painter Toulouse-Lautrec.

This property is locally owned, and contributes to the unique reputation New Orleans enjoys for small luxury hotels.

The decorative ironwork in the French Quarter is an irresistible subject for photographers.

MARIE ANTOINETTE

827 Toulouse St.   Map, pg. 159   525-2300
Luxury   800/535-9111

At 93 rooms, the Marie Antoinette is one of the best of the elegant small hotels for which the French Quarter is famous. The property dates from 1970, but its architectural detail makes it indistinguishable from its well kept historic neighbors.

Standard rooms here are large and reflect the commitment to excellence in decor and furnishings. Many former guests request one of the eight Slave Quarter rooms which are hidden away with their own private courtyard and pool. Half the rooms in the hotel have balconies. Inside room balconies overlook a courtyard pool surrounded by flowers and greenery.

The extras include terry cloth bathrobes, evening turn-down service, free newspapers, and 24-hour room service. Valet parking is guest paid. The Marie Antoinette is the home of the Louis XVI French Restaurant, a highly regarded gourmet room. There is also a function room which caters to small private parties and banquets.

THE MONTELEONE

214 Royal St.   Map, pg. 71   523-3341
Deluxe   800/535-9595

Antonio Monteleone, a Royal Street cobbler, started this hotel tradition in 1888 as the 14 room Commercial Hotel. In 1908, with the addition of 200 rooms, the Monteleone name and its crest was established. In 1928 another 200 rooms created a trend with private baths, closets, and central steam heat. By 1930 the hotel was the first in the city to offer air conditioning. Third generation hotelier Billy Monteleone expanded the hotel in 1956 to 600 rooms, and then directed its complete renovation in the 1960's.

Today, the Monteleone is the French Quarter's largest hotel. Its 16 meeting rooms, six restaurants and lounges, and 17 stories have perhaps created more memories than any other property in the city. One of the authors spent his honeymoon here in a room that then contained a great rarity: a king sized bed. The Carousel Bar, innovative then, still attracts a happy clientele to its revolving stools and sophisticated piano showroom.

The Sky Terrace was one of the South's first roof top pools and sun decks. Its nightclub has a memorable view of the crescent in the river. The Penthouse Suite, with its $10,000 bathroom, and the Presidential Suite, with its private balcony and access to the pool, are very desirable addresses. There are exceptional views from all of these high level locations.

Meeting wise, the Monteleone caters to regional affairs up to 500 participants. There are 15 elegantly traditional spaces for groups of all sizes and requirements.

Parking is guest paid. Barber and beauty shops are on premises.

OLIVER HOUSE

828 Toulouse St.   Map, pg. 159   525-8456
Moderate

Claire Tully hosts this 40 room property which is operated in the tradition of a guest house. A lively pet parrot greets guests in the foyer of a townhouse that was built in 1836 for a Madame Oliver and her 50 grandchildren. Her large house was built adjacent to the Opera House because the widow's passion was L'Opera.

Rooms here are individually decorated. Some capture the era of Madame Olivier with canopied beds, polished wood floors, and ornate chandeliers. There is no lack of modern conveniences, however. There is even a pool nestled in the lushly green courtyard.

Guests may enjoy a complimentary continental breakfast on the second story gallery or in the antebellum courtyard. Parking is nearby and guest paid. Some rooms have kitchenettes. Although the Olivier House has a "moderate" rating, the scale of its more elaborate rooms runs through the deluxe and luxury categories.

PLACE D'ARMES

625 St. Ann St.   Map, pg. 159   524-4531
Deluxe   800/535-7791

There is much hidden beauty behind facades in the Quarter, and the Place D'Armes is a good example. Only one building removed from the busy Jackson Square, its large patio is a secluded environment for enjoying the old architecture and the residential life style of the city amid magnificent magnolia trees.

Like many of the small hotels, the 67 room Place D'Armes is a collection of buildings, some new construction, and others restorations of historic structures. Slave Quarter Suites here, for example, open onto the patio. Second story rooms have private balconies. Another restored structure has high ceilings with overhead fans. These rooms are not large, but very well decorated, comfortable, and a good value. Many rooms have the original brick walls. The large double-double is a demi-suite, and by opening its sofa bed it becomes a family accommodation.

There is a restaurant on premises, and a function room off the patio for parties of up to 60 persons. Indoor parking is extra.

PRINCE CONTI

| 830 Conti St. | Map, pg. 71 | 529-4172 |
| Deluxe | | 800/535-9111 |

The portrait of Prince Armand Conti in the lobby honors the hotel's namesake who was a sponsor of Bienville's expedition to Louisiana. The hotel has some striking rooms containing original Louisiana plantation era furniture. Carved and canopied beds, dressing tables, chests, mirrors, and velvet covered chairs are a few of the antiques which appear in many of the hotel's 49 rooms.

Not all the rooms are done in antiques. One modern decor is done in an East Indian style with a large circular skylight. The pull of a shutter cord opens the room to moonlight.

In the European service tradition, a complimentary continental breakfast is served to each room on a silver tray. Like its sister property, the St. Ann, the Prince Conti has a lot of service extras.

The hotel lounge, La Galerie, is a comfortable spot which features for-sale art on its walls. New Orleanians pronounce Conti as con-tie (as in bow tie).

PROVINCIAL MOTOR HOTEL

| 1024 Chartres St. | Map, pg. 237 | 581-4995 |
| Moderate | | 800/535-7922 |

The Provincial offers a variety of accommodations in three separate buildings on a quiet street only two blocks from Jackson Square. There are five isolated patios lush with trees and plants and lit by gaslights.

The high ceiling rooms in the 1830's Chartres St. building are individually furnished in authentic antiques. Other rooms open onto long balconies overlooking one of the verdant patios. This 95 room property shows the class and concern of local ownership. Its small lobby illustrates the distinctive style that can be achieved by the tasteful use of Creole period antiques and French Quarter architecture.

Suites here are unusual and cost less than a single room at many hotels in the area. The location and on-site parking make this a good choice for those who intend to use their cars for touring. The hotel restaurant serves breakfast, lunch, and drinks from the cocktail lounge to the pool and patio areas.

THE ROYAL ORLEANS

| Royal and St. Louis | Map, pg. 159 | 529-5333 |
| Luxury | | 800/535-7988 |

The royal Orleans traces its spiritual heritage to one of the legendary hotels in New Orleans history, the St. Louis Exchange Hotel, built in 1836, and rebuilt in 1841. Being close to the Opera House, Jackson Square, fine restaurants, and the levee, the handsome Roman Revival styled building soon became the center of Creole social and business life. The St. Charles, built in the same year, was the showcase hotel of the American municipality on the other side of Canal Street.

The original hotel on the site housed the City Exchange where commodities, and even slaves, were auctioned. The rush of businessmen from this exchange to the Cabildo to register sales, and then to the Merchants Exchange (on Royal near Canal where the Holiday Inn now stands) established the famed Exchange Passage, a quick-step improvised route for men who needed to avoid the ladies and their petticoats on the streets. The need to refresh these harried businessmen who could not pause for a full course lunch prompted the St. Louis Bar to invent "the free lunch". It became an American institution until Prohibition.

The St. Louis later saw duty as a hospital for both Confederate and Union troopers, and as the capital building for the post war Carpetbagger Legislature. It was finally destroyed by hurricane in 1915.

The opening of the Royal Orleans in 1960 marked the modern day revitalization of the French Quarter, and thus New Orleans, as an international visitor attraction. A decaying area, devoid of serious hotel investment interest until then, was suddenly rejuvenated with grandeur and dignity. The presence of the Royal Orleans once again made the French Quarter desirable as a social center.

The hotel today epitomizes for many what is best in New Orleans hostelry. The ratio of service staff, for example, is nearly one to one with guests. Fine marble, polished brass, giant crystal chandeliers, live flowers and plants, and precious antiques surround visitors with elegance. Born of tradition, the hotel creates its own modern epoch of hospitality. It established the standards in the city toward which later luxury properties have had to strive.

The 362 rooms and numerous suites are spread over seven floors. An extensive guest room renovation (1981) continues to keep the hotel at the top of its class in room decor and furnishings. A new innovation is the creation of 16 luxury Semi Suites done in the style of a contemporary designer which feature a round marble tub-for-two open to the bedroom.

The dining, lounge, and public areas reflect the hotel's good taste. The Rib Room, The Cafe Royale, The Touche Bar, and the Esplanade Lounge are all popular with the local and visiting gentry. La Riviera, the 7th floor sundeck-pool and observation area is also a very fashionable day and evening cocktail place.

The Royal Orleans has 13 flexibly tasteful meeting spaces. Its Grand Salon can host 700 for a reception or 320 for a formal gourmet dinner. One of the most inviting rooms opens onto a shrubbed and flowering courtyard. It is especially sought for wedding receptions, and candlelight dinners.

Guests at the Royal Orleans pay for parking and local telephone calls. A barber shop and florist are on premises. Its location is the premium spot in the French Quarter.

ROYAL SONESTA

| 300 Bourbon Street | Map, pg. 71 | 586-0300 |
| Luxury | | 800/~~343-7170~~ |

766-3782

This classy 500 room hotel had a major impact on the redevelopment of the French Quarter when it was opened in 1969. Although the construction was new, the architecture and design reflected the essence of what is special about New Orleans.

A unique 3rd floor Pool Deck with its red canopied service bar can be reached directly by two levels of balconied rooms. A railing at the end of the pool deck area overlooks a large courtyard that abounds in tropical greenery. Cafe tables with pagoda-like umbrellas accent the lavish jasmine and hibiscus scented garden which has a marble fountain at its focal point.

The public rooms of the Royal Sonesta are equally impressive. Its Grand Ballroom, seating 450 for a banquet, and its 17 flexible meeting rooms are regally appointed. The OPEC oil ministers chose these facilities for one of their secret international gatherings in the mid 1970's. There are four restaurants and four lounges in the hotel including the award winning Begue's. The Mystic Den showcases one of the city's major entertainers, Elario.

For V.I.P.'s there are 30 rooms and suites in the Sonesta Tower on the 7th floor. Check-in and out is automatic, and Tower guests have a key activated, private-access elevator. A special Tower staff provides concierge services, and room service is available 16-hours a day. Tower rooms have a lot of extras including a refrigerator stocked with beverages, and in-room movies.

Another special accomodation is one of the few split-level Slave Quarter Suites. The lower level is the parlor with a wet bar. A spiral stair leads to the deluxe bedroom. The suites open onto a private patio.

The Royal Sonesta is in the middle of the Bourbon Street action, but once you pass the uniformed doorman, and see the cadre of professional bellmen, you have entered a separate world.

SAINT ANN

| 717 Conti St. | Map, pg. 71 | 581-1881 |
| Deluxe | | 800/535-9730 |

This is one of the small charming French Quarter properties which makes New Orleans such a unique hotel city. Pride in the housekeeping, and quality furnishings with a residential feel add to the enjoyment of its 58 rooms.

There is a decidedly romantic atmosphere in its semi-tropical patio, and the room balconies overlooking its fountain. The intimate decor and setting of the hotel's lounge also adds to the tranquil ambience. A small dining room serves breakfast and brunch on the patio.

Extras here include terry cloth bathrobes, evening turn-down service, and complimentary newspapers. The staff emphasis is on personal service, the kind you expect in a well run European hostelry.

Suites at the five story St. Ann have wet bars, and most have courtyard balconies. A function room can serve small parties and diners. Parking is guest paid.

ST. LOUIS

730 Bienville   Map, pg. 71   581-7300
Luxury   800/535-9706

The St. Louis is one of the best small hotels in America. Its street facade resembles other French Quarter structures, but its interior is regal. The elegantly formal French decor lobby, and its jewel-like central courtyard indicate the splendor and tradition of this unique 66 room hotel.

Rooms and suites are individually decorated with French period furniture and antiques featured in many of its decors. Many rooms have balcony views of the impressive, lushly tropical courtyard. Suites enjoy the additional luxury of a private courtyard where cocktails or meals can be served. There is no pool.

The extras at the St. Louis include personal terry cloth bathrobes, daily newspapers, evening turn-down service, and the attention of a concierge who can arrange tours, dinner reservations, and a myriad of other personal services. Parking on premises is a separate charge.

In late 1981, the St. Louis completely renovated its restaurant and kitchen spaces, and imported one of France's most celebrated chefs to attend the 50-seat L'Escale room. Classic French cuisine is the fare of this posh "port-of-call". The hotel also hosts private parties, dinner, and receptions with great style in its new function room on the courtyard.

Elario, one of the city's favorite entertainers.

△ ATTRACTIONS

1. Chalmette National Historical Park, pg. 93
2. De La Rond Oaks, pg. 93
3. Jackson Barracks, pg. 95
4. Steamboat Houses, pg. 95
5. The Faubourg Marigny, pg. 94
6. Metairie Cemetery Heritage Trail, pg. 107
7. City Park, pg. 109
   Duelling Oaks, pg. 110
   New Orleans Museum of Art, pg. 110
8. Longuevue House and Gardens, pg. 111
9. Pitot House, pg. 112
10. Fair Grounds Racing, pg. 112
11. Lake Shore Drive, pg. 127
12. Pontchartrain Beach Amusement Park, pg. 127
13. West End Lake Shore Park, pg. 128
14. Fat City, pg. 129
15. Lake Front Airport, pg. 23

☐ ACCOMMODATIONS

1. Rodeway Inn Downtown, pg. 201
2. Superdome Motor Inn, pg. 201
3. Best Western Patio, pg. 201
4. Quality Inn Midtown, pg. 202
5. Fountain Bay Club, pg. 202
6. Holiday Inn Fat City, pg. 202
7. Best Western Gateway, pg. 203
8. Landmark Motor Hotel, pg. 203
9. Holiday Inn East Hirise, pg. 206
10. Howard Johnson's East, pg. 206
11. Campgrounds, pg. 207
12. St. Charles Inn, pg. 199

◯ RESTAURANTS

1. Le Ruth's, pg. 258
2. The Caribbean Room, pg. 263 at the
   Pontchartrain Hotel, pg. 199

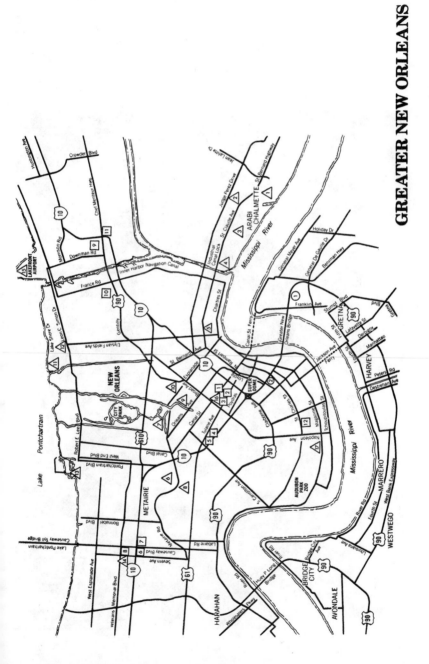

GREATER NEW ORLEANS

A jazz band parades through the French Market.

"Papadu" and "Thelma" from the cast of One Mo' Time.

Al Hirt means New Orleans to music lovers all over the world.

A cornstalk iron fence in the Garden District.

Alvin Alcorn in the kitchen at Commander's Palace.

Audubon Park Zoo

Artist rendering of the Convention and Exhibition Center.

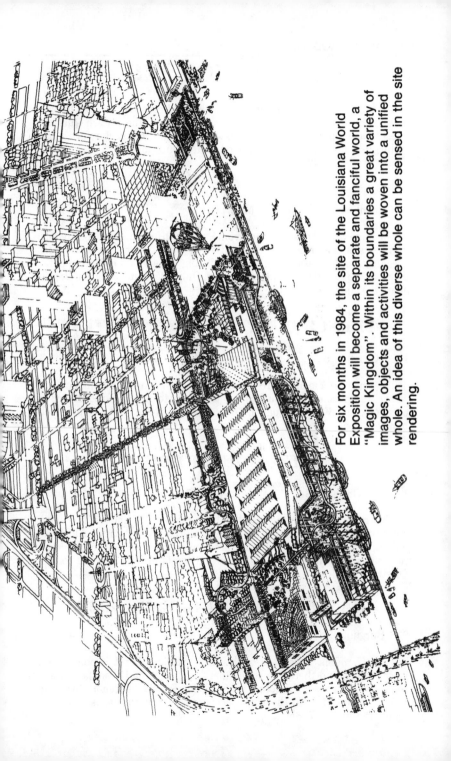

For six months in 1984, the site of the Louisiana World Exposition will become a separate and fanciful world, a "Magic Kingdom". Within its boundaries a great variety of images, objects and activities will be woven into a unified whole. An idea of this diverse whole can be sensed in the site rendering.

GUEST HOUSES

Guest House accommodations are a viable alternative in New Orleans because of its hostlery traditions. Especially within the French Quarter, guest house rooms are among the few at moderate rates. Here are some of the guest houses which enjoy good local reputations.

CORNSTALK HOUSE

915 Royal St.   Map, pg. 159   523-1515

The large white house set back from Royal with its remarkable cornstalk iron fence is in a prime Quarter location. Antique decor, free continental breakfast, and access to the columned front gallery and off street patio make this a comfortable place to stay. Only 14 rooms. Pay parking is nearby. Major credit cards.

FRENCH QUARTER MAISONNETTES

1130 Chartres St.   Map, pg. 237   524-9918

The seven rooms in this 1825 townhouse are in constant demand. The street is quiet, and fresh, modern rooms look out to a beautiful courtyard or carriage drive. Free newspaper. One of the few places that accepts "well behaved" pets.

FELTON GUEST HOUSE

1133-35 Chartres St.   Map, pg. 237   522-0570

This early Creole townhouse has been restored to contain ten units, some rooms with bath and kitchenette, and others with a parlor. All rooms and suites open via a balcony to the gracious courtyard. Each accommodation has a working fireplace. Coffee and tea is provided in the rooms. Offstreet parking.

HANSEL & GRETEL GUEST HOUSE

916 Burgundy St.   Map, pg. 159   524-0141

The 37-rooms here makes this a borderline hotel. Rooms have kitchenettes, and there is a complimentary continental breakfast. Many rooms have views of the courtyard and pool. Parking is free. Babysitting can be arranged. And the house accepts major credit cards. Toll free number: 800/535-7785.

LAFITTE GUEST HOUSE

1003 Bourbon St. Map, pg. 237 581-2678

This three storied restored 1849 townhouse is on the quiet, residential end of Bourbon. There are 14 rooms here with exposed brick walls, fireplaces, high ceilings, and a mixture of modern and antique furnishings. Balconies on the 2nd and 3rd floors. Free continental breakfast. Telephones in the rooms. Guests pay parking. Major credit cards.

LA MOTHE HOUSE

621 Esplanade Ave. Map, pg. 237 947-1161

This 14 room accommodation is in a restored 1800 mansion with its wide center hallway, winding staircases, flagstone courtyard, and antique furnishings. Guests meet around a formal dining room table where a complimentary breakfast is served each morning. Free parking. Valet services. Major credit cards. Closed July and August.

ST. PETER GUEST HOUSE

1005 St. Peter St. Map, pg. 159 524-9232

Rooms here have balconies, or open onto the courtyard. Color TV, telephone, and private bath are included in each accommodation. Accepts major credit cards.

COLUMNS HOTEL

3811 St. Charles Ave. 899-9308

This 100 year old white columned mansion is on the St. Charles Streetcar line and especially convenient to Tulane University and Audubon Park uptown, and the Garden District which has its boundary within four blocks away. Guest rooms have private baths, and some have balconies. Coffee and the morning paper are complimentary. Recently renovated to include a small Creole restaurant, the Columns is still more guest house than hotel.

PARKVIEW GUEST HOUSE

7004 St. Charles Ave. 866-5580

The Parkview is a rambling Victorian mansion that is appropriately named since Audubon Park is just across Walnut Street from its corner location. The Streetcar passes on St. Charles, and the Broadway bus to Uptown Square shopping and the Zoo is only two blocks away. Tulane University is equally close, within walking distance.

The public rooms are impressive with chandeliers, stained glass, and antique furnishings. Guest rooms are comfortable, and some have balconies. A complimentary continental breakfast is served weekdays in the formal dining room with a view of the park. There are 25 rooms. A few have connecting baths.

Interior of the Gallier House decorated for the warm weather months.

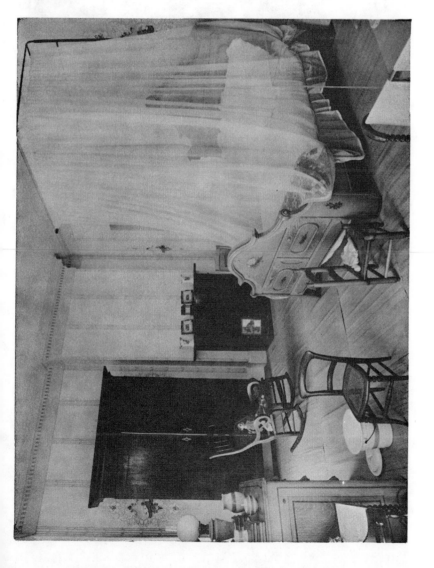

Audubon Park Zoo

CENTRAL BUSINESS DISTRICT

DOWNTOWN HOWARD JOHNSON'S

330 Loyola St.   Map, pg. 105   581-1600
Deluxe   800/654-2000

Overlooking the gardens of the Civic Center, this 17-story 300-room Howard Johnson's is at the center of CBD activity, and within a few blocks of the Superdome. Rooms are modern, spacious, and offer petite balconies for views of the city, or the 8th floor pool deck.

The Audubon Room, the hotel's restaurant, displays some of the most famous prints from the naturalist's "Birds of America" series. Additional art can be seen throughout the hotel. Group facilities include five meeting rooms which serve banquets from 24 to 210 persons. The St. Maxent Room, 2,368 sq. ft., can be subdivided into three parts.

Guests self-park their vehicles free in the lower level parking garage. In-room movies are also free.

FAIRMONT

University Place   Map, pg. 105   529-7111
Luxury   800/527-4727

The hotel tradition on this site dates back to The Grunewald, erected in 1893. The old hotel introduced showroom entertainment to the city with its elaborate night club, the Cave. In 1923, the hotel became the Roosevelt, named in honor of Theodore Roosevelt, and expanded into a new building on Baronne Street in 1925. The hotel changed ownership in 1934 and continued to expand, remodel, and redecorate. Seven floors in the adjoining Shell Building were taken in 1954. In November, 1965, the hotel became one of the select properties to carry the Fairmont Hotel name.

Today, the Fairmont has 750 rooms and all the ambience, and services of a "grand hotel". The three interconnected buildings that now comprise the hotel offer a variety of accommodations. There are rooms and suites with high ceilings and unique traditional and antique furnishings; and others with contemporary decors. Extras include shoe buffers, alarm clocks, bathroom scales, 24-hour room service, and evening turn-downs by the floor staff.

The hotel has a rooftop pool-sundeck, and two tennis courts for outdoor enthusiasts. For indoor attention there are two famous public rooms to peruse. The Sazerac Bar is celebrated for two New Orleans originals: the Sazerac cocktail, and the Ramos Gin Fizz. The bar's legacy dates to 1850. It has been located off the hotel's lobby since 1949. The senior mixologist here has served its exclusive drinks for nearly 40 years.

The second room to see is The Blue Room, a supper club par excellence since New Year's Eve, 1935. The big bands, and the big names have entertained here, and the tradition continues. Check the playbill to see what star is in town when you are.

The hotel also has an award winning gourmet restaurant, The Sazerac, and a 24-hour informal, multi-level restaurant called Bailey's.

The Fairmont is a major meeting and convention hotel. Its uniquely theatrical gala banquets are highly regarded. There are four ballrooms which can serve dinners to 1800, 1300, 800, and 400 persons respectively. More than 20 meeting rooms provide flexible and attractive spaces for smaller groups.

The Fairmont's location is close to Canal Street shopping, and the French Quarter. Guests pay for valet parking. A concierge desk, barber shop, and beauty salon are available for guest convenience.

HILTON & TOWERS

Poydras St. at the River   Map, pg. 105   561-0500
Luxury

Towering over the river and adjacent to the Rivergate and the International Trade Mart, the Hilton is a modern 29-story complex with 1200 guest rooms. It is one of the city's principal convention facilities.

Most Hilton rooms have panoramic views of the river and the city including the Superdome. Decors are tasteful, and furnishings reflect Hilton's quality standards. For those who desire exclusive accommodations, the Tower occupies the top three guest floors. These 132 rooms and 12 suites are lavishly decorated and consitute a hotel within a hotel. Tower guests by-pass downstairs check-in, have a private club with an honor bar and continental breakfast service, use key activated elevators to their floors, and get V.I.P. treatment from a select Towers staff.

The Hilton has a riverside 3rd level pool deck with bar service. It also offers access for guests to the Riverside Tennis Club, a private club within the hotel complex. Pro Vic Seixas directs activities on eight indoor, and three outdoor tennis courts, eight racketball courts, a quarter mile jogging track, saunas, whirlpools, Universal Gym rooms, and a tennis pro shop.

For dining and entertainment the Hilton has seven varied opportunities. Winston's is the place for award winning nouvelle cuisines served in an Edwardian setting on the lobby level. Le Cafe Bromeliad, located under the 9-story lobby atrium, is for less formal dining. Its luncheon buffet, special nights, and Sunday champagne jazz brunch are popular.

The Rainforest, on the top floor of the hotel, is a room of many moods. Amid its knarled cypress trees and lavish tropical greenery its days see it as a place for the Computer Diet Buffet. The idea is that each of the 60 beautifully presented items has a count that can be totaled up at the patrons convenience. The extravagance of the presentation, and low cost, make this one of the best lunchtime experiences in the city, dieter or no. At night, the Rainforest becomes a light-show disco dancing place with thunder, lightning, and rain effects punctuating the tropical environs, and the city and river lights spread out below.

This is also the hotel for seeing Pete Fountain who moved his jazz club from Bourbon Street to the Hilton's third floor. Great clarinet is played there Tuesday through Saturday beginning at 10 p.m.

The Hilton's meeting spaces are impressive. There are 31 individual rooms including the street level Grand Ballroom seating 4000 theatre-style or 2800 for banquets. The third floor has another Convention Center, opened in 1980, which includes two elegant, chandelier enhansed ball-rooms. The Napoleon Ballroom seats 850 for dinner, or serves a reception of 1500. The Versailles Ballroom hosts 550 and 1000 for similar functions. All of the major function rooms are divisible for small occasions. A major exhibit area is located on the street level.

Guests pay parking at this always busy riverfront address.

HYATT REGENCY

500 Poydras Plaza	Map, pg. 105	561-1234
Luxury		800/288-9000

The architecture of this property was designed to impress, even amaze. The 32-story Hyatt Regency is connected to the Louisiana Superdome by a 60-foot-wide concourse. It is an integral part of an 11-acre complex that includes the Poydras Plaza Shopping Mall. The hotel itself has nearly 1200 guest rooms in its high-rise structure, and in a 5-story mid-rise with rooms overlooking the swimming pool and terrace.

The hotel lobby is a garden atrium 24-stories high. Its north and south exposures are dramatic glass space frames which allow views of the Superdome as guests look from their atrium access balconies, or from the glass elevators as they glide up and down.

Guest rooms here are furnished in two contemporary decors; one in soft browns with upholstered furniture, and floral print draperies, and the other in tropical greens with cane and rosewood furniture accents. There are 100 suites. Deluxe suites have a sunken marble bathtub and a parlor styled as a conference room.

Guests can also elect accommodations in the 27th floor Regency Club. For about 15% extra, the Club guest is issued a Passport Elevator Key for entry to the Club floor. A concierge staff, complimentary continental breakfast, newspaper, turn-down service, velour bathrobes, and a private club with an honor bar are just part of the V.I.P. treatment.

The Hyatt Regency has three resturants and a lively jazz lounge. The Top of the Dome overlooks the Superdome by some 87 feet and revolves 360 degrees every hour. It is a spectacular view day or night for drinks at the lounge, or for formal dining.

The Hotel's Regency Conference Center was designed with flexibility to service board meetings, training sessions, and conferences of up to 400 people. Its eight rooms ranging in size from 500 to 4000 sq. ft. are away from the mainstream of hotel people traffic. This is a new facility.

The Regency Ballroom, with 24,525 sq. ft., can seat 2000 for dinner, or serve 4,300 for a cocktail reception. The huge room divides into eight sound-proof sections for meetings of any type. The French Market Exhibit Hall has over 25,000 sq. ft., space enough for 150 ten by ten booths. There are additional spaces for groups of 30 to 380 persons.

Guests pay parking. Specially designed rooms for the handicapped are available.

INTERNATIONAL

300 Canal St.	Map, pg. 105	581-1300
Deluxe		800/535-7783

For a hotel that has positioned its services and facilities for the corporate patron, the 16-story, 375-room International still has the Mardi Gras spirit. It's one of the few hotels remaining on the Carnival parade route, and it has a regular following for its guest ball on the night preceeding Fat Tuesday.

The Liuzza family, a well known New Orleans name, operates this property which opened in 1973. It is adjacent to the Rivergate, and also convenient to the CBD and the French Quarter. Rooms here are modern in decor, and have a clean, functional, masculine feeling. This is the kind of hotel that brags about the speed of its computer controlled elevators, and its ten Seco (Murphy-type swing away beds) double queen sized rooms that are a traveling salesperson's delight. The doors are even extra wide to facilitate small equipment display.

The Penthouse is reserved for chief executives who mean business. The huge living room has a fireplace and overlooks the Rivergate, the ITM Building, and the river. There are phones everywhere, and a butler in morning suit to provide personal service. It comes with two bedrooms, one formal and the other for fun. Other suites distinguished by hallway treatments are on each floor, and are custom decorated. Other suites are available on the 4th floor pool deck, health club, sauna area.

The International Ballroom on the top floor commands an exciting view of the river and city lights. It can seat 550 for a banquet, or serve a meeting or reception of 700. There are a total of 25 meeting spaces, including two ballrooms. An acoustical engineer is employed to insure quality sound controls.

The International has a lobby restaurant, coffee shop, and a bi-level lounge with live entertainment. A barber shop and beauty salon are also on premises.

INTERNATIONAL CENTER YMCA

936 St. Charles Ave.	Map, pg. 105	568-9622
Economy		

Realizing that there was a need for economy accommodations in New Orleans that were suitable for families, the A.B. Freeman International

Center YMCA has assumed the role as a clearing house for inexpensive hotel rooms and youth hostels within the city. The Center, located on Lee Circle, is the place to go when your only requirements are a clean, safe place to stay.

With the addition of 50 new double rooms, the Center has a total of 225 rooms. It also can refer travelers to seven other economy locations, and hostels. The new family doubles at the Center are deluxe by YMCA standards. The rooms are attractively decorated, have TV and telephone, and are air conditioned. A family of five can stay in this accommodation for about $45 a night. Regular rooms at the Center are spartan. Some have private baths, but many share common facilities on each floor. A tired stranger can still find a clean room at the Y for under $10.

In addition to having an excellent location, the YMCA has a coin operated laundry, full service restaurant, and a tour desk. For a small fee guests can use the pool, gymnasium, indoor jogging track and sun deck. The Center annually hosts more than 60,000 guests from some 25 foreign countries. It even offers a Mardi Gras package.

MARRIOTT

| 555 Canal St. | Map, pg. 105 | 581-1000 |
| Luxury | | 800/228-9290 |

The Marriott is one of the city's major convention hotels. Its meeting and banquet spaces cover over 80,000 sq. ft. The Grand Ballroom can host a reception for 4000 or a banquet for 2200. The Mardi Gras Ballroom, a separate facility, can seat 1000 for diner. On another level of the hotel the 30,000 sq. ft. Exhibit Hall is space enough for 200 booths. There are 35 total meeting rooms which provide flexibility for all types of functions.

The 41-story River Tower was built in 1973 and then linked to the 21-story Quarter Tower in 1978. On the 5th floor level, above the parking garage, a large Pool Deck lies between the two towers. There are excellent views of the river and the Quarter from many upper level rooms. The new (1981) Riverview Restaurant and Lounge on the top floor provides exciting vistas both day and night.

The New Orleans Marriott is being upgraded in room decor and furnishings as part of a corporate policy to upgrade all Marriott properties. Entire floors have been redecorated in sophisticated earth tones. The red and black traditional Marriott colors will soon be a thing of the past.

There are 100 suites in this 1354 room hotel. Deluxe suites have a large parlor with a formal dining area and wet bar with bar stools. The Presidential Suite has a "house beautiful" picture book $150,000 contemporary decor in large rooms commanding expansive views of the river below.

Guests pay for on premises parking at this convenient location. The Lobby Bar, with its comfortable sofa groupings and extensive plantings, is a popular meeting place. Other amenities include barber, beauty, and gift shops.

INTERNATIONAL AIRPORT

△ ATTRACTIONS

1. Jefferson Downs, pg. 129
2. New Orleans International Airport, pg. 19

☐ ACCOMMODATIONS

1. Airport Hilton, pg. 204
2. Ramada Inn Airport, pg. 205
3. Airport Holiday Inn, pg. 204
4. Airport Sheraton, pg. 205

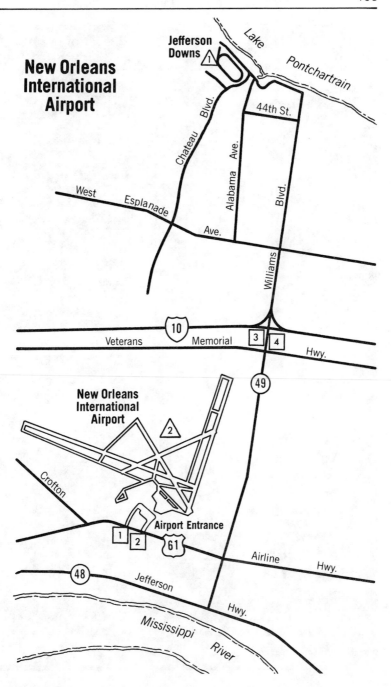

New Orleans
International
Airport

Jefferson Downs 1

Lake Pontchartrain

Chateau Blvd.

44th St.

Alabama Ave.

Blvd.

West Esplanade Ave.

Williams

10

Veterans Memorial 3 4 Hwy.

49

New Orleans
International
Airport

2

Crofton

Airport Entrance

1 2 61

Airline Hwy.

48

Jefferson Hwy.

Mississippi River

Gallier House

LE PAVILLON

Baronne and Poydras   **Map, pg. 105**   581-3111
Luxury   800/535-9095

The original hotel on this site was opened in 1907. The land deed can be traced back over 200 years to Bienville, the city's founder. In 1970, the grand structure was gutted, and 18 months and $8 million later, it was reborn as Le Pavillon. Its owners had searched the world for artifacts to create a classic showplace property. Pewter decorations displayed in the Chateaubriand Dining Room were found in Spain and Italy. The marble columns and statues at the Poydras Street doors came from Italy, and the magnificent lobby chandeliers are Czechoslovakian. The marble railing in the lobby is from the Grand Hotel in Paris.

The 226 guest rooms and suites at Le Pavillon are large and have high ceilings. Furnishings are traditionally tasteful with a decided French influence. Bay window rooms have a view of the nearby Superdome, and deluxe suites have a wet bar, living room, and formal dining area.
The Versailles Ballroom is a palatial room with Italian marble floors and crystal chandeliers which can seat 240 for a banquet. Five other function rooms service parties from 20 to 400 persons.

Hotel amenities include a rooftop sundeck and pool, restaurants, and a cellar lounge with staggered arches and candlelight reminiscent of a French country inn. Guests pay for parking at this location close to the Civic Center and Superdome.

SHERATON

Canal and Camp St.   **Map, pg. 105**   525-2500
Luxury   800/324-3535

New in 1982, the Sheraton is one of the major new properties which will support the New Orleans Convention and Exhibition Center due to open in 1984.
Located directly across Canal from the Marriott, the Sheraton will add 1200-rooms to the city accommodations inventory, and 33 meeting rooms to its facilities base. The Grand Ballroom will seat 2090 persons for a banquet. A separate exhibit hall, some 13,827 sq. ft., can seat another 1430.
The hotel offers a variety of restaurants and lounge experiences. The top floor has a health club facility with an outdoor rooftop running track.
The Sheraton has quality rooms and suites, and also special Tower accommodations for those who desire extra luxury, privacy, and security. Off street parking is guest paid.

The International Trade Mart at the end of Canal Street.

WARWICK

| 1315 Gravier St. | Map, pg. 105 | 586-0100 |
| Deluxe | | 800/535-9141 |

The Warwick, a long time apartment-hotel, has recently been renovated and redecorated by New Orleans hotelier Olav Lambert. The feeling of the new ornate lobby, and the restaurant, which is a popular mid-day CBD spot, is English continental.

The rooms are extra large, and all have a dressing room, fine linens, walk-in closets, and two telephones. There are 24 suites, two on each of the 12 floors, with wet bars. The decors are tastefully traditional, and the rate is very favorable when compared to similar facilities.

The 171-room Warwick is across the street from the Louisiana Supreme Court, and is especially convenient to the Civic Center, the L.S.U. Medical Center and Charity Hospital. It attracts a corporate and professional clientele. Its private dining club, Churchill's, a 40-seat room, numbers the Mayor and other city VIP's among its membership.

Parking is guest paid, but a valet is available. Free morning newspaper, and in-room movies are provided. The hotel has two small function rooms for parties of 20 to 60 persons. No pool.

AVENUE
PLAZA

in the heart of New Orleans
Garden District

· 144 guest rooms
· Cocktail Lounge
· Room Service
· Wet bar in all rooms
· Courtyard Swimming Pool
· Parking provided on premise
· Sidewalk Cafe

2111 St. Charles Ave.
New Orleans, La.

Telephone (504) 566-1212

GARDEN DISTRICT AND UPTOWN

THE PONTCHARTRAIN HOTEL

2031 St. Charles Ave.   Map, pg. 170   524-0581
Luxury   800/323-7500

This 100-room hotel at the front door of the Garden District is recognized as being one of the finest small hotels in the world. All of its rooms have been individually decorated with a style and grace worthy of the most elegant of private residences. Some of the suites contain over $100,000 worth of antique furnishings and outstanding examples of decorative arts.

The hotel began in 1927 as an apartment hotel. Its founder, E. Lysle Aschaffenburg, established a tradition for unqualified excellence that is carried on today by his son, Albert. Many staff members have served hotel guests for more than 25 years. The same man, for example, has provided room service for 48 years. Turn-down service is still provided each night.

The dedication to redecorating and remodeling at the Pontchartrain has kept its rooms fresh and its facilities modern. Mary Martin, Richard Burton, and Henry Stern have had magnificent suites named in their honor after long residences in the hotel. The Manhattan suite, complete with grand piano, is a favorite of distinguished conductors and musical artists who visit the city.

The exceptional accommodations at the hotel are equaled by its multi-award winning restaurant, the Caribbean Room. The hotel also has a Cafe serving three meals daily, and a fashionable, but comfortable, Bayou Bar.

Meeting space is limited, although the hotel is popular for wedding receptions, and dinner parties of less than 65 persons. There is a charge for parking. No pool.

ST. CHARLES INN

3636 St. Charles Ave.   899-888
Deluxe

This comfortable 40-room hotel is on the edge of the Garden District. The St. Charles streetcar passes in front of its canopied entry, and it is especially convenient to St. Charles General Hospital, the Touro Infirmary, and the uptown universities.

Rooms are large and contemporary in decor. A continental breakfast and morning newspaper are served complimentary. Room service is available from the Que Sera Lounge and Restaurant. There is a daily parking charge.

The St. Charles Inn gets booked early for Mardi Gras because it is one of the few hotels actually on the St. Charles Avenue carnival parade route.

AVENUE PLAZA

2111 St. Charles   566-1212
Deluxe   800/535-9575

This 'Garden District address until recently (October, 1982) was a convenient residential apartment building. Now, after major renovation, it has been transformed into a new deluxe hotel and Time-Sharing condominium. The location is next door to the Pontchartrain Hotel, and the St. Charles Street Car passes by to provide scenic transportation either Uptown or to the French Quarter.

The 100-plus guest rooms at the Avenue Plaza are tastefully furnished, and each accommodation has a wet bar. Suites are equipped with a kitchenette for light housekeeping, and remind us of the Guest Quarters concept: the appointments of apartment living. An additional 100 rooms and suites have been reserved for condominium ownership on a time-sharing basis, that is owners purchase the use of the unit for a specific period and pay only for their percentage of ownership.

Amenities at the Avenue Plaza include a Sidewalk Cafe restaurant, the Empire Lounge, a courtyard swimming pool in the setting of a Garden District home, on-premise parking, room service, a beauty salon, and a 12th-floor sundeck.

The rich French furnishings in the lobby, and the renovation investment evident in the rooms, mark this property as a significant arrival in the hotel roster. The accommodations are especially welcome as rooms needed in the Garden District.

MID-CITY

RODEWAY INN DOWNTOWN

| 1725 Tulane Ave. | Map, pg. 170 | 529-5411 |
| Moderate | | 800/228-2000 |

The Rodeway Inn has 150 rooms in two bi-level buildings which are raised for parking underneath. The location is excellent, and the rooms are well kept, and comfortable. There is an outdoor pool area for sunning and cooling off.

Although there is no antebellum charm or noteworthy architecture here, an acceptable moderately priced room so close to the French Quarter and the Superdome deserves consideration. A restaurant and lounge are on premises for further guest convenience.

SUPERDOME MOTOR INN

| 2222 Tulane Ave. | Map, pg. 170 | 821-2812 |
| Moderate | | 800/535-8636 |

Located on busy Tulane Avenue, a few blocks beyond the Central Business District and Charity Hospital, this three story motor inn is a good choice for the budget conscious.

Many of the 100 comfortable rooms open onto a bi-level courtyard. The upper level is reached by a twin, plantation style iron staircase from the pool area. The Inn has a full service restaurant and a lounge with access to the pool. The spacious bedrooms here are all kings or double-doubles.

The Superdome Motor Inn is not adjacent to the Louisiana Superdome as its name may imply, but it's only a short cab ride away. For families on tour, the presence of a laundry machine, and a babysitting service are real conveniences.

BEST WESTERN PATIO MOTEL

| 2820 Tulane Ave. | Map, pg. 170 | 822-0200 |
| Moderate | | 800/528-1234 |

Tulane Avenue, US Route 90, is the New Orleans "motel strip". The Patio Motel is one of the budget accommodation alternatives within a mile of the French Quarter and Superdome.

Guests drive under the raised second and third level rooms. There are two pools, a washerteria, and an adjacent restaurant which provides room service to the motel. The 76 rooms and suites are modern, comfortable, and have all the basics you expect from a Best Western property.

QUALITY INN MIDTOWN

3900 Tulane Ave.   **Map, pg. 170**   486-5541
Moderate   800/228-5151

If the street were not Tulane, you could imagine that this property was in the French Quarter. The style and construction of brick and lacy ironwork on balconies put you in the New Orleans spirit.

This is a family owned 102-room inn, and the attention to detail shows. Rooms are well appointed in the multi-storied buildings which surround the courtyard pool. Most of the second and third level rooms have balconies.

The Regency Room restaurant features many of the city's favorite traditional dishes plus live Maine lobster. The lounge also gets a lot of local patronage.

The Inn's meeting facility is named Bonaparte Place. It has a separate entrance, and foyer, and was designed to cater to weddings, parties, and business meetings up to 450 persons. The three function rooms are served by their own kitchen. A spacious VIP suite accessible from the foyer by a carpeted staircase is a hidden asset at this attractive property.

FOUNTAIN BAY CLUB

4040 Tulane Ave.   **Map, pg. 170**   486-6111
Moderate   800/327-3384

Before the Interstate highways, travelers arriving from the west knew that they were in New Orleans when they saw the huge sign announcing this motel-hotel complex, then known as the Fontainebleau. Today, the combination of low and mid-rise structures houses 454 rooms, many with balconies. Decors are traditional in style. The 12 meeting rooms can serve functions as large as 650 for a banquet. The Pelican Room, at 5157 sq. ft., can host a reception of 875.

The large outdoor recreation area between the main buildings has three pools, four lighted tennis courts served by a tennis club staff, and a tropical patio for relaxing. The entire complex covers eight acres.

Inside the hotel are two restaurants and two lounges. There is also service to the pool areas. Casual and formal dining, and nightly entertainment are offered. A barber shop, and beauty salon are on premises.

HOLIDAY INN FAT CITY

I-10 & Causeway   **Map, pg. 170**   833-8201
Moderate   800/238-5400

The Metarie location, just off the Interstate, is close to the restaurants and night life of Fat City. There is courtesy service to the airport, a full service restaurant, and a popular lounge with live entertainment.

Many of the 196 rooms have balconies overlooking the hotel pool. Two banquet and meeting rooms can serve diners to 240 persons, or host receptions for up to 275. Room taxes in Metarie are 7%, a saving over the 10% tax in Orleans Parish. This is a good location for drivers who want to be close to Lake Pontchartrain attractions and Jefferson Downs racing.

BEST WESTERN GATEWAY

2261 N. Causeway Blvd.   **Map, pg. 170**   833-8211
Moderate   800/528-1234

A tall high-rise near the I-10 Causeway Blvd. Exit, the 203-room Gateway is convenient to Fat City, and only seven miles from the French Quarter.

Rooms and suites here have recently been redecorated so they appear fresh and inviting. The Metairie location has 12 meeting rooms for parties up to 500 persons. Courtesy scheduled transportation to the airport, and to downtown, is provided. Dining at the Gateway is in the style of an Old English Pub with prime rib and local seafoods as specialties.

LANDMARK MOTOR HOTEL

2601 Severn Ave.   **Map, pg. 170**   888-9500
Moderate   800/535-8840

The Landmark is a 17-story circular tower located near I-10 and Causeway Blvd. in Metairie. There are 207 rooms that are comfortable, although some are beginning to show their age and need redecorating to restore their freshness. This was once a deluxe property, and there are still touches of excellence in its public spaces.

The Top of the Wheel Lounge, for example, is a lively happy hour place with entertainment and a view of both the lake and the distant downtown skyline. The hotel's restaurant, also on the top floor, specializes in US Prime steaks.

There are seven function spaces accommodating receptions up to 450, and banquets up to 350 persons. Courtesy airport transportation is provided.

AIRPORT WEST

AIRPORT HILTON

901 Airline Hwy.   Map, pg. 193   721-3471
Deluxe   800/452-8703

The Hilton is almost directly across from the airport entrance. More than a transient orientated property, the hotel has resort amenities which include an Olympic-size pool set within a huge expanse of lawn landscaped with trees, flowers, and shrubbery, a putting green, shuffleboard courts, and two lighted tennis courts.

Many of the Hilton's 284 rooms front on the recreational area which is a quiet retreat removed from the highway. All rooms are king or double-doubles and up to the Hilton standards for quality decors. There is a restaurant appreciated for its buffets, an Oyster Bar, and a stylish Casablanca lounge with live entertainment.

The hotel has extensive meeting spaces which can serve parties from 10 to 780 guests. The Plantation Ballroom and the Rosedown rooms combined can seat 700 for a banquet. Courtesy airport transportation, free in-room movies, and room service are available.

AIRPORT HOLIDAY INN

I-10 & Williams Blvd.   Map, pg. 193   722-5611
Moderate   800/238-5400

This Brock Hotel Corporation franchised Holiday Inn is unusual: it is a Holidome. A Holidome is an indoor recreation center with an Olympic size pool and much more. The 70-foot dome covers a climate controlled playground for children and adults. A children's activity director plans day long events; anything from face painting to scavenger hunts. Adults can enjoy the hot whirlpool, Polynesian styled hut bar, ping-pong, shuffleboard, etc. The Jockey Club restaurant, lounge, and disco provides evening diversions.

Many of the 306 rooms open onto the Holidome. The functional furnishings meet or exceed national Holiday Inn standards. There are seven meeting room combinations which can service conventions or trade shows of up to 400 persons. The airport, Jefferson Downs Race Track, and Fat City are convenient to this location. Bourbon Street is only 20-minutes away via I-10.

RAMADA INN AIRPORT

1021 Airline Hwy.   Map, pg. 193   721-6211
Moderate   800/228-2828

The Ramada is a comfortable alternative among accommodations near the airport. The four levels of rooms surround the pool area, and there is a well appointed restaurant, and cozy lounge with a residential library atmosphere.

Four ground level meeting rooms can serve banquet groups from 10 to 150 persons. All 160 guest rooms are either kings or double-doubles. Courtesy transportation to the airport is provided.

AIRPORT SHERATON

2150 Veterans Memorial Hwy.   Map, pg. 193   467-3111
Moderate   800/325-3535

This modern 8-story, 250-room hotel is 2.5 miles from the International Airport and 15 miles from the French Quarter. Its amenities include an outdoor pool, four lighted tennis courts with a resident tennis pro, a full service restaurant, oyster bar, and a contemporary lounge with nightly live music for dancing.

The Sheraton has two major meeting rooms on the ground level and three others on the second floor. Its Louisiana Ballroom can seat 500 for a banquet. Rooms and suites conform to Sheraton's quality standards. Free 24-hour service to the airport is provided for guests.

EAST I-10
&
RT. 90

HOLIDAY INN EAST HIRISE

6234 Chef Menteur Hwy.   Map, pg. 170   241-2900
Moderate   800/238-5400

Located off I-10, this is a good stopping place for families on tour. The French Quarter is only five miles away, and the Inn provides free daily transportation. Free rides are also provided to the general aviation Lake Front Airport.

There are 210 rooms, many with balconies. A full service restaurant, and a separate lounge with nightly entertainment add to guest convenience. The Inn has three meeting rooms with a great deal of flexibility for small and medium sized groups.

HOWARD JOHNSON'S EAST

4200 Old Gentilly Rd.   Map, pg. 170   Map, pg.944-0151
Moderate   800/654-2000

If you stay on the east side of town, this 160-room Howard Johnson's is just off I-10 and convenient to driving downtown or to the Fair Grounds via Gentilly Blvd. This is a standard roadside facility with dependable chain quality rooms, and a full service restaurant. Free courtesy transportation is provided to the Lake Front Airport.

CAMPGROUNDS
Map, pg. 170

Recreation vehicles, mobile homes, and tenters will find space and facilities in travel parks within 10-miles of the French Quarter. Most parks provide free scheduled transportation to the historic area. Bus and cruise tours originate and return to most campgrounds, too.

With the exception of one westside location, the concentration of travel parks is near the I-10 and US Route 90 junction on the east side of the city. To avoid disappointment, make reservations for campground accommodations well in advance of arrival.

KOA NEW ORLEANS WEST

11129 Jefferson Hwy.   721-0246

This location on LA Rt. 48 is the most convenient travel park on the west side of the city. It is a large site that welcomes both RV's and tenters. Full hook-ups, TV, lounge, and store available. Tour arrangements, and free transportation to and from the French Quarter.

PARC D'ORLEANS I

7676 Chef Menteur Hwy.   241-3167

A modern park with paved streets, picnic tables, pool, and showers. RV's and tenters welcome. All hook-ups. Free French Quarter rides, and daily tours departing from the site.

NEW ORLEANS TRAVEL PARK

7323 Chef Menteur Hwy.   242-7795

Close to the I-10 and US Rt. 90 junction, there are full hook-ups, two pools, game room, laundry, and showers here. Most of the 150 sites are shaded. Bus service to downtown, and daily tour departures available.

RIVERBOAT TRAVEL PARK

6232 Chef Menteur Hwy.   246-2628

This park is close in, and relatively new. Located within the southwest cloverleaf of I-10 and US Rt. 90 junction, it has full hook-ups, sauna, game room, laundry, and showers. Free transport to the French Quarter, and on site tour departures are available.

* Incomparable French Wine

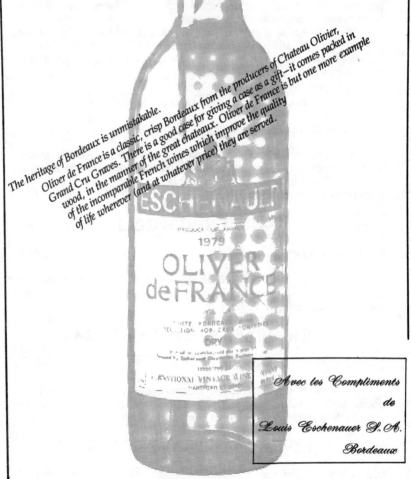

The heritage of Bordeaux is unmistakable. Oliver de France is a classic, crisp Bordeaux from the producers of Chateau Olivier, Grand Cru Graves. There is a good case for giving a case as a gift—it comes packed in wood, in the manner of the great chateaux. Oliver de France is but one more example of the incomparable French wines which improve the quality of life wherever (and at whatever price) they are served.

Avec les Compliments de Louis Eschenauer S.A. Bordeaux

*OLIVER DE FRANCE is served as house wine at some of New Orleans' most incomparable restaurants.

Imported by International Vintage Wine Co., Hartford, Ct.

EATING OUT IN NEW ORLEANS

The great restaurants of New Orleans evolved from a food conscious society whose tastes border on gormania. Native New Orleanians patronize culinary artistry in their own city perhaps more than any other community in America. Good restaurants maintain their reputations not by pleasing the passing tourist, but by meeting the rigorous criteria of their critical local patrons. The true New Orleanian gladly pays the bill for excellence in food and beverage.

The creole cuisine that is celebrated in this city is a polyglot creation. It began with the French colonists who learned from the Choctaw Indians about the bounty of their new world. The Indians revealed the native mirlitons, plantains, yams, okra, and the secret of the file powder. The land abounded in seafoods and game, and as the port developed, fresh produce arrived from up-river farms on flat boats, and ships came through the Gulf with ingredients from the West Indies, Mexico, and South America.

The 34-year Spanish rule introduced another food tradition based on spicy seasonings. Acadians came to settle the bayous and produced sausage and other country delicacies. A substantial immigration of Italians introduced cooking oils, and generation after generation of Negro plantation cooks contributed an almost magic ability to make tasty dishes from the most humble provisions.

The combination of these ethnic tastes and the accessibility to so many ingredients produced a cuisine tradition that is distinctive. Creole cooking is often imitated, as are many of the world's great cuisines, but it is never better than when it is prepared in its native city.

Students of Louisiana cuisine appreciate the differences between Creole cooking and that of its rural cousin, Cajun fare. More subtle however is the distinction between these styles, and another tradition which should be called New Orleans Style. The New Orleans Style is to Classic Creole what the Nouvelle Cuisine is to Classic French, a hybrid which has developed into a category of its own. New Orleans Style can be haute cuisine or just something traditional from home kitchens. It is represented by Oysters Rockefeller, Bananas Foster, Mile High Ice Cream Pie, Bread Pudding, and the many distinctive ways New Orleans cooks treat fish, shrimp, and oysters. Even the "French" bread tastes different here. Some say its the water, and the effect of humid air when the bread is rising. Whatever, there is a great deal to enjoy in New Orleans that is unique to the city and is apart from the Creole and Cajun traditions. We refer to this cuisine as New Orleans style.

The owner-operated restaurants of New Orleans are peopled by individuals who are passionate about the quality of their food and service. Families pass the legacy of their recipes and preparations to the next generation. Each restaurant has its specialties, its traditions. Many members of the inheriting generation are sent to France to study cuisine and wine before they take roles of responsibility in the family restaurant.

The food traditions of New Orleans seem to inspire everyone in the restaurant business here. There are only a few cities in the world who can claim to have so many good places to eat. From Po-Boy shops and oyster bars to gourmet rooms, New Orleans is **lagniappe**, that little something extra which shows its class.

THE FAMOUS FOODS OF NEW ORLEANS

The following descriptions of dishes and preparations are especially associated with New Orleans. They are either distinctive victuals like boudin and jambalaya, or famous restaurant preparations like Eggs Hussarde and Bananas Foster.

The descriptions are not meant to serve as recipes. We recommend that you invest in one of the many excellent cookbooks available on Creole and New Orleans cuisine if you want to try to duplicate these dishes at home. You should be aware, however, that there are many recipes for the same dish. Each chef has his special insight into what tastes best.

A friend of ours, for example, set out to reproduce the perfect Oysters Rockefeller in her home kitchen. The wife of a Navy pilot, she did her research thoroughly over many weekend trips to New Orleans and came away with almost 80 separate recipes. Fortunately she lived near a natural supply of oysters, and made Oysters Rockefeller a weekly item on her menu for nearly two years. She never duplicated the New Orleans taste to her satisfaction, and got pregnant twice during the attempt. Whether this was a result of the romance of the city or the legendary powers of oysters is still unknown.

Nevertheless, since one of the primary reasons for being in New Orleans is the enjoyment of its unique cuisine, here is a guide to some of the things that you should try to sample.

APPETIZERS

Oysters Rockefeller Antoine's originated this preparation which is now served worldwide. Curiously, the original recipe does not utilize spinach. The secret to the spinach mixture covering the oyster is "absinthe". The spinach-topped oysters are cooked on the half shell under the broiler, and then are served on a bed of hot rock salt.

Oysters Bienville Arnaud's "invented" this original. The thick complex sauce covering the baked oyster on the half shell contains shrimp, mushrooms, white wine and many other ingredients.

Crabmeat Lorenzo Many restaurants offer special crabmeat appetizers by various names which are served on toast. The Lorenzo is served at Commander's. It arrives as a ball with two strips of anchovy on a toast round. The fresh crabmeat has been cooked with about ten ingredients including shallots, parsley, and sherry. It is sprinkled with grated Parmesan cheese and browned under the broiler just before coming to the table.

Oysters on the Half Shell Step up to the oyster bar and watch a professional shucker open you a dozen fat raw oysters. The couple on your left may be in formals. The guy on your right may have his taxi parked at the curb. All of society meets at the oyster bar. The dipping sauce is a mixture of horseradish, lemon, ketchup, and hot sauce. There is more lemon and Louisiana hot sauce on the side.

SOUPS

Crawfish Bisque This soup is rich in crawfish and seasonings in a tomato base. The heads of the small fresh water crustacean, really an empty shell after cooking, appear in the soup stuffed with a spicy dressing made from French bread. Local people will sometimes pick up the pointed end of the head and suck out the succulent contents.

Gumbo This is **the** staple among Creole and Cajun cooks. There are thousands of recipes utilizing shrimp, chicken, sausage, fish, and game as the primary ingredient. Add okra, and the dish becomes a Shrimp-Okra Gumbo or a Chicken-Okra Gumbo. Add file powder just before serving, and it becomes a File Gumbo. The secret to making gumbo is the preparation of the roux, a dark paste made from cooking flour and shortening. Tomatoes form the base of many seafood gumbos where roux may not be used. At its best, the soup is not only wonderful to taste, but it is a hardy dish worthy of an entire meal. Rice is often served on the side and added to the hot soup. Make the soup a bit thicker and you have a stew. Gumbo is both the dish of the common man and the gourmand. It can have great variety and finesse.

In recent decades Gumbo in restaurants has evolved from an entree to a soup. Some believe that it has lost some of its flavor and texture in the process.

Courtbouillon This is a fish soup or stew usually made with the filets of redfish or red snapper and using tomatoes, onions, and spices. Served in bowls with French bread.

Turtle Soup Turtle meat is a natural resource in Louisiana, and restaurants vie for excellence in its preparation. The best soups are dark and meaty. Sherry is either added by the chef or served on the side. The soup is usually garnished with lemon and chopped hard-boiled eggs.

EGGS

Eggs Hussarde At Brennan's, this presentation begins with a slice of ham across a Holland Rusk covered with marchand de vin sauce. Then a slice of ripe tomato and a poached egg are added. The finishing touch is Hollandaise sauce and a garnish of paprika. The restaurant uses one million eggs and Rusks annually.

Eggs Sardou This creation was named for French playwright Victorien Sardou at Galatoire's. Boiled fresh artichoke hearts are filled with creamed spinach and topped by a poached egg and Hollandaise sauce. At other restaurants, the artichoke hearts may be stuffed with other ingredients. Hollandaise sauces are always individual to the respective restaurants.

SANDWICHES

Po-Boys They began as a "poor boy's" nickel lunch. To call them "subs" or "hoagies" indicates a failure to recognize the New Orleans mania for food. Po-Boys start with French Breach and then delicious things are added on a base of mayonnaise. Fried oysters, soft shell crabs, and roast beef with gravy are some of the variations.
    A Po-Boy by any other name might be called a shrimp Boat or an Oyster Loaf. In this sandwich some of the bread is hollowed out to allow for a generous cargo of seagoods.

Muffuletta A muffuletta is a gigantic Sicilian/Creole sandwich which is as filling as any sandwich can be. At Central Grocery (famous for the best Muffulettas) an olive-oil based salad is prepared in advance. Then large circular buns are dipped in the mixture and some of the salad sprinkled over the wet bread. Layers of Italian meats and sausages are then added and the entire concoction is topped off with some aged Italian parmesean cheese. The muffuletta is then quartered and sometimes served with pickles. If you can finish the whole thing, all the better. Many before you have tried and failed.

SEAFOODS

Buster Crabs The crab sheds its shell each time it grows. At the moment it breaks out of its old shell, it is a "buster" and it is totally edible and especially rich in taste. The "soft shell" stage follows as the crab begins to grow a new shell. Busters are usually fried or broiled and served with lemon butter.

Crawfish Etoufee The tails of the small, fresh water crustacean which is a relative of the lobster are served in a spicy tomato-based sauce. Usually accompanied with hot fluffy rice.

Shrimp Creole   If you have eaten it a dozen times anywhere else but New Orleans, you haven't tasted the real thing. Every chef has his own special recipe for the spicy red sauce. Maybe the secret is boiling the shrimp in Mississippi River water. Whatever. If you like big Gulf shrimp and a sauce with finesse, try it in at least two restaurants. Served with rice.

Red Snapper   It's fresh from the Gulf, and it is an especially "meaty" fish that lends itself to sauces. It is often sauted in seasonings, and always seen with a sauce that is the pride of the house.

Redfish   This fish is a relative of the Atlantic Rockfish. It is plentiful in the waters of Louisiana, and is very versatile for poaching, broiling, and baking. Fillets of redfish appear in hundreds of Creole recipes. Baked whole, it can be eaten hot or cold with the appropriate sauce. Redfish and Red Snapper are often used interchangeably in many preparations. You will see it on most restaurant menus in New Orleans.

Pompano En Papillote   This is Antoine's classic preparation of a noble, tasty fish with a little help from his friends, the shrimp and the crab. The sauce for the pompano fillets, involving his seafood friends, wine and other supporting flavorings is prepared in several complex stages. The sauted fillets are married to the sauce in well oiled parchment-paper hearts (yes, hearts) and baked. The paper bag is cut open at the table. The aroma is a gourmet's delight; the taste his ecstasy. Franklin D. Roosevelt and Cecil B. DeMille were among the patrons of this particular culinary extravaganza.

Oyster Brochette   Oysters are wrapped in bacon and placed on a skewer for sauteing. They are usually served on toast triangles with lemon butter. They are eaten both as an appetizer or a main course. Masson's is well known for this presentation.

Frogs' Legs   Early American arrivals in New Orleans called the Creoles "Johnny Crapauds" because they enjoyed eating frogs legs. (Crapaud in French means toad. The appelation is not exactly flattering.) Nevertheless, with Louisiana bayous abounding in big edible Anuras, it is natural that the culinary minds of New Orleans made the most of them. Frogs' Legs are usually sauted in butter with garlic, shallots, mushrooms, wine and other variations on the flavoring ingredients. At their best, they are tender as a young chicken, and delicate in taste. Don't be afraid to order Frogs' Legs at any of the city's gourmet rooms. You won't be disappointed. (And you won't be called a Johnny Crapaud!!)

MEATS

Grillades   In restaurants, grillades may be squares of beef sirloin browned in a skillet and then simmered in a brown roux gravy with onions, tomatoes and spices. In Creole homes, the meats are the left-overs of a beef or veal dinner that are recooked in the morning for breakfast and served over fried grits. Grits and grillades is a Creole breakfast food.

Boudin This is country Cajun food. It is a mixture of pork, cooked rice, onions, and spices stuffed into a sausage casing. Boudin can be hot or midly seasoned. It is eaten hot, not because it cannot be eaten cold, but because the people standing in line for it to finish cooking eat it in the car before they get home.

Andouille The hard, salty country sausage you see in your Cajun gumbo is probably andouille. It has a unique smoked taste, and is used in Cajun cooking to flavor soups and beans. It is also great off the grill.

Jambalaya The name means "clean up the kitchen". It's another testament to the ability of Louisiana cooks to make something wonderful from simple foods. The meats can be ham, shrimp, sausage, or bits of pork, chicken or beef. The vegetables are chopped onions, celery, bell pepper, and parsley. Spices include garlic, thyme, cloves, and cayenne. It all comes together with tomatoes and cooked rice. A meal in a skillet. Leftover jambalaya makes an excellent stuffing for green bell peppers.

Veal Fillets and cutlets of baby veal have always been in demand by gourmets, and the French influence in New Orleans has led to some elegant veal preparations. **Veal Lafayette** at Commander's is a milk-fed veal cutlet in a wine sauce and cheese filled crepe topped by the Lafayette glaze, a mixture of Hollandaise and Bechamel sauces.

Boeuf Robespierre Created by the 16-year-old Antoine Alciatore, the founder of Antoine's, in a meal prepared for Talleyrand, Napoleon's Foreign Minister.

FOWL

Pigeonneaux Squabs were a popular plantation delicacy. You can still see pigeon coops standing behind some of the restored plantation houses.

Pigeonneaux Acadiens at Brennan's are roasted squabs stuffed with a dressing made with chicken livers, gizzards, ham, and other good things.

Pigeonneaux Paradis at Antoine's are roast squabs topped with a wine, red currant jelly sauce containing grapes and truffles.

VEGETABLES AND SALADS

Souffle Potatoes   The great French chef Collinet taught the future founder of Antoine's how to make Pommes Soufflees. Chef Collinet "accidently" created the fried potatoes that are miraculously puffed up like balloons for a late arriving King Louis Philippe. The secret is carefully selected potatoes, two different oil temperatures, and a lot of luck. The ones that come out perfectly are still served at Antoine's.

Stuffed Eggplant   Bon Ton and Galatoire's are among the restaurants which stuff the shells of boiled eggplants with shrimp and lump crabmeat and bake it with other ingredients for a beautiful and taste enriching presentation.

Mirliton   This is a vegetable pear with a hard shell and eatable inner pulp. It is prepared like acorn squash and generally stuffed with shrimps and a spicy French bread dressing.

Plantain   It's like a banana, but New Orleanians like to serve it as a vegetable. Baked in a sugar sauce like yams, or fried and then simmered in a sherry fortified syrup, plantains are excellent as a meat accompaniment. Order it as a side dish if it is offered on the menu.

Red Beans and Rice   Thsi dish was traditionally served on Mondays when mothers had their stoves occupied heating water for the weekly clothes washing. The kidney beans were soaked overnight and then boiled with onions, garlic, bay leaves, and a salt meat, either ham or sausage. Some of the beans are mashed to make a gravy, and the hot beans and meat bits are served over rice. It is a hardy meal that can still be enjoyed in New Orleans today.

Dirty Rice   Leftover cooked rice is put into a skillet of sauteed onion, celery, green peppers, meat essence and giblets. The result is a hardy side dish that is worth of a good Chinese fried rice.

SAUCES

Remoulade Sauce   Every great New Orleans Restaurant has its own recipe for Remoulade Sauce to serve with shrimp and other seafoods. Parsley, shallots, celery, garlic, Creole hot mustard, horseradish, and paprika are some of the common ingredients. Remoulade here is not like its mayonnaise based Paris ancestor. In New Orleans, the sauce has fire! Judging the qualities of the various Remoulade Sauces served in the city could be the excuse for a restaurant tour, or a culinary graduate paper.

DESSERTS

Bread Pudding With Whiskey Sauce   Day old French bread has a second chance at glory when soaked in milk, crushed and mixed with eggs, sugar, vanilla and raisins, and then baked and served with a butter-sugar-egg based whiskey sauce. It's another New Orleans tradition of using all your resources creatively. Small restaurants and even famous ones take their versions of bread pudding seriously.

Crepes Fitzgerald   This dessert crepe contains Philadelphia cream cheese and sour cream over which a flaming sauce of strawberries, butter, strawberry liqueur and kirsch is poured. Famous at Brennan's.

Sabayon   A thick, rich sherry custard served cold in ramekins. It is an old Creole adaptation of Italian Zabaglione, and is often spelled "zabayon". It can be served hot.

Mile High Ice Cream Pie   The original, and still best version of this often imitated dessert can be found at the Caribbean Room of the Pontchartrain Hotel. Layers of vanilla and chocolate ice cream are placed in a pastry shell, topped by a tall meringue, and drizzled with a very special chocolate sauce.

Bananas Foster   This is another flaming dessert which is associated with Brennan's. It is usually prepared in a tableside presentation. A ripe banana is basted with flaming banana liqueur and rum, in a sauce of cinnamon and brown sugar. The restaurant usees 35,000 pounds of bananas for this dessert every year.

Beignets   The square yeast dough doughnuts, sprinkled with powdered sugar are perhaps better suited to coffee breaks than to elegant dinners. The traditional place to enjoy them is at the Cafe du Monde in the French Market. Open 24-hours a day.

Pralines   A city rich in sugar is rich in candy. Pralines are a candy confection of cooked sugars, both white and brown, which are poured into thin round patties. Pecans are the most common extra ingredient, although you will find many varieties of pralines in New Orleans gift and candy shops.

THE SAN FRANCISCO WINE EXCHANGE

MARKETERS OF FINE CALIFORNIA WINES

Presents

CALIFORNIA'S FINEST WINERIES

Louis J. Foppiano Wine Co.
David Bruce Winery
Lytton Springs Winery
Martin Ray
Navarro Vineyards
Baldinelli Vineyards
Monterey Peninsula Winery
M. Marion & Co.
Quady Ports
Bandiera Winery
Gemello Winery

**Available at Finer Restaurants and
Wine Stores in New Orleans**

442 Tehama Street, San Francisco, California 94103, (415) 546-0484

RESTAURANTS

In providing a guide to one of the world's great restaurant cities, we are conscious of the difference between eating and dining; the former is a pleasant daily experience, the latter is a special event. We acknowledge the many variables in the food service profession, but our experience tells us that there are obvious telltales of excellence within each type, or genre, of restaurant operation.

For our readers convenience we have established four categories as a guide to menu prices, and a three-star system of identifying award caliber establishments.

The cost guidelines are based on a meal for two persons which includes appetizers, entrees, two vegetables or side dishes, desserts, and coffee. The calculation for each restaurant was based on a la carte items at evening prices. Luncheon specials and other common sense factors can lower the basic check total just as cocktails, wine, and flaming tableside desserts can increase it.

Restaurateurs with pocket calculators can easily challenge our best intentions in offering menu price guidelines. A meal may be obtained in many places below the cost line especially at better places serving lunch. Inflation and menu changes will also come into play. But our dining-out attitude is to enjoy our favorite offerings on the menu and be prepared to pay the bill.

Here are the guidelines that are reflected in the restaurant profiles to follow:

INEXPENSIVE   A basic meal for two under $22.

MODERATE   A check for two of $22 to $28.

EXPENSIVE   Over $35 for two.

VERY EXPENSIVE   Over $45 for two.

The above cost do NOT include gratuities (15 to 20 percent depending on service), and the 7-percent tax on restaurant meals imposed in New Orleans. Thus a $36 meal (Expensive), plus tip of $5.50 (about 15%), plus tax of $2.52 (7%) runs the total tab to $44.02. Now if you add two cocktails each ($12 including tip), and a bottle of wine (let's say $15 including tip), you've hit $71 for the evening.

The three-star rating system is our attempt to recognize excellence within several genre of restaurant operations. We have also named selections for **Best Suburban Neighborhood Restaurant**, and **Best New Restaurant.**

Here are the award criteria:

THREE STARS	Absolutely one of the finest restaurants in America. A magnificient dining experience.
TWO STARS	A truly superior restaurant worthy of special acclaim.
ONE STAR	An excellent restaurant in its genre which serves distinguished food.

There are a few discouraging reviews of restaurants in this section. Our general policy is to ignore places that we cannot recommend, and that is not to say that some worthy places were not included in this edition. However, when a restaurant is widely advertised, or overrated because of its ancient history, we feel justified in warning you away from spending your food dollars there. Many visitors come to New Orleans for only two or three days. There should be no excuse for a second-rate experience when there is so much excellence among the city's eating establishments.

The authors continue to evaluate the area's restaurants on almost a daily basis. We take our responsibility to critique seriously, and we are saddened when we feel it necessary to give a negative report. As our guide goes through respective printings and annual editions, we have the opportunity, however, to up-date our observations. We'll be at the table to monitor changes and to reflect them in our future profiles. Just like you, we always hope for a good eating or dining experience at a fair price.

As users of our information, and our recommendations, we urge you to communicate your own restaurant experiences to us. Share with us your own observations. Tell us about the good as well as the bad that you encounter. Your opinions are important to us. If enough of you turn thumbs up, or thumbs down on a particular establishment, and our own investigation confirms the points, our future up-dates will reflect that input in print.

Most restaurants in our profiles accept major credit cards. Exceptions are noted. Most places accept reservations, and it is wise to reserve early to avoid disappointment. Parking can pose a problem in the French Quarter and in the Central Business District. If possible, take a taxi to your restaurant destinations in these areas.

The restaurants profiled in this guide are arranged alphabetically by area. For example, all the French Quarter spots are together. Each location is keyed to a detailed strip map for your further convenience.

THE 1982 INSIDERS' GUIDE
RESTAURANT AWARD WINNERS

THREE STARS
★★★

Commander's Palace	Arnaud's	La Louisiane
Le Ruth's	Willy Coln's	Visko's

TWO STARS
★★

Agostino's	Antoine's
Bistro Steak Room	Brennan's
Broussard's	Butcher Shop
Caribbean Room	Chez Helene
Christian's	Crozier's
K-Paul's	La Provence
Louis XVI	Maison Pierre
Mayer's Old Europe	Moran's Riverside
Peppermill	Sazerac
Versailles	Vincenzo's

Winston's

ONE STAR
★

Andrew Jackson	Anything Goes	Bon Ton
Augie's	Begue's	Drago's
Bozo's	Delerno's	Georgie Porgie's
Fish Market	Galatoire's	Gumbo Shop
Impastato's	Imperial Palace Regency	La Riviera
Jonah's	Kolb's	Lido Gardens
Le Bon Creole	Lido	Marti's
Little Cajun Cuisine	Mandina's	Mr. B's Bistro
Masson's	Mittendorf's	Parkers
Mosca's	Navia's	Rib Room
Pascal's Manale	Ruth's Chris Steak	Stephen & Martin's
Restaurant Jonathan	Royal Oak	Tony Angelo's
Ro-je's	Tchoupitoulas Plantation	Sal & Sam's

FRENCH QUARTER

ACME OYSTER HOUSE

724 Iberville Street   **Map, pg. 71**   523-8928
Inexpensive

Looking very much the same as it always has, the Acme is another of those traditional eating and watering holes which never seems to age nor diminish in popularity. Here the proud oyster steps to center stage in the specific American city where his presence seems most appreciated. Most New Orleanians tend to enjoy their oysters on the half shell, where pure taste separates this worldly mollusk from his billowy counterparts.

Acme prepares a number of different oyster dishes, with the fried oysters surpassing other preparations for consistency and taste. There are shrimp dishes also, and a marvelous selection of sandwiches from which to choose. Best are the tasty Shrimp Loaf and the rich Roast Beef Poor Boy, which are both made in the style of old New Orleans.

Fresh french bread holds some of the secret to these dishes which have contributed a great deal to the city's culinary reputation. There is also always plenty of cold beer on hand (both on tap and in bottles) at the Acme, a site whose convenient location can also serve as a brief respite from the full-service facilities which dot the French Quarter and the downtown area. Closed Sundays.

ANDREW JACKSON

221 Royal Street   **Map, pg. 71**   529-2603
Expensive

This pleasant restaurant has been a dependable part of the French Quarter dining community for the past two decades. Even though it occupies a tourist-oriented location directly opposite the Monteleone Hotel, its trade is mostly New Orleanians as evidenced by its large luncheon volume.

Fare here is typically New Orleans, with a few classic Creole dishes thrown in for variety. The kitchen's output, while not often of the spectacular variety, is quite steady and worth the prices. The Andrew Jackson's most celebrated single dish is the Veal King Ferdinand VII which has won lasting critical acclaim. The dish combines baby veal, a large portion of hand-picked lump crabmeat, and an exquisite sauce bernaise. There are other good dishes, but the Veal Ferdinand is in a class by itself.

We recommend the Puddin du Pain and the Lump Crabmeat Lafitte as excellent examples of old-style New Orleans cooking where seasoning emphasis tends to portray individual flavors rather than the conglomeration of flavors more prominent in regional cooking. Closed Sat. and Sun. for lunch.

ANYTHING GOES

727 Iberville Street   **Map, pg. 71**   561-8251
                                    Moderate

At Anything Goes, everything usually does, and that's the fun of it all! This newish (1978) establishment fulfills even the wildest fantasies of both its customers and service personnel. Built along the lines of the successful Magic Time Machine theme chain, Anything Goes has been wildly popular since its inception.

Numerous theme settings in the multi-level building offer some innovative attention getters for the prospective diner. A vintage MG sportscar serves as a soup and salad bar. A spirited kookoo's nest bypasses a giant Budweiser can. Anything Goes never ceases to amaze. Waiters and waitresses can choose their own costume, suited, of course, to their own fantasy life. Baby Huey, Tarzan, Wonder Woman, Zorro, take your pick, they are all part of Anything Goes' carnival air.

The fare here is continental and decidely consistent. The main emphasis is on steaks, chicken, and lobster combinations. A children's menu is available. Everything in sight is for sale including soiled and unsoiled menus and T-Shirts. It's all for fun, so come prepared to smile. Closed Mondays and Tuesdays for lunch.

ANTOINE'S

713 St. Louis Street   **Map, pg. 159**   581-4422
                                    Expensive

Like a grand dame of the stage, this lovely relic of by gone days grows older gracefully. Proprietor Roy Guste IV is the fourth generation owner of Antoine's which dates back to 1842, making it the oldest restaurant at the same address in the United States.

Oysters Rockefeller was created here as were many other marvelous dishes. Today's Coq au Vin is simple and rewarding. Several items which locals take for granted have won worldwide acclaim. The Pommes de Terre Souffles (Puffed Potatoes) is an incredibly-conceived appetizer in which the potatoes are fried at 400 degrees and served piping-hot at tableside. The glorious Pompano en Papilotte is an institution at Antoine's and the Omelette Alaska Antoine (Baked Alaska) is the epitome of dessert.

Antoine's means something different to each diner which is perhaps the secret of its success. Her grandness is finesse itself, and as the elder matron she is, she holds herself proudly. Closed Sundays.

ARNAUD'S

813 Bienville Street   **Map, pg. 71**   523-5433
Very Expensive

When Archie Casbarian bought Arnaud's in 1978 from Germaine Wells (Count Arnaud's daughter) many knowledgeable eyes around New Orleans took notice. As one of ageing matrons of the New Orleans restaurant community, Arnaud's had quite simply seen better days.

At this time it is our pleasure to report that the renaissance of Arnaud's is now complete. Casbarian has returned the place to its lofty perch as one of the top restaurants in the city. Indeed, Arnaud's might be the finest restaurant in the entire city at this point.

The main impetus in Arnaud's rise to culinary excellence is the incredible balance between kitchen and service, the basic necessity *any* restaurant who attempts greatness must achieve. Pay special attention to the menu items which are underscored in red. All are house specialties worthy of consideration by even the most astute gourmets. Of particular note are the Oysters Bienville (which was originated here decades ago), and the marvelous Shrimp Arnaud.

Entree-wise, the fish dishes surpass even great expectations. Finest are a superlative Trout Meuniere (the way New Orleanians love it) and a more arty Pompano en Papiliotte. From fowl selections, try the marvelous Rock Cornish Hen Flambe Twelfth Night for a festive touch or the delicate Veal Scallopini Claude which is Chef Claude Aubert's crowning veal masterpiece.

A new innovation, Sunday Jazz Brunch, features musican Alvin Alcorn, Jr. and his group in a most memorable setting.

BRENNAN'S

417 Royal Street   **Map, pg. 71**   525-9711
Expensive

True to the American "melting pot" tradition, this wonderful restaurant was conceived in 1945 by an Irishman, Owen Brennan. Today, his three sons, Pip, Jimmy and Teddy, continue the pioneer restaurant traditions which have brought the French Quarter location worldwide acclaim. This is the exact spot on which breakfast was elevated to the grand experience which is "Breakfast at Brennan's". The egg reaches its zenith in both Eggs Sardou and Eggs Hussarde, two traditional breakfast items at Brennan's which never disappoint.

After dark, Brennan's assumes another personality with soft lights and service that makes for a truly memorable gourmet dining experience. Superb entrees like Veal Kottwitz and Redfish Perez must be experienced to be believed. Those who consider Brennan's only for breakfast miss many of its great menu items. For desserts (daytime and nightime) Brennan's simply can't be touched. Masterful creations like Crepes Fitzgerald and Bananas Foster are the tops, but Maude's Peanut Butter

Pie is a sleeper which has won a boisterous following.

Brennan's interior and patio setting is exquisite and considered by many to be the Quarter's most accessible location. A finely tuned bar makes waiting even more of a pleasure at this renowned spot. Reserve early, for Brennan's tends to become crowded at the drop of a hat even during normal times. It is just that sort of a place.

BEGUE'S ★

(Royal Sonesta Hotel)

300 Bourbon Street   **Map, pg. 71**   586-0300

Expensive

In its impeccable Royal Sonesta location, Begue's is one of the most conveniently located restaurants in the French Quarter. About four years ago, management decided to offer a buffet luncheon and a regular continental dinner selection in the evening. The decision proved very successful and ever since, Begue's has been a crowded place.

Of particular note are the fifty-odd buffet items which feature an assortment of thoughtfully conceived dishes in a splendid setting. Seafood, Veal, and Chateaubriand appear on the generous table. On warm evenings and weekends, the verdant patio (without a doubt one of the finest in the city) is put to practical use as the setting for outdoor parties. The food is remarkably consistent for a hotel which has employed several executive chefs during the past few years.

Private parties are quite special at the Sonesta and several gourmet functions have received rave notices. Next door, the dominant singing personality Elario (See Nightlife section) holds forth in the Mystic Den. At Begue's main entrance, the city's first wine bar beckons the oenophile. Not surprisingly, it all fits together at the Sonesta.

BENIHANA OF TOKYO

720 St. Louis Street   **Map, pg. 71**   522-0425

Moderate

Japanese restaurants have appeared on the horizon for the past few years, so it seems only natural that the French Quarter should have one of its own. The emphasis here is on the culinary show, or the performing cooks. Semi-private partitions divide the large dining room. The center of each is the grill, or stage, where the meal is prepared. The chef enters stage right, and the play begins. The chef's meticulous art of stripping, cutting, balancing, and frying is a masterpiece of timing and in some cases, a little luck.

Best items are the Hibachi Shrimp, which are cut to resemble roses, and the Sukiyaki Steak, shaped to resemble hearts and arrows. A selection of Japanese beers and sakes is available and also a diminutive wine list.

Prices are well within reason and the entire production makes the time pass quickly. Good entertainment, great fun! Closed Sat. and Sun. for lunch.

BROUSSARD'S

819 Conti Street **Map, pg. 71** 581-3866

Moderate/Expensive

Each of Broussard's three dining rooms is an exquisite jewel and the entire facility a necklace adorning New Orleans' sparkling culinary reputation. After five years of operation, Broussard's continues to be one of the city's most successful restaurant restorations. Much of Broussard's success can be traced to Chef Nathaniel Burton who developed most of Broussard's original recipes and to his recent successor, Chef Gerard Thabuis.

While Burton's creations set the standard for pure New Orleans taste and style of cooking., Thabuis' innovations and presentations have propelled Broussard's into recent national limelight. Masterful Duck a la Novelle Orleans is about as good as duck can taste. It is served over a bed of dirty rice and presents an imposing picture. An excellent fresh Trout Louis Phillipe and a classic Chicken Clemenceau give some insight as to the kitchen's style as opposed to either Creole or Cajun, and the subtleties must be understood to be enjoyed. A great deal of research into New Orleans' earlier dishes and recipes has made this lavish setting a leader around town.

Desserts, too, are incredible. A wonderfully rich Crepes Brulatour features strawberries, whipped cream and whole pecans and challenges even the heartiest diner. The more simplistic Creme Caramel and the delicate Lemon Ice are also wonderments to the palate. Service is elegantly attentive. Valet parking is a plus in the crowded French Quarter. Broussard's is a most intriguing place, both historically and commercially. It is a spot which shouldn't be missed. Dinner only.

CAFE MASPERO

811 Decatur Street **Map, pg. 159** 523-8414

Inexpensive

When Maspero's moved from its original site which was an old slave auction house, thank goodness they remembered to take their marvelous recipes with them. Today the home of New Orleans' foremost deli-style combination sandwich and plate emporium is on Decatur Street but little has changed. It's entirely possible Maspero's provides you with too much sandwich for the price, for that's the only complaint Maspero's usually receives. Best of the sandwiches are the Corned Beef on rye and the Pastrami on anything. Maspero's Hamburgers, while also of the giant variety, are not really equal to their specialty sandwiches and should be left for the uninformed.

Maspero's new location, directly across from the Jax Brewery, is one of the pioneers of the Decatur rehabilitation effort and well within most foot traffic patterns for the French Quarter. Long lines prevail even during slack periods, so we suggest takeouts whenever possible. While service sometimes tends to be tardy and seemingly unconcerned, the end product certainly outweighs any inconvenience. In a city such as New Orleans, a people place like Maspero's is a large part of the fun. Recently, catfish and oyster selections and some soups and salads have been added to enhance Maspero's limited menu.

CAFE SBISA

1011 Decatur Street   **Map, pg. 237**   561-8354

Expensive

Dating from 1899, Cafe Sbisa (pronounced saBEEsah) was renovated and reopened by its present owners in 1979. Its interior is a masterful decorating feat and the massive dominant bar/oyster bar is well-placed. Although referred to as a Grill on its menu, Cafe Sbisa is a serious restaurant which could conceivably gain real stature.

The menu is marvelously New Orleans and leans heavily toward fried seafoods and an assortment of grilled entrees that are prepared open-hearth. Cafe Sbisa's Pate Maison is well-textured but more a terraine that a true pate. Several fried appetizers, Oysters Brochette (a different style than usual), Fried Dill Pickles, and Fried Eggplant were all light, crispy and should be well received. Best bet on the seafood side of the menu is the Special Seafood Mix which features shrimp, scallops, crabs and/or oysters, either sauteed or deep fried. Another house special, New Orleans Bouillabaise, is a watery version of its French cousin with distinct white pepper and cayenne undertones. Redfish with Crabmeat Sauce is light, delicate, and fills the tastebuds. Duckling a la' Orange was dried and lacked any real punch. One wonders why the duck is attempted in restaurants of this type?

Cafe Sbisa's new lease on life seems destined for longevity and continued progress. The Sunday Champagne Brunch is among the best with a large choice of Table d'Hote menu items and unlimited champagne. Closed Mondays.

CASTILLO'S

620 Conti Street   **Map, pg. 71**   581-9602

Inexpensive

There is an explosion of Mexican fast food outlets around the country which tends to give one a rather negative view of what is involved in really good Mexican cooking. While New Orleans doesn't possess a top-flight Mexican establishment, Castillo's must certainly rank among the top three in existence. Conveneintly located on Conti between Royal and Chartres, Castillo's is comfortable and attractively styled and fits in nicely with the French Quarter's cosmopolitan attitudes.

The Menu is basic Mexican provincial, with more on the plus side than the minus. Guacamole at Castillo's is one of the finest offerings around, and is in keeping with New Orleans' deep-rooted affair with avocado. A spicy Mexican soup Caldo Xochi combines vegetables and avocado, and a home grown herb named Culantio to good effect. The Chili Conqueso is another impressive entree when accompanied by a hearty Mexican beer like Carta Blanca or Dos Eques.

A spot like Castillo's is a welcome haven after prolonged partying in the Quarter. Its spicy dishes are just what the doctor ordered for heavy heads, and the process puts only a modest dent in the pocketbook.

CHART HOUSE

801 Chartres Street   Map, pg. 159   523-2015
Moderate

While Chart House is part of a national chain, the interior furnishings and food produced by this convenient French Quarter corner location make it worthy of special mention and consideration. Located at the busy St. Ann/Chartres Street intersection. Chart House's second floor balcony commands a truly spectacular view of Jackson Square, with its historic setting and ever-changing cast of people. Chart House's interior is comfortable with touches of Southern graciousness.

True to the chain concept, small loaves of bread are offered upon seating. That's about where the chain similarity ends however at this Chart House. Salads are big production affairs. There is an excellent Beef Kabob and several fine steak selections (the filet is an unusually large piece of prime meat) as well as continental items designed to please the average palate.

For dessert, a glorious throwback to total Southern decadence, the Mud Pie is unmatched anywhere in the city. Wines are generally Californian and quite reasonably priced. For an extra treat, try to time your arrival just as the sun begins to set over Jackson Square. It is a picture postcard experience.

COURT OF TWO SISTERS

631 Royal Street   Map, pg. 159   522-7261
Expensive

Movies have been made in this famous courtyard and thousands on their honeymoon have had their first meal together at the "Court". Reeking of southern hospitality and charm, the Court of Two Sisters could easily be one of the most romantic locations in the entire world. Food here tends to be New Orleans style of the purely commerical variety owing to the place's large annual tourist business.

Owned by the Fein Family, the Court of Two Sisters has always specialized in group and tourist business. A year or so ago, a new brunch concept, focused around two giant pirogues filled with a variety of buffet-style food items, went into effect and has been quite popular with the Court's clientele. Such a concept gives the French Quarter spot greater flexibility but really doesn't interfere with private parties or the like which tend to make up a large part of its business. The setting here is quite spectacular and the bar well-stocked. One would wish for more elevated cuisine to match such surroundings, but that's simply not the case. A daily Jazz Brunch has also been added which tends to keep the court very lively.

DESIRE OYSTER BAR
(Royal Sonesta Hotel)

300 Bourbon Street   **Map, pg. 71**   586-0300
                            Inexpensive

This attractive niche is a prime example of a hotel attempting to be all things to all people. The Desire Oyster Bar location (Bourbon and Conti) is the best corner in the French Quarter with crowds flowing by both day and night. Ambiance is near-perfect and the prices charged are in line with most oyster bars. But the Desire's main offering, and supposedly the reason for its existence, is sadly neglected. Desire's oysters run the gauntlet between very good and very bad. On occasions, they are served almost warm due to the staff's opening the oysters prematurely. The oysters themselves are inconsistent, both in size and taste.

Running an oyster bar in New Orleans is something of an art and tradition, and it seems to us that the Royal Sonesta is at somewhat of a disadvantage. Some of Desire's other items tend to be above average, but an establishment named an oyster bar must be judged by its oysters. Most tourists don't seem to mind (or really aren't aware of the subtle differences in oysters) for the Desire Oyster Bar is well-attended most of the time; a tribute to the eternal people-watchers who live in and visit New Orleans.

EL LIBORIO

334 Decatur Street   **Map, pg. 71**   581-9680
                            Moderate/Expensive

This is one of the few pure Cuban establishments still operating in a city where Cuban food was once quite popular. The menu is standard island fare, with a couple of fairly consistent stuffed steak items emerging as the best choices on a rather large menu. The big push is for El Liborio's Paella which sometimes tends to be mushy and quite drab, as good Paellas go. Other menu items which should be tried include a stuffed steak (either shrimp, crab or lobster) and a variety of sandwiches (roasted pig is best) for the not-so-hungry.

The service here fluctuates, as does the food, and it is hard to determine why. The location is right across from the city's largest fire station on Decatur Street, a little off the beaten track, but there is ample parking nearby. El Liborio has never caught on with the large local Cuban community and they realistically should be aware of significant Cuban cooking if it does indeed exist. Closed Mondays.

EMBERS STEAK HOUSE

700 Bourbon Street   **Map, pg. 159**   523-1485
                            Expensive

Long underrated in restaurant circles, the Embers continues to thrive on a proven format of consistent meat in convival surroundings with excellent portions and acceptable prices. True, the clientele is mainly tourist, but a good number of French Quarter regulars dine frequently at this cozy place in the heart of Bourbon Street. The menu is strictly middle-road steaks, but the specialties like Broiled Lamb Chop and Broiled Trout are very well prepared. When the cook is in a good mood, he is capable of an entertaining show—as befitting a permanent resident of Bourbon Street. The Embers is a comfortable stopover amidst the rigors of the famous strip.

FATTED CALF

727 St. Peter Street   **Map, pg. 159**   523-8425
                              Inexpensive

Popular with local residents and tourists alike, the Fatted Calf provides a pleasant atmosphere, strong mixed drinks, and a variety of the most unusual (and creative) hamburgers to be found anywhere. Menu items include a large Chef Salad, a variety of steak selections, and Red Beans and Rice. What separates the hamburgers of the Fatted Calf from their more commerical cousins is the variety of 16 toppings. Sour cream and caviar, fresh mushrooms, horse radish, and even red beans are on the list.

The fatted Calf is so laid back that its owners don't even advertise in the Yellow Pages. It is one of the places where the Jackson Square artists eat and relax.

FELIX'S

739 Iberville Street   **Map, pg. 71**   522-4440
                              Inexpensive

This unpretentious little niche fills one of the prime needs of the French

Quarter—a late night seafood house with a transcending sense of humor. Felix's can be (and usually is) loud and boisterous owing to its relaxed clientele and absolute down home atmosphere. Many Quarterites consider a weekly visit here part of the New Orleans ritual.

This hangout has one of the area's finest oyster bars which is locally rumored to be a Guiness record holder for number of oysters opened and served on the half shell during a given period. Other local seafood specialties are featured along with a smattering of Italian items. At Felix's however, the oysters still reign supreme.

If the main dining room seems filled, venture in anyway, for there is an elongated annex, capable of accommodating large numbers, connected by an inner passageway. Be prepared for a continuing din, for crowd noise here is as much a part of the place as the delicious salty oysters which have brought Felix's such wide acclaim. Closed Sundays.

GALATOIRE'S

209 Bourbon Street | Map, pg. 71 | 525-2021
Expensive

The reason for the ever-present line on Boubon Street in front of this oft-storied establishment is simply due to the fact that Galatoire's still continues the practice of accepting no reservations, a fact we find hard to accept. However, if the humidity and dust aren't particularly disheartening, the food and surroundings of this old epicurean niche are often well worth the wait and the inconvenience.

Galatoire's kitchen is most certainly at home with fish and poultry, and the Trout Almandine here sets the standard for the rest of the city. The end product is lightly crisp, delicate and perfectly enthroned in a pool of nutty deliciousness. Most food people consider Galatoire's fry station as the area's best and hence the accolades.

Tables here tend to be placed too close together and thus conversations carry to other diners. The dining room is a mirrored throwback to Bourgeoise dining in an era when this type of restaurant seems to have been forgotten. To beat the reservations game, try odd times (after 2, before 6:30) and you may get lucky. Oh yes, don't forget the Oysters en Brochette, a marvelous creation which tends to transcend Galatoires more obvious shortcomings in today's modern restaurant world. No credit cards are honored here, another inconsistency which casts a pall on what could easily be one of New Orleans' top restaurants. Hours 11:30 a.m.-9 p.m. Closed Mondays.

GIN'S MEE HONG RESTAURANT

739 Conti Street   **Map, pg. 71**   523-8471
Inexpensive

Gin's might be New Orleans' oldest Chinese restaurant. Located just off Bourbon Street's crowded sidewalks, Gin's is a well-kept secret of locals who enjoy Chinese food. Gin's was refurbished a few years ago, but has maintained most of its kitchen magic, oriental style.

Gin's celebrated Almond Duck, a cousin to the more widely accepted Mandarin Duck, is an oriental taste adventure. Add the marvelous Chinese mixed vegetable selection and the Cantonese-style Lobster and you've ascended to occidental heaven.

Prices are reasonable and the place is seldom crowded. A real sleeper among New Orleans' better restaurants. Closed Mondays.

GUMBO SHOP

630 St. Peter Street   **Map, pg. 159**   525-1486
Moderate

It is indeed fitting that one of the superb food creations which has helped shape the reputation of New Orleans as a premiere city of cuisine should have an entire restaurant dedicated to its preservation and betterment. It is even nicer when the end product of this particular establishment proves to be incredibly good and consistent.

The Gumbo Shop's real secret lies in the fact that its cooks follow traditional recipes and methods to produce truly original and distinctive, quality foods. Gumbos are prepared in large iron pots (in earlier times, these were the only pots available to produce sufficient amounts of Gumbo necessary to feed the large numbers) and cooked for hours at moderate temperatures. This method of cooking preserves the flavors and results in a rich and lavish combination of regional vegetables, seafoods, okra, and shellfish. There is also a selection of sandwiches available and daily special luncheons and dinners.

Bistro-like in scope and personality, the Gumbo Shop is one of those marvelous little spots which make you feel comfortable by simply doing what it knows best. During convention time, the Shop tends to crowd up easily, especially during the luncheon rush. It would be prudent to plan accordingly. A second location at 4932 Prytania (899-2405) near the Garden District, offers top food without the problems of French Quarter traffic and parking.

HOULIHAN'S

315 Bourbon Street   **Map, pg. 71**   523-7412
                                Moderate

When the prestigious Gilbert Robinson Co. of Kansas City decided to
open its New Orleans Houlihan's unit, its decision to alter the normal chain
menu proved wise. In addition to some innovative food planning, the New
Orleans Houlihan's has proved profitable and ranks among Gilbert
Robinson's top earners around the country. Houlihan's middle-of-the-
road continental menu has been complimented with a variety of excellent
New Orleans specialty items to provide some appetizing adventures
within Houlihan's relaxed dining atmosphere and convivial surroundings.

Salads are enormous, with the Spinach a real treat if you opt for
Houlihan's distinctive house dressing. An excellent Oyster Bar provides
fresh oysters year round, while several tasty seafood dishes on the menu
rate quite high. Of course, there are sandwiches and poor boys designed to
fit the whims and needs of its clientele. The bar is also well stocked and
contains several traditional New Orleans drink varieties which makes the
entire operation come together.

What Houlihan's has accomplished is to make a chain operation seem
quite local, a feat in which few other national franchisers have succeeded.
The wine list is predominantly Californian and able to carry the menu with
ease. Food prices are reasonable and designed to fit the occasion.
Houlihan's is a welcome addition to the French Quarter, an area which has
heretofore taken a rather dim view of national chain food businesses.

JOHNNY WHITE'S

733 St. Peter Street   **Map, pg. 159**   523-6153
                                Inexpensive

This smallish spot caught fire some years ago on Mardi Gras day and
nearly burned to the ground due to the fact that fire engines simply
couldn't penetrate the dense crowds. Johnny White's is tucked neatly
within the French Quarter, and today caters to a mostly local crowd (during
days) and at night to Bourbon Street's varied workers and entertainers.

The kitchen's emphasis is on fried seafood (try the shrimp, they fare best
overall) and an interesting poor boy selection which proves to be better
than the commerical variety one generally finds in this section of town. At
times the daily specials are worthy of attention and should be tried, but we
suggest this only at times Johnny White's is uncrowded.

On weekends and during heavy traffic times service tends to become
quite haggard, and the diner usually comes out on the short end. Still,
Johnny White's is one of the offbeat little French Quarter sites where one
will put up with food inconsistency and inconvenience to be part of a
genuine atmosphere and way of life which is truly New Orleans.

K-PAUL'S LA KITCHEN

416 Chartres Street   **Map, pg. 71**   524-7394
Moderate

In mid-1979, this charming little nook opened with little fanfare and a great deal of underlying background. True, K-Paul's is a tad musty and is possessed of an incredibly miniscule kitchen, but the tiny spot has nevertheless blossomed into a respectable restaurant and has already received wide critical acclaim for its culinary mastery. K-Paul's is owned by Chef Paul Prudhomme, former Executive Chef at Commander's Palace, and his wife, Kay. Prudhomme is responsible for the creation of the food dishes and guidance of the kitchen staff while Kay runs the front side with a careful, yet relaxed hand.

What Prudhomme has attempted here is his own particular style of Louisiana cooking, not Creole, not Cajun, just totally Prudhomme. There are no fancy tablecloths or fancy silverware, no tuxedoed waiters. What is in evidence is some incredible food at moderately low prices. K-Paul's daily specials should be tried. Both vegetables and seafood are bought fresh daily. There are such superbities as the Sauteed Seafood Platter, where the fish are battered and everything else is sauteed to perfection. The Trout with crabmeat butter is a luscious concoction which is richer than you can imagine. Traditional New Orleans Red Beans and Rice are cooked in ham hocks with regional andouille sausages thrown in for good measure.

A sense of adventure permeates K-Paul's where there is little emphasis on decor and almost complete dedication to food excellence. There is also little dependence on tourists, witness the closed days of Saturday and Sunday.

LA LOUISIANE

725 Iberville Street   **Map, pg. 71**   523-4664
Moderate/Expensive

After the fabled Elmwood Plantation burned down in 1978, its owners acquired this venerable New Orleans institution as a vehicle to continue their well-established reputation. After a magnificent restoration and enlargement, La Louisiane has quickly ascended into restaurant hierarchy and has again become one of the city's finest dining places.

Chef and co-owner Nick Mosca has an international following to compliment his formidable local reputation. His Oysters Mosca is considered a classic dish, on par with the regal Oysters Rockefeller, and other widely celebrated shellfish creations. Other Elmwood carryovers, including an inspired Cornish Hen, and a most rewarding Fresh Trout can also be found on La Louisianne's menu along with several dishes conceived in honor of the new French Quarter location.

La Louisiane itself is steeped in local restaurant tradition and personality.

FRENCH QUARTER III

△ ATTRACTIONS
1. Old French Market, pg. 68
2. Old U.S. Mint, pg. 84
3. Archbishop Blanc Memorial, pg. 69
4. Beauregard-Keyes, pg. 69
5. Gallier House, pg. 75
6. Gauche House, pg. 84
7. Streetcar Named "Desire," pg. 46
8. Haunted House, pg. 37
9. Cabrini Doll Museum, pg. 76

□ ACCOMMODATIONS
1. Provincial Motor Hotel, pg. 165
2. French Quarter Maisonnettes, pg. 182
3. Le Richelieu, pg. 160
4. Felton Guest House, pg. 182
5. Chateau Motor Hotel, pg. 156
6. Lamotte Guest House, pg. 183
7. Lafitte Guest House, pg. 183

○ RESTAURANTS
1. Fish Market, pg. 245
2. Cafe Sbisa, pg. 228

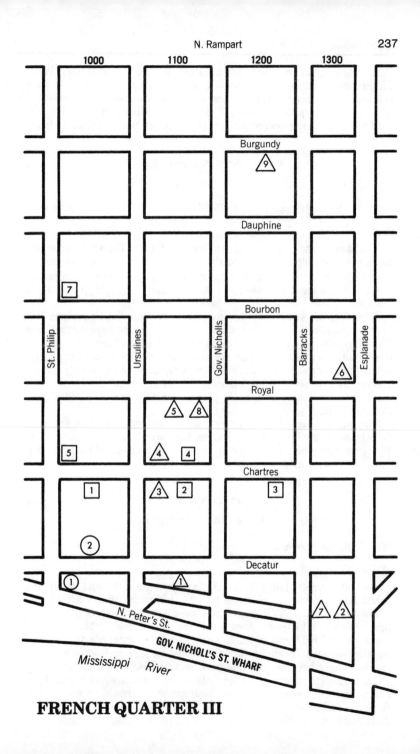

FRENCH QUARTER III

Service is stylish and intimate as befitting such a gracious setting. Prices offer an excellent value and the wine list exceeds expectations. At times this grand old place tends to become a bit clamorous, but in actuality, this is all in keeping with the owners' design of a relaxed and comfortable setting for both regulars and visitors alike. Closed Sat. and Sun. for lunch.

LE BON CREOLE
(Maison Dupuy)

1001 Toulouse Street   **Map, pg. 159**   586-8008
Expensive

The Maison Dupuy is one of the newer hotels in the French Quarter, and from many standpoints, one of the loveliest. Its enormous fountain is practically unmatched and creates a marvelous atmosphere in its courtyard. Le Bon Creole is a nattily attired restaurant resplendent in varying shades of pastels.

Foodwise, the kitchen mainly adheres to specific Creole recipes. The food served is very consistent, and at times is elevated to real excellence. The Maison Dupuy caters to Europeans and Le Bon Creole's food gives those visitors a true taste of the city's famous regional cuisine. Leading the menu items is an articulate Crabmeat au Artichauts which literally sings its praises by combining lump crabmeat in an exquisite chablis sauce. A manicured Veal Maison usually pleases, as does an excellent Crepes Pontchartrain.

The wine list here is much better than average with particular emphasis on whites, both imported and from California. Service tends to be European-oriented also, so one can expect a lengthy meal with plenty of time for conversation.

LOUIS XVI
(Marie Antoinette Hotel)

829 Toulouse Street   **Map, pg. 159**   581-7000
Very Expensive

Just off the main lobby of the Marie Antoinette Hotel sits the opulent Louis XVI, a haven for classical purists of French culinary art. Since it opened, the Louis XVI's accomplishments have dwarfed those of its pretentious hotel surroundings, a fact which still holds true.

Executive Chef Daniel Bonnet is a multi-award winner whose talents are equally virtuoso in all facets of culinary endeavor. Bonnet's Souffle creations have become his trademark, and rank with the finest anywhere.

The house specialty is the Filet de Boeuf Wellington which reeks of pate charm and true pastry crispness. Your attention should be given to the Rack of Lamb as well as the assortment of Soups du Jour which are never disappointing.

All dishes are tastefully presented by the salon's expert service personnel, most European, and all deft in full French table service. The wine list needs depth and expansion, but this seems the only real drawback. Reserve early, for the Louis XVI's seating capacity is quite limited.

MAISON PIERRE ★★

430 Dauphine Street　　Map, pg. 71　　529-5521
Very Expensive

This intimate French Quarter spot is the lushest in town, and with good reason. Besides truly elegant napery, expensive settings and opulent surroundings, Maison Pierre provides complete personal and professional service. It is indeed the haunt of the well-heeled lover of culinary excellence and ambiance.

"When guests enter Maison Pierre," says owner Pierre Lacoste, "it is our sincere wish to make them feel they are entering our home." Lacoste carries forth this ideal with great vigor, having gathered (mostly from Europe) a collection of period pieces and decorative items which collectively provide for the ultimate in gracious dining and enjoyment. The kitchen excels in regional seafood and shellfish dishes, many of which are Pierre's personal creations.

Of particular note is the Redfish Madame Pierre, a marvelous taste adventure and Lacoste's best single dish. The Tournedos Henry IV are the highest calibre, and the classical Shrimp Scampi reaches lofty heights at Maison Pierre's.

For years, Lacoste has spent time studying the sea creatures which are local to the Gulf and Louisiana areas, and his handling of these creatures is quite imaginative. Maison Pierre's is undoubtedly the most expensive restaurant in town, but the food served and the fuss made over you by the highly professional staff make the experience well worthwhile. Closed Mondays and Tuesday.

MARTI'S ★★

1041 Dumaine Street　　Map, pg. 159　　524-6060
Inexpensive

Reminiscent of the small, intimate bistros and brasseries which abound around Paris' opera district, Marti's is home for many of the arty types which populate the French Quarter. Located directly across from the Theatre for the Performing Arts/Armstrong Park complex, Marti's is a perfect blending of good taste and great food which produces a restaurant with true inner soul and feeling.

Its cuisine is pure Creole and very edible. House specials are changed often and offer excellent values. On nights when an event is booked at either the TPA or the neighboring Municipal Auditorium, a pre or post dinner at Marti's has become a tradition for many New Orleanians. The bar area is a true American brasserie, perfect for a quick drink and filled with colorful personalities. It is truly a world of its own.

Marti's possesses natural charisma and has become the darling of both the symphony and opera sets as well as many of the city's finest Carnival organizations. To accommodate its clientele, Marti's will stay open late on theatre nights if reservations to that effect have been made.

MESSINA'S

200 Chartres Street   **Map, pg. 71**   523-9225
                                     Inexpensive

Among the French Quarter's better neighborhood spots, Messina's ranks extremely high in honesty and unpretentiousness. Messina's is something of a tradition with locals and its half shell oyster bar ranks in line with Felix's and Acme; impressive company. Messina's sandwiches are near legend, particularly the traditional Roast Beef poor-boy and the fried Oyster Loaf.

The regular menu includes a number of Sicilian-style dishes which are sure to raise eyebrows. These dishes, mainly seafood-based, are rich and filling, so one should order accordingly. The extensive menu also includes broiled and fried versions (shrimp and oysters are always great) which vary according to how busy the place is i.e. the lighter the crowd, the better the frying, etc.

Messina's is a local hangout which reeks of personality and thrives on the neighborhood types which frequent its premises. It is fun to just sit and watch. Closed Monday.

MORAN'S RIVERSIDE   ★★

14 French Market   **Map, pg. 159**   529-1583
                                 Expensive

Perched atop a building in the renovated French Market, Moran's Riverside provides a spectacular view of the main crescent of the Mississippi River. Moran's menu mirrors owner Jimmy Moran's remarkable penchant for Creole/Italian cuisine.

The kitchen, after several personnel changes during the past few years, has stabilized and is most at home with a classic Fettucini Alfredo (comparable to the original in Rome). An excellent Veal Moran which is a throwback to old-style New Orleans preparation gives additional insight to Jimmy Moran's culinary genius.

Moran's dinner setting is elegant, discriminating, and perfect in its surroundings. The wine list is well above average and reasonably priced. It is a truly intimate and satisfying spot to enjoy the seaport of New Orleans and Moran's always seems to rise to the culinary occasion. As a regular gathering place for professional (and retired) athletes, there seems to be an air of celebration here throughout most of the year.

MR. B'S BISTRO ★

201 Royal Street   Map, pg. 71   523-2078
                          Moderate

The fact that Mr. B's chose to utilize its enormous working kitchen as a focal point gives an insight as to just how forward-thinking this food operation is. No longer is a diner offered bare walls and distant decorations to view during mealtime. At Mr. B's a complete kitchen operation featuring wood-burning stoves, a utilitarian pasta station and drying racks, not to mention plenty of old-fashioned elbow grease makes for a most interesting side show.

This adventuresome concept is the product of Ella and Dick Brennan, members of the famous Brennan restaurant family. The Brennan's gave former Executive Chef Paul Prudhomme free reign here and his mark is still quite evident. In order for the open kitchen to work in the eyes of the public, it has to be meticulously maintained, and Mr. B's staff certainly sees to that.

The menu, an engaging combination of items designed to fill any number of needs, includes Fettucine, a delightful melted Camenbert appetizer, a long list of grilled specialties, and fresh Louisiana seafood. Through it all, Mr. B's is amazingly adept and distinctly consistent. The place is huge and the bar is polished and finely stocked. Wines are practically all California and expertly selected to compliment the food. Mr. B's is an excellent addition to the French Quarter as well as an enterprising look into the future. Breakfast is served with style on weekends only from 9-12.

PARKER'S ★

One Canal Place   Map, pg. 71   525-5050
                          Expensive

It is difficult to understand why Parker's hasn't been a success since its opening several years ago. Its location in the imposing One Canal Place complex is easily accessible, with available parking. Its decor, elegant and easy on the eye, makes dining a really enjoyable experience. The three-level dining area affords a wide selection of menu items and prices. And yet, Parker's as a top dining experience, has never quite caught on.

The extensive menu is laced with Continental, classic French, local Creole and New Orleans Style dishes and even selections specifically designated as Cuisine Nouvelle. Frankly, the eating public is missing out on this one. Corn and Crab Bisque (a soup du jour) is incredibly spicy and true to taste. There are other daily specials, including Quiche (a beef-

The garden dining area at the Court of Two Sisters.

broccoli combination with cheese topping was highly imaginative) which help lift Parker's kitchen to high standards. For the adventuresome, try the Shrimp Dijonaise, or the Lobster Pernod which are both excellent, Also, Parker's Aubergine (Cuisine Nouvelle) should not be missed.

RALPH AND KACOO'S

215 Bourbon Street   **Map, pg. 71**   523-0449
Inexpensive

This attractive seafood operation originated around the Baton Rouge area a number of years ago and was extremely successful in its upriver location. The new spot on Bourbon Street is now several years old and has also proven rewarding for its owners, Ralph and Kacoo Olinde. The Olindes seafood tends to be mostly fried but this type of cooking is not uncommon in high volume seafood operations. Freshness abounds in most dishes, including crabmeat combinations, shrimp platters, and the catfish and trout offerings.

The kitchen is best when frying, and most servings are plentiful. When in season, crayfish delicacies are featured and prove to outshine Ralph and Kacoo's year-round specialties. Another location at 601 Veterans Blvd. (831-3177) is a carbon copy (food wise) of this French Quarter restaurant.

RESTAURANT JONATHAN   ★

714 N. Rampart Street   **Map, pg. 159**   586-1930
Expensive

Restaurant Jonathan is an Art Deco experience. It is an adventure into restaurant decor which is stunning even to the casual art lover. Practically all the Deco masters (Brandt, Icari, Lalique and Sabini) are represented at Jonathan. Erte's famous touch is especially apparent. Each floor has its own unique personality.

While initial attention is always focused on Jonathan's deco, there is equal creativity in the kitchen. Executive Chef Tom Cowman is a culinary veteran with a flare. His best entrees include a Sauteed Liver l'Orange and a Filet Mignon accompanied by cold Bernaise Sauce which is picture perfect. There is also an excellent mild Lamb Curry. Try the Homemade Ice Cream for dessert.

Cowman's leadership has rocketed Restaurant Jonathan into serious culinary consideration. Today it must be considered as one of New Orleans' brightest restaurant newcomers. Closed Sundays.

RIB ROOM
(Royal Orleans Hotel)

621 St. Louis St.   **Map, pg. 159**   529-5333
Moderate/Expensive

Since the Royal Orleans is one of the premiere hotels in the city, it stands to reason that the Rib Room should also have a similar elevated status. Right? Right! The Rib Room is good and the house specialty, Prime Rib, is just about the best to be found anywhere. The dining room is run with great professionalism by Maitre d' Ernst Fischer whose staff shows true discipline and class.

Lunch time finds many city political figures, attorneys, and businessmen at neighboring tables enjoying the Rib Room's continental offerings. Little private rooms, such as the one which houses the wine room a flight downstairs, are available for private parties.

The continental menu features some remarkable Northern Italian delicacies which gives some insight as to the Executive Chef's heritage and training. Among the Quarter's most convenient meeting places, the Rib Room is a consistent treat and sure to please. During rush periods, reservations are an absolute necessity.

RISTORANTE PASTORE

615 Bienville Street **Map, pg. 71** 524-1122
Expensive

This Northern Italian restaurant is at the corner of Exchange Alley and Ibervile, off the beaten Quarter track by about one-half block. In operation for several years, Pastore's features an extensive classic Italian selection sprinkled with French, Creole, and even Spanish specialties. The interior is masterfully conceived and manages to capture much of the spirit and feeling of its French Quarter surroundings.

Ristorante Pastore's food tends to be heavy by Northern Italian standards and the mostly a-la-carte menu provides a formidable obstacle when trying a number of different dishes. Of the antipastas, Granchi alla Lombarda, a sauteed crabmeat creation, is rich and flavorful. Oysters Bienville and Oysters Rockefeller are pale however in comparison to some of its Quarter neighbors. Tortelloni Allitaliana far exceeds expectations; the pasta shells are stuffed with spinach and tangy cheese to produce excellent results. Several special rice dishes are also available at a fixed price if you are willing to allow for extra preparation time. Braciola D'Angello (baby lamb) is sometimes overcooked but the Vitello Santa Maria achieves near perfection.

Once Pastore overcomes some minor problems in its kitchen, and its slightly obvious commercial attitude, it could easily ascent to the ranks of a top Quarter restaurant.

STEAKS UNLIMITED
(Monteleone Hotel)

214 Royal Street **Map, pg. 71** 524-1044
Expensive

This restaurant within the Monteleone Hotel has utilized a specific plan to develop a large local following. Top grade meats are served in a rustic, relaxed atmosphere with certain old-style New Orleans side dishes designed to please the palate of the visitor (and local alike) who has had his fill of rich French dishes and sauces.

Meats are all Chicago prime, the Porterhouse cut is best, and the 2-2-2 oysters selections (Bienville, Rockefeller, and Monteleone) proves to be the best appetizer. Lyonnaise Potatoes and Broiled Mushrooms are excellent side dishes while the Special Cheese Cake and Homemade Bread Pudding make it wise to save a little room for dessert. The Monteleone's location is one of the busiest in the city, so you should plan accordingly. Peak times and special events tend to see Steaks Unlimited reserved early.

THE FISH MARKET ★

1000 N. Peters   **Map, pg. 237**   523-7418
Moderate

When the Red Stores building was restored during 1976 in the French Market, it offered an excellent opportunity for a first class, New Orleans-style seafood restaurant. One was quickly built, but remained in business for just a short while. The site was taken over in 1980 by two experienced New Orleans restaurateurs, renamed The Fish Market, and it has proved to be an unqualified success ever since.

The fish Market's seafood is about as fresh as possible and covers a wide variety of local treats. Completely a-la-carte, the menu spans the entire fried seafood spectrum, and even delves into areas once reserved for restaurants with high aspirations. The appetizers' list features shrimp, oyster, and crab dishes and is complimented by an excellent Fried Calamari, a definite plus. The batter is light, crusty, and golden brown. A meticulous Gumbo serves as The Fish Market's only soup. The Gumbo is a traditional one, with a big okra overtaste and subtle undertones of oregano, sweet basil, and thyme. The fried selections are quite consistent with a wonderful catfish filet standing out. Several market specialties are also rewarding, including a fabulous BBQ Shrimp which certainly equals, if not surpasses Manale's dominant dish. These are absolutely delightful, less garlicky than Manale's, and capable of becoming a legendary offering.

Open 11 a.m. to 10 p.m. daily. A complete variety of seafood is also available on a takeout basis which is good news to Quarterites and those of us whose homeward route takes us through the French Market and past The Fish Market's inviting doors.

TONEY'S

212 Bourbon Street   Map, pg. 71   523-9261
                           Inexpensive

Recently renovated, Toney's is still a busy, noisy place, the type which can be found in and around New York's theatre district. The dining area is large, and caters to the myriad of people who work on or around Bourbon. Necessity dictates that Toney's remain open for long hours, and the crowds who frequent Toney's never disappoint an ardent people watcher. Barkers, strippers, musicians, hotel people and businessmen mingle with ever-present tourists for some bona-fide Italian cuisine which has always been sold on pure strength (a situation where garlic predominates).

Toney's features pizzas (extra good after a night walking the French Quarter), and an autocratic spaghetti and meatballs (regal and rich), which, to many of Toney's regular customers, is a true staple of life. Toney's homemade biscuits are light and fluffy, and a variation of Creole Red Snapper soup also deserves special praise.

Toney's owners are intently serious about their business and keep the establishment practically spotless. Good honest food fare here, at prices which makes inflation look as if it took a holiday. Closed Saturdays.

TORTORICI'S

441 Royal Street   Map, pg. 71   522-4295
                          Moderate/Expensive

Located on one of the best corners in the French Quarter (Royal and St. Louis), this attractive establishment has never lived up to its potential or local reputation. The third generation of the Tortorici family operate the business, but Tortorici's kitchen has proved too inconsistent to warrant serious study or consideration by ardent food lovers.

On one occasion, Shrimp Scampi proved classically delicious, with butter and garlic evenly balanced. On the very next visit, a similar dish couldn't compare. Pastas too, are inconsistent, and apparently not always freshly made. Fettucine is the best offering, with an excellent cheese flavoring balanced in cream. Service personnel here are always neat and attentive, which tends to make the outing a great deal more palatable. Closed Sundays.

TRUJAQUE'S

823 Decatur Street   Map, pg. 159   523-9462
                          Inexpensive

Sadly, this once fine restaurant is but a worn-out relic of bygone days. Reputed to be the site of the second oldest restaurant (Madame Begue's) in the city, Trujague's has fallen on some very hard times. The once marvelous Brisket of Beef, long the kitchen's bellweather dish, is but a shadow of its former self.

Everyone connected with the place seems to just be going through the motions. Tujague's seems quite drab inside which tends to deepen the disenchantment with the food. It is still possible to walk in and order a drink at the bar and reflect on Tujague's past glories, but as far as restaurant acceptability is concerned, Tujague's is a tired old friend in need of help.

VIEUX CARRE

241 Bourbon Street   **Map, pg. 71**   524-0114
Expensive

The Vieux Carre Restaurant has been bounced around so much in past years that it must certainly be compared to the proverbial Mexican jumping bean. Too bad, for the establishment is well-apportioned and its location (Bourbon and Bienville) is ultra-prime for attracting visitors and local residents alike. The problem stems from many management and ownership changes along with blatant kitchen inconsistency which have tended to turn off the Vieux Carre's local trade completely. This factor usually sounds the death knell for many restaurants, but for some reason the Vieux Carre is still in existence.

Through the years, the Vieux Carre's menu has become quite elaborate and under the circumstances, unbelieveably pretentious. While there are probably a sufficient amount of tourists to keep Vieux Carre in business, one hopes for the emergence of some sort of permanency to stabilize it. The basics are there for a type of operation which could develop nicely under the proper set of circumstances.

CENTRAL BUSINESS DISTRICT

GEORGIE PORGIE'S ★

601 Poydras St.
(Poydras Plaza)

Map, pg. 105
Expensive

566-0000

If this attractive place has any faults, it would be Georgie's location within the city's best discoteque. For some unknown reason, Georgie Porgie's food operation has always played second fiddle to the disco.

The continental dining room's reputation has been developed by providing top meat and fresh seafood dishes on a dependable basis for some time. Rather than attempt the exotic, Georgie's kitchen has concentrated on a limited number of time-tested favorites. The Red Snapper with Crabmeat is distinguished and imaginative. It's cream sauce is worthy of a master chef's hand. The middle-of-the-road items, such as Stuffed Lobster (with crabmeat) bathed in melted butter are incredibly popular. The Lobster is simple, tasteful and deliciously delicate.

Since Georgie's location is so close to the Louisiana Superdome, you must reserve very early on event days. If you are running late (or just plain thirsty), the large bar is well-manned and competent. Georgie Porgie's is somewhat of a rarity in New Orleans, for it combines excellent food and entertainment that somehow never seems to lose its attractiveness. Its large following draws from a wide variety of city types who enjoy its convivial atmosphere and urban sophistication.

BAILEY'S
(Fairmont Hotel)

127 Baronne Street

Map, pg. 105
Moderate

529-7111

This inviting spot is exactly what the doctor ordered for the American side of Canal Street. Open long hours, Bailey's caters to both visitors and locals alike. After touring Bourbon Street for what might seem like eons, this charming continental setting just a half block off Canal Street becomes an oasis.

Bailey's features an excellent pouring bar (in keeping with the international reputation of the hotel's other bars), and a menu geared to anytime hunger. For instance, the fried oysters and shrimp are on a par with many of the area's better restaurants, and a couple of local specialties (Red Beans and Rice is the best of the lot) are truly excellent. This does not mean that Bailey's constitutes a really first class dining experience. Rather, it is a pleasant place where food is served under relaxed conditions at reasonable prices anytime, day or night. The fact that its kitchen often excels is a plus which should be recorded in one's memory bank.

BON TON CAFE

401 Magazine Street   **Map, pg. 105**   524-3386
                             Expensive

As cafes go, the Bon Ton is something akin to a palace. The setting is neat, airy, and a perfect showcase for founder Al Pierce, one of the city's most outspoken food personalities. Although recently turning over the daily controls to his nephew, Wayne, Pierce remains fiercely proud of his Cajun food heritage. To be authentic, Cajun cuisine must be utterly simple. Bon Ton is one of only three real Cajun restaurants in a city where many purport to embrace the food culture of Southwestern Louisiana.

Jambalaya, golden in its creative glow, is always excellent here. Pan-broiled Oysters and Turtle Soup are basic items which are always consistently satisfying. Lunches are madness, but dinner time offers a more relaxed atmosphere and a chance for some rare insight into this unique food style. Reserve for dinner, for Bon Ton as a nighttime restaurant, has finally caught on. Closed Saturdays and Sundays.

HUMMINGBIRD GRILL

804 St. Charles Avenue   **Map, pg. 105**   561-9229
                            Inexpensive

If there ever existed a typical down-home type New Orleans restaurant and bar (slightly more elevated in stature than a greasy spoon), then the Hummingbird Hotel and Grill is the place. Located in the middle of New Orleans' skid row district, the Hummingbird has nevertheless become a food mecca for a respectable clientele. Press and media-types, police, professionals and blue collar folks, as well as a smattering of Uptown socialites, consider the Hummingbird an "in" place to be.

The best single item offered on the menu is the fresh-baked Corn Bread, whose fragrant odors work wonders for the entire neighborhood. Other substantive features are a splendid Spaghetti and Meatballs combo, and the local favorite, Red Beans and Rice. The Hummingbird's daily specials should be enjoyed off the old chalk board. These items are almost always fabulous values, and equally important to the hungry diner, they are served in the Hummingbird's famous oversized portions.

There is little need to feel intimidated by the area, for as mentioned above, a large number of policemen frequent the Hummingbird. It adds a little to the charm of the spot, which is totally unique in New Orleans.

IMPERIAL PALACE REGENCY ★

601 Loyola Avenue

Map, pg. 105
Expensive

522-8666

To understand this oriental showcase, it is necessary to remove all previous preconceptions concerning Chinese restaurants. The Imperial Palace Regency is, first and foremost, the ultimate in Eastern decor. Furnishings are authentic and have been painstakingly acquired and placed by proprietress Lorraine Lee. The fact that food here rivals and sometimes exceeds the surroundings is a plus for lovers of Szechuan and Cantonese cuisines.

Lemon Chicken, light and tartly succulent, and the Szechuan Shrimp, rich and luxurious, lead a varied menu. These dishes are house specialties which are imaginative and worth trying. If anything within the Imperial Palace could be considered a departure from the norm, it must be the bar and dancing area.

Prices tend to be slightly higher than other oriental spots, but portions are large and service excellent. This opulent spot has proven immensely popular since it opened and usually requires reservations. On weekends and during special events at the nearby Louisiana Superdome, the Imperial Palace Regency is justifiably crowded. Closed Sundays.

JONAH'S
(Hyatt Regency)

500 Poydras Plaza

Map, pg. 105
Expensive

561-1234

This cozy spot is located just off the second (or is it third) floor atrium of the New Orleans Hyatt Regency. From inception, Jonah's was never meant to compete with the city's prestigious restaurant community, but was simply intended to provide convenient food for the hotel's guests who preferred in-house dining.

Jonah's has, however, proven to be a distinct surprise to many food practitioners. The food served is a decided notch above standard hotel fare. Of particular interest are the numerous seafood items which are conceived with a continental flair. The Five Star Duck comes at its roasted best and is flamed at the table in a rich orange sauce. Shrimp Scampi is good and there is even a Bouillabaisse available which smacks of a strong regional hand. Probably the best single dish is the Rack of Lamb, which many restaurants attempt and few succeed.

Pricing here is reasonable and service steady. Since the food is more assertive than one would imagine, Jonah's must be considered as one of the real sleepers. For convenience to Superdome special events, it has few equals.

CENTRAL BUSINESS DISTRICT SHUTTLE ROUTES

Convenient transportation for convention
delegates and downtown shoppers

ROUTE ONE

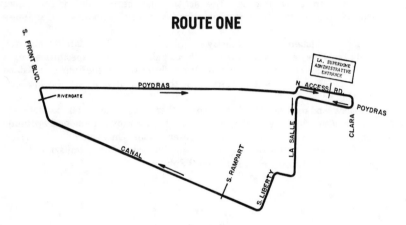

ROUTE TWO

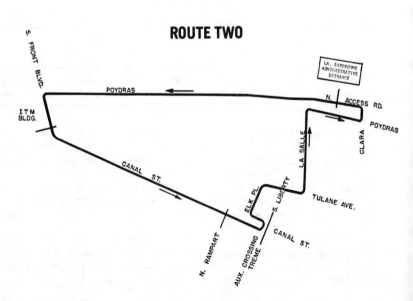

KOLB'S GERMAN RESTAURANT ★

125 St. Charles Ave.　　　　Map, pg. 105　　　　　522-8278
　　　　　　　　　　　　　　Moderate

While the setting and accessories are definitely Tuetonic, there are only a few top German dishes still on the bill of fare. The restaurant's true culinary direction embraces rather the Creole and old-style New Orleans cooking. A combination of a steady kitcken force, and some excellent recipes and direction provided by the late General Manager, Bill Martin, won Kolb's a large local following, and a reputation as one of the CBD's most popular luncheon spots. The violin and accordion duo which provides evening atmosphere by touring the tables at Kolb's is a fond memory for couples now scattered all over the country.

The Brisket of Beef here is always good, not too fatty or overcooked. Shrimp and fish items seldom disappoint. The excellent German Sausage and Sauerkraut is the best found locally. Prices at Kolb's are among the most reasonable in town, and the service is always attentive. The mood is chatty except during Kolb's annual Octoberfest. Then a bit of Bavaria is captured within these rooms in songs, strolling musicians, raised beer steins, and special German food offerings. It is a very popular event requiring reservations well in advance. Closed Sundays.

MAYLIE'S

1009 Poydras Street　　　　Map, pg. 105　　　　　525-9547
　　　　　　　　　　　　Moderate/Expensive

To have one of New Orleans' oldest establishments still operating in the very shadow of the Louisiana Superdome might require some consideration, but Maylie's still seems quite unaffected by the nearness of the giant colossus. Maylie's is truly a throwback to old-time New Orleans dining from the gracious golden era which has since passed. At one point, Maylie's was one of the finer restaurants in the entire city, but sadly, Maylie's best days are far behind.

A group of hard-core regulars still frequent this aging matron and swear by her Brisket of Beef. In actuality, the dish is but a mere shadow of its former self. The kitchen still produces a predominance of typical New Orleans dishes, but for most intents, the food is void of any real substance. Soups and desserts are probably the most consistent items available, but it is a sad proposition when side dishes become any restaurant's principal forte. Closed Saturdays & Sundays.

SAZERAC ROOM ★★
(Fairmont Hotel)

University Place   Map, pg. 105   529-4733
Very Expensive

In a city of free-standing restaurants, this post hotel dining room continues its tradition of fine French and continental cuisine in scarlet ambience and elegance. Amid strolling classical musicians, diners enjoy full French table service and an excellent varied menu. For many locals, the Sazerac Room is still very much part of a grand night out on the town.

Of the menu items, Steak Tartare, Tournedos Rossini, and live Maine Lobster are superb traditional fare well worth the trip. So too, are the flaming desserts which have become so synonymous with New Orleans.

Over the past few years, the Executive Chefs here have changed often (this is not altogether uncommon in hotel properties) and so have the restaurant's overall specialties, but through it all the Sazerac has remained a top-calibre operation. Service here is among the best in the entire city and food presentations are quite rewarding. The Sazerac will always attract a very high calibre clientele and will seldom disappoint.

ST. CHARLES RESTAURANT

333 St. Charles Avenue   Map, pg. 105   522-6600
Moderate

Restaurants on the American side of Canal Street tend to concentrate largely on breakfasts and luncheons, and the St. Charles is no exception to the rule. Well into its second year of operation, this conservatively decorated establishment fills a specific luncheon need in its area. Located ideally in the center of the city's Central Business District, it caters to bankers, lawyers and other professionals from nearby office buildings.

A wide variety of luncheon items including incredible Oysters Jaubert (oysters with Canadian bacon on an English muffin topped by a creamy Tarragon sauce), and a delightful Soft Shelled Crab Lafite (features a house-special crawfish sauce), is well suited to both the professional clientele and to the Creole kitchen staff. Owner Hank Vosbein transitioned from the catering-oriented Saxony Restaurant to this restaurant with much ease and a measure of success.

The restaurant is neatly divided into a main dining area and several additional smaller private rooms which accomodate from six to twenty diners comfortably. These smaller rooms are extremely popular with professional clientele as business/dining settings. Closed Saturday and Sunday.

WINSTON'S
(New Orleans Hilton)

2 Poydras Avenue   **Map, pg. 105**   561-0500
Expensive

Cleverly designed as an interior open-air dining area within the New Orleans Hilton's gigantic atrium, Winston's has been immensely popular since it first opened. Featuring a changeable verbal menu and continental table service, Winston's sometimes creates a test for service personnel. The process is carried off smoothly however, and the entire verbal sequence tends to add to the total dining experience.

There is always a choice of entrees, consisting of meat, poultry or seafood, and a number of specified accompanying side dishes. Period furniture and elegant napery set an elegant tone for the format initially conceived at the Atlanta Hilton. Food here is generally well-above normal hotel fare and can be compared to some of New Orleans' best restaurants.

When the hotel is crowded and guests fill the ground floor area, the clamorous noise from below can distract from the dining. At the same time however, jazz music from the party below can provide a carnival atmosphere which resolves some of these unpleasantries.

THERE'S A NEW FRY IN TOWN.

Visko's Fish Fry is the best thing that's happened to Louisiana tastebuds since oysters learned to loaf.

Tested and perfected at Visko's, Louisiana's most popular seafood restaurant, this is the fry that lightly seasons, but never hides the flavor of fish, oysters, shrimp, crabs — all the great Louisiana favorites.

If you love seafood, you're gonna love this new fry.

Mail Order Form:

VISKO'S FISH FRY
516 Gretna Blvd.
Gretna, Louisiana 70053

WEST BANK

BISTRO STEAK ROOM

1098 Fourth Street   341-1061
Westwego   Expensive

When we first wrote about Bistro and its personable owner-chef Maurice Bitoun, city officials in the West Bank town of Westwego were chagrined that we expressed incredulity over the location of a major French restaurant in their particular city. Well, after six years, little has changed to sway our opinion, and we feel it's still quite far-fetched to find an establishment of the calibre of Bitoun's Bistro in its particular setting.

Bitoun is a native of Lyon and that says a great deal. His unpretentious manner and style of operation has propelled the Bistro into the ranks of the area's top eating locations. He is famous for his marvelous Bistro Bread (which he bakes), a deep-pan golden loaf certainly designed without dieters in mind. He deep fries parsley in his own secret batter for an added touch. On his menu, the Catfish Hawaiian is a romantic adventure into absolute taste perfection encompassing a meuniere and pineapple sauce combination which entices and excites.

True to its name, the steaks are rewarding and meticulously prepared. Best is the Steak au Poivre, presented in a manner only understood by a true master of French cuisine. The Prime Chicago Strip and the engaging Ribeye are also well worth trying. Side dishes are a curious blending of local specialites (crab claws), classic French (snails) and traditional Creole (oysters) which are generously proportioned and distinguished in themselves.

Bistro's staff is courteous and well-attuned to service. Prices are reasonable and reservations are a real must on weekends. The drive from downtown takes about twenty minutes via the Greater New Orleans bridge. It is a drive well worth making. Closed Sundays.

DOS GRINGOS

932 Westbank Expressway   367-7977
Gretna   Moderate

It is sometimes hard to believe this establishment is part of a nationwide chain, but then, that is part of the beauty of Mexican food. When Dos Gringos was new and still under its initial ownership, its food was just about the best Mexican fare in the city, but of late Dos Gringos seems to have slipped a bit. Not that there is anything negatively tangible to be seen in the food or operation, but rather commercialism seems to have gotten the better of the restaurant.

The best items featured are the Tortillas which have proved to be consistent, spicy, and much too generously portioned. The Chili Rellenos, a personal favorite, is Dos Gringos' best individual dish, worthy of distinctive note.

Service is attentive, if not altogether professional, and the typical check makes one's pocketbook cheer when there's little to cheer about the national economy. There is a family air about the entire surroundings and seldom more than a token wait for tables. Dos Gringos is still a nice place to try something different.

MOUNT FUJI

3042 General Collins Ave.
Algiers   504/392-2920

Many Japanese specialty restaurants follow the lines of showy, theatrical decors where fanfare generally outshines the cuisine. Mount Fuji, at least, departs from this norm and offers an insight into authentic Japanese cooking. Located directly across the Greater New Orleans bridge in Algiers, Mount Fuji is a pleasant enough setting with little, if any, cosmetic side effects.

For the serious diner, Mount Fuji offers a formal Teishoku Dinner at a fixed price which includes a number of Japanese staples, the likes of which are seldomly seen in the United States. The meal proves to have its ups and downs, depending on one's appreciation of true Japanese cuisine. The Otoshi appetizer, mostly marinated bamboo shoots with a few salmon eggs, was tasty and well-done. Next came a marvelous Sunomono, the highlight of the meal. Here, paper thin medaillons of octopus are served with a mixture of slightly vinegared vegetables. The entire concoction is somewhat dill-flavored and absolutely increadible to taste. Three authentic Sashimi portions, raw fish, were pungently genuine, if not particularly attuned to American minds. A candied ginger root added to the dish. Yakitori, skewered chicken with Teriyaki sauce, was next and was well-conceived and delivered.

Mount Fuji also offers an excellent Steak Teriyaki complete with a luxurious sauce and some unusual side dishes. These accompaniments illustrate the creative talents in the kitchen and the authority of its ethnic specialization.

LE RUTH'S

636 Franklin Avenue   Map, pg. 170   362-4914
Gretna   Expensive

If a single person is responsible for New Orleans' restaurant revitalization, Warren Le Ruth must be that person. Le Ruth opened his out-of-the-way

West Bank operation in 1966 and in the short span of nearly fifteen years, his efforts and creativity have made Le Ruth's world-renowned in international restaurant circles. Smallish (120 seating capacity), the establishment is mirrored and muralled with original paintings and period pieces.

The menu is inspired and makes adaptive usage of many regional metiers, particularly fresh trout, chicken, and avacado. Le Ruth's superbities are almost too numerous to mention. From the classic Crabemeat St. Francis and the incomparable Potage Le Ruth as appetizers, our lump crabmeat, a marvelous Rack of Lamb (perhaps the finest in the entire United States), a finesseful green House Salad with avocado dressing or possibly an Avocado Tropique and a taste-defying Melon Ice.

Le Ruth's standing within local restaurant circle is non-pareil and in his generosity, Le Ruth has helped numerous other restaurants in a consulting capacity. Of course, reservations here are paramount, and should be made at least three weeks in advance. Le Ruth's is the complete dining experience with a polished professional service staff and a wine list which offers a rare combination of value and quality. Closed Sundays.

LIDO

1019 Avenue C   347-8203
Marrero   Moderate/Expensive

Not long ago, the two families which operated this very successful West Bank Northern Italian food operation decided to end their association and go their separate ways. (See Lido Gardens for associated review). Josie and Pietro Calliagaro have continued to operate the Lido with the same verve and competency which propelled the smallish establishment into restaurant respectability. Pietro was always the front or outside man in the old Lido operation, but he has managed the changeover to the back of the house quite well.

The same great specialties are still on the menu and offer a true insight into the delicacy and polish of real Northern Italian cuisine. Pastas here are freshly made and worth ordering. A marvelous Stuffed Artichoke is resplendent in the company of a generous homemade salad with Lido's distinctive house dressing. The Veal Involtini is available accompanied with its masterpiece companion called Polenta, Northern Italy's corn side-dish. There is also an assortment of Italian cheeses, sausages and meats, along with an interesting Creole Bread Pudding variation which makes Lido's Cappucino a joy to experience.

Prices are moderate and portions generous. A reasonable wine list is available and plenty of tender, loving service. It is fitting that this business has continued to thrive after the partners chose to split.

MOSCA'S

Highway 90   436-9942
Waggaman   Moderate/Expensive

When Momma Mosca passed away not so long ago, New Orleans and the entire world lost a wonderful personality and one of the most competent cooks and restaurateurs around. In making Mosca's a legend in her own time, Momma Mosca exceeded even her own optomistic aims. To her, Mosca's was a family and her hours were when her family gathered. With the support of her son John and others, she made the foods she knew so well—her native Sicillian cuisine and the local Creole dishes of the region.

Since her death, little has changed at Mosca's, and one doubts that anything of substance will ever change. The tantalizing Italian Crab Salad is still at its piquante best, and the renowned Oysters and Shrimp Mosca remain legendary wonders of the culinary art. The Mosca variation of Barbeque Shrimp is a tad too olive-oily for some palates, but for others the dish has become a prerequisite for Crustacean enjoyment.

Reservations are still rather indefinite at best, so the wise should prepare for this eventuality. Mosca's is one-of-a-kind dining experience which should never be taken lightly. Its character, ambiance and remarkable effect on the city will be felt for sometime to come. Closed Sundays & Mondays.

ROYAL OAK

Oakwood Shopping Center   362-4592
Gretna   Moderate/Expensive

The ancient cuisine of Greece is featured at this spot in the Oakwood Mall across the Mississippi River from downtown New Orleans. The John Newsham's are your hosts in this family run restaurant. Mrs. Newsham is a native-born Greek who has transported her considerable culinary skills into a setting which permits her complete freedom and versatility. One of the great secrets of Greek cooking is correct food pre-preparation, which often dictates consistency, and ultimate food integrity. At the Royal Oak, much of the food pre-prep is done at the Newsham home and finished off at the restaurant.

Many local Greek food fanciers swear by the place and we must add our agreement. Mrs. Newsham is immortal (it would be un Greek to word it differently) Baklava is a most proficient example of masterful Greek technique and finesse. The Spinach Pie is a genuine ethnic treat. Lamb dishes are done in the traditional manner, slightly more done than their French counterparts, and the salads proliferate with fresh, briney Feta cheese taken from a huge jar.

Prices are reasonable and the fact that the Royal Oak is one of the few really successful mall restaurants speaks for itself. Closed Sundays.

VISKO'S

516 Gretna Blvd.   368-4899
Gretna   Moderate

The Vuscovich family who owns Visko's are of Yugosalavian origin and were once fishermen plying the rich Gulf waters off the mouth of the Mississippi River. Those earlier efforts are the key factor in this fantastically busy spot's meteoric rise to supremacy as the city's outstanding seafood establishment. Visko's sources of fresh seafood are legend around town, but that's only part of the story.

Recipes at Visko's are carefully planned and mirror the soul and feeling of true New Orleans tastes. Some dishes, such as the Oysters Meaux or other Visko's Special, are superbly versatile and innovative. In the Oysters Meaux, fresh Louisiana oysters are immersed in a virtuoso sauce which utilizes Moutarde de Meaux as the base. The result is a tangy, tasty oyster concoction without parallel. The Fried Shrimp also have a legion of local followers who claim Visko's shrimp are the best anywhere. There are also distinctive salads and side dishes, particularly the Fried Zucchini.

A second facility, known as the Steam Room, is located adjacent to the main restaurant, and features steamed seafood and vegetables. The Steam Room has also proved to be extremely successful. Reservations are accepted for the Steam Room only. Traditionally, local seafood establishments have operated on a first-come basis. Closed Sundays.

WILLY COLN'S

2505 Whitney Avenue   361-3860
Gretna   Expensive

Cologne-born owner-chef Willy Coln brings much-needed Germanic expertise to the New Orleans area. His masterful menu combines German, Swiss, Creole and certain continental innovations, but his forte is his native German cuisine. Willy Coln's possesses a great natural ambiance. Add to that fact that Willy does all the cooking himself, and you have a rare restaurant treat. His annual Octoberfest celebration is the finest in the city and should be reserved quite early.

Menuwise, a creation with particular allure is the Veal Shank (for two), properly fatty and served with a bedding of fresh vegetables. The dish is consistently satisfying and absolutely unique in the area. Another masterpiece is Coln's Bahamian Chowder, which combines numerous vegetables and meats to produce a taste experience surpassing most soups or bisques we have every tasted. The list of culinary accomplishments goes on and on.

Service personnel are adroit and keenly aware of the needs of their customers. Appointments in the restaurant itself are tasteful and in keeping with the overall German/Swiss character of the cuisine. Willy Coln's is one of New Orleans' truly great dining experiences. Closed Sunday and Monday.

Lee Barnes hosts classes in New Orleans cuisine at her school in the Riverbend area.

GARDEN DISTRICT AND UPTOWN

CAMELLIA GRILL

626 S. Carrollton Ave.   866-9573

Inexpensive

New Orleans is a city of fabled eating institutions and this Uptown nook must be considered one of the most revered. Located just off the junction of Carrollton and St. Charles Avenues, the Camellia Grill has satisfied generations of hungry New Orleanians. With a menu consisting of a curious mixture of burgers, sandwiches, omelettes, dinner plates and desserts, the Grill literally appeals to any sort of appetite any hour of the day or night.

The fact is, Camellia Grill's food actually trancends its immediate surroundings; a facaded mini-replica of an ante-bellum mansion. It is possible to catch the St. Charles street car along its route and step out practically at Camellia Grill's front door. The meal which will ensue will provide a fond recollection of one of New Orleans' most unique offsprings. It is a quaint haven with food offerings which are extremely consistent and rewarding to the palate. Of particular note are the fresh homemade pies (with ice cream topping, of course) and a marvelous creamy cheesecake which is a masterpiece. No reservations here; reservations would tend to ruin the effect of the Grill. Again, no credit cards accepted.

CARIBBEAN ROOM
(Pontchartrain Hotel)

2031 St. Charles Avenue   **Map, pg. 170**   524-0581

Expensive

This graciously appointed hotel dining room is as popular with local diners as it is to its star studded list of international clientele. For years, the Caribbean Room has served as the darling of the city's Garden District, a role still cherished and untarnished.

The regal Trout Veronique reigns here, in a truly grand and luxurious setting. Another unique creation, the famous Mile High Pie, was invented here and has been consumed by marathon dessert eaters ever since. This is one setting where the specialties are indeed special, and should not be missed. The innovative Crabmeat Biarritz combines the finessful taste of lump crabmeat with a slightly piquante sour cream dressing with impressive results. There are also several oyster and shrimp dishes which excel and are usually quite consistant.

The test of such an establishment and distinguished institution is its consistency. At peak times, service and quality may suffer, or when Executive Chef Louis Evans steps away from the kitchen. Still, the Caribbean Room stands as the standard of an era in New Orleans dining history which one would hope would last forever. It is the embodiment of creativity and taste. A superior hotel dining room operation.

CASAMENTO'S

4330 Magazine Street   895-9761
                          Inexpensive

If you are ever in the Uptown area with visitors who would appreciate a taste of the classic flavor of a true New Orleans bar and restaurant, then Casamento's should not be missed. At this streetcar barn hangout, oysters and their shuckers are both storied. In the hands of these characters, the craft of opening oysters has been developed to a fine art. Casamento's is more a bar than a restaurant, but the food served surpasses its humble surroundings.

Casamento's renowned Oyster Loaf has no local peer and the assorted fried seafoods rank with the very best neighborhood fare in the city. Devoid of pomp and ceremony, food and relaxation are paramount to Casamento's.

The locals who lounge here are a bit noisy, but the clamor adds to the charm of the place. During the long, hot summer, Casamento's closes completely. No credit cards. Closed Mondays.

CHARLIE'S STEAK HOUSE

4510 Dryades   895-9705
                          Moderate/Expensive

Charlie's steaks are often maligned locally, for they are inevitably compared to Ruth Chris' and that always seems a bit unfair. Charlie's is probably the most comfortable, most casual steak house in the city and deserves consideration.

Charlie's steaks are notably consistent, well-prepared and served in an unsophisticated, family-like atmosphere. The salad accompanying the meal is large with a generous dressing on top. One great surprise is the French Fried Onion Rings, crisply fried to perfection and a dish which ranks among the best in the city. The beer here is always well-chilled and happily the best possible accompaniment to the wonderful onion rings.

The staff is courteous, and seems to have been employed at Charlie's forever. Charlie's is a place to relax, let your hair down and enjoy your friends. Dinner and accompaniments will always reach a respectable level, and therefore provide a most satisfying evening's enjoyment. Closed Sundays.

COMMANDER'S PALACE ★★★

1403 Washington Ave.   Map, pg. 269   899-8221
                                    Expensive

Commander's Palace has emerged in recent years as one of the city's finest overall dining experiences. Snugly located in the heart of the old Garden District, Commander's maturity is a result of meticulous direction on the part of the Brennan family (Ella, Dick, John, and Adelaide). The Brennan's ability to correctly diagnose the pulse and heartbeat of their clientele is unmatched in New Orleans.

Commander's large seating capacity (around 400) makes comparison between it and other first class restaurants difficult. That the venerable old place can accomodate as many daily and nightly seatings as well as it does is remarkable. It is a fitting tribute to the entire staff.

The menu is the real heart of Commander's success. A delightful oyster or soup appetizer choice (each is called 2-2-2) can start your meal off with great variety. Turtle Soup au Sherry is from Commander's original 1880 menu and well worth trying. Entree-wise, Crabmeat Imperial, Redfish Grieg with Sauteed Lump Crabmeat and the Trout with Roasted Pecans are absolute wonders from the sea. On the meat side, the Filet Debris is a superb creation and the Veal Lafayette (in a crepe filled with a myriad of seasonings) cannot be matched in any large-scale operation. Traditional desserts (flaming and otherwise) close out a most memorable dining occasion.

Commander's Palace is a charming, affectionate experience, which tends to mean something different to each diner. The Jazz Brunch was begun here and today is widely copied. In a word, Commander's is special, very special indeed.

COMPAGNO'S

7839 St. Charles Ave.   866-9313
                                  Inexpensive

Near to Uptown's Riverbend section (at the corner of Fern Street) is an unpretentious little neighborhood bar and restaurant that is easily overlooked. Compagno's does its own culinary thing with first rate oysters and fried seafood. The dining room is bare and somewhat seedy, but this adds to its color. Food quality is consistent and the prices reasonable.

At certain times, Compagno's surpasses itself. When buster crabs are in season, for example, Compagno's comes alive and the pace around the restaurant really quickens. Crabs are juicy, well-fried and a real treat. Fried oysters and shrimp are house delights and a variety of Italian standbys are also available. Best are the Spaghetti and Meatballs and the Veal Parmesan. Sandwiches are also on the menu, but do not rise above the ordinary.

Parking is non-existent except along the sidewalks, but the group of Compagno's faithful never seem to mind. Closed Mondays.

CORINNE DUNBAR'S

1617 St. Charles Avenue   525-0689
                          Expensive

For the past few years, the decline of this faded relic of bygone times has been a major disappointment to local food partisans. Rumors of a food renaissance at Corinne's have proven totally inaccurate and Corinne Dunbar's has retired to its current status as a masterpiece of indifference. Frankly, there is no real talent emitted from the kitchen. What is more, the meals are expensive and service marginal. The whole situation is indeed unfortunate, for at one point in time, Corinne Dunbar's was a gracious dining spot capable of competing with any of the finest restaurants in the city.

Perhaps the best advice we can offer the prospective diner is to steer a wide course around this St. Charles Avenue location. There are simply too many quality restaurants in New Orleans more capable of superior food and service to choose from. Better to save your time and money. Closed Sunday and Monday.

DANTE BY THE RIVER

723 Dante Street   861-7610
                        Moderate/Expensive

Nestled comfortably between the Mississippi River and the Riverbend Shopping Center is tiny Dante by the River. Dante is housed in a smallish shotgun cottage which reeks of charm and simplicity. Miniscule rooms accommodate a select clientele with a variety of continental and New Orleans style dishes.

Although the kitchen staff has undergone several changes since inception, a few successful dishes have emerged. Best is the solid Veal Oscar, a staple on many continental menus which is well-conceived and presented here. an excellent Redfish Pontchartrain (sauteed crabmeat and green onions topped with a combination Meuniere and Hollandaise sauce) is a good example of productive local cooking.

Dante's service and overall standing are still in need of a lift, but real restaurant respectability is just around the corner. Closed Sundays.

DELMONICO'S

1300 St. Charles Avenue   525-4937
                        Moderate/Expensive

A pair of absolutely charming ladies, Angela Brown and Rose Deitrich, combine to run this traditional New Orleans Creole restaurant located on the very fringe of the city's Garden District. The fare here is consistent and the easy-going pace of things is reflective of fine New Orleans dining of bygone days. That these sisters are able to maintain this sort of establishment is remarkable in this day and time, and is a tribute to their hard work and dedication.

Delmonico's features a really strong appetizer selection topped by a fantastic Turtle Soup done in the old style. There's much to choose from among the entrees. Frog Legs Meuniere (a real delicacy), several fish selections, and a fine Beef Cordon Bleu, a variation which is delicious. The Table d'Hotel menu always affords an opportunity to try something extra.

Don't miss the fresh homemade Apple Pie for dessert. Delmonico' has elevated the dish and it easily surpasses other city restaurants with it. If possible, say hello to Delmonico's charming owners, who make dining out in this city something personal and quite rewarding for their guests.

ENRAGED CHICKEN

1115 St. Mary Chicken   524-8636
                              Moderate

This unique operation located smack in the middle of the city's Irish Channel district seeks to provide a forum for student chefs who actually prepare the restaurant's daily meals. The customer is offered no menu choices. The offering changes depending on the dishes being taught. Diners become fair game for the amateur chefs while the chefs are exposed to the comments of the customers.

Admirably, the food is produced to very high standards, and one can always count on an extraordinary amount of creativity in the individual dishes. Physical aspects of the Enraged Chicken tend to fit the restaurant's concept and achieve an intimacy which is quite charming for all involved. The first few times we attempted reservations to this smallish spot, the Enraged Chicken was booked, so a word to the wise.

Operations like the Enraged Chicken offer the only real chance amateur chefs receive to cook in a semi-professional atmosphere, and we wholeheartly endorse this particular pioneering group's initial efforts and achievements. Closed Sundays.

LA CARIDAD

4210 Magazine Street   899-4839
                              Moderate

This establishment is located in a seedy part of Magazine Street, not far from a grouping of antique shops. For some time, La Caridad has assumed the position of the area's most consistent if not always spectacular, Central American eating spot. Featuring surprisingly low prices and a constantly changing selection of daily specials, La Caridad enjoys a large

☐ ATTRACTIONS

◯ RESTAURANTS

GARDEN DISTRICT

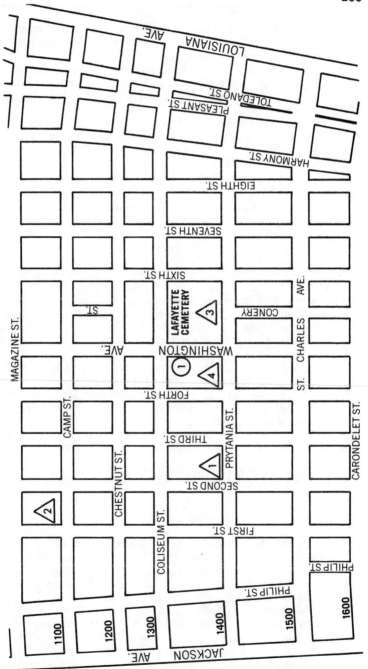

following. While La Caridad draws mostly from New Orleans' burgeoning Central American population, there is a growing number of New Orleanians who seem to find this food style enjoyable.

Meat items on the menu are the best bets. Look for stuffed offerings, and meat with unusual accompaniments. An unusual Lobster a la Caridad is delightful. Beans, of course, are predominant, while other fresh vegetables tend to be slightly undercooked.

La Caridad can be enjoyed when you're feeling expansive, relaxed, and possessed of a great deal of time for your meal. Everything tends to happen a bit slower down South, and La Caridad fits into that stereotype quite nicely. Closed Wednesdays.

PASCAL'S MANALE

1838 Napoleon Avenue   895-4877
Expensive

This frantic establishment caters to New Orleans' Uptown crowd who prefer to dine in somewhat noisy, informal surroundings. Manale's, as it is locally know, is a model of food stability and consistency, but not necessarily culinary superiority. While an excellent oyster bar and some well-conceived Creole/Italian dishes add to its allure, Manale's somehow fails to attain the pre-eminence one expects from such a celebrated and oft-storied location.

Its best individual items are the Pan Roast, Stuffed Tufoli, and BBQ Shrimp. The BBQ Shrimp made Mandale's reputation and it is indeed a great dish in conception and presentation. However, there is more to a dining experience than food. Manale's success has evidently encouraged an attitude of indifference among its host and table service staff. Reservations carry no force and there is a lack of control and finesse that should be evidenced in a restaurant enjoying a good reputation.

ROCCAFORTE'S FISHERMAN'S WHARF

1121 St. Mary Street   525-1701
Moderate/Expensive

It is ironic that the Irish Channel's best seafood restaurant is Italian, but that's the way it is in New Orleans. Roccaforte's Fisherman's Wharf (what a mouthful) possesses a long-standing reputation and numbers among its patrons an unusually large number of tourists for a predominantly neighborhood restaurant. This is due in part to the excellent press Roccaforte's has received over the years.

The best food here isn't necessarily the most pretentious, and everyday seafood items prove to be the real winners. Oysters at Roccaforte's are something special and the Crabs (in season) are delightful and achieve unusual levels of perfection. The dining area is kept meticulously clean and the service personnel are proven veterans who greet you with warm, no-nonsense service and advice on what to eat.

Prices are reasonable and the beer is kept really cold to accompany the seafood. Some of Roccaforte's Italian creations are gems in the rough if the seafood menu doesn't meet your fancy. There is also an excellent Gumbo on the menu and a wide selection of poorboy type sandwiches. Roccaforte's has much character and must be enjoyed by coming early and staying late. Closed Saturday and Sunday.

STEPHEN & MARTIN'S

1613 Milan Street   897-0781

Moderate/Expensive

Located in the same building with St. Charles Avenue's popular disco, 4141, fashionable Stephen & Martin's has emerged as a serious food bastion serving an uptown clientele seeking a relaxed, leisurely meal. Stephen & Martin's accomplishes this with a bright, springy interior of green colors, garden lattice work, and mirrors.

Of the menu items, a continental assortment is headed by an aristocractic Veal Reginald, sauteed to perfection and topped with fresh mushrooms over a Hollandaise base. Another interesting combination is the Spaghetti and Oysters, where the pair is brought together in a white sauce laced with fresh aromatic vegetables. An excellent Broiled Trout with Crabmeat shows the kitchen's deft hand with seafood.

Recently enlarged, Stephen & Martin's now seats approximately 185 (twice its old capacity) and hosts private parties in an upstairs room located directly above 4141.

This rising star among the city's better restaurants bears further watching.

T. PITTARI'S

4200 S. Claiborne Avenue   891-2801

Expensive

Long a New Orleans landmark on Claiborne Avenue near Napoleon, T. Pittari's has recently received a new lease on life. The reason for this pleasant happening is the fact that Tom Pittari, Jr. returned to run the family business after a year's hiatus in the hotel world. Tom is young, personable and perfectly attuned to the needs of his customers.

Pittari's has always specialized in live Maine Lobsters and a variety of big game dishes (we once tried a tiger steak) which add unusual flair to the menu but little else to the operation. Today, Tom is concentrating on the old-style Italian and continental dishes that the restaurant originated years ago and which prompted its initial success. Pittari's Hot Crabmeat a la T. Pittari is extremely popular and with good reason. It is flavor-filled, tantalizing and delivers on the palate. A stuffed Pompano fulfills that great fish's promise and the combinaion Lobster/BBQ Shrimp is the sleeper on the menu.

By the way, the convenience of the Claiborne Avenue location before or after a Louisiana Superdome activity is without equal.

TURCI'S

3218 Magazine Street   899-3463
Expensive

At its former downtown location within the Central Business District, Turci's was a widely respected and well-attended restaurant. Its move to the present Magazine Avenue location some years ago was by necessity, and the meticulous job of restoration done by Turci's new owners was nearly perfect. What has been lacking since Turci's took up new quarters is a kitchen consistent enough to carry out the old-time Turci's recipes which had brought it so much attention during its heyday. This is not to say that Turci's is incapable of producing some extemely creditable food on occasion, for at times the fare has been of extremely high calibre.

As one would expect, the menu is predominately Italian with some local New Orleans specialties available. Best of the entrees are the **Veal Scallopini** and **Veal Piccata**, with hearty meatballs and spaghetti available for the really hungry. An interesting Stuffed Eggplant combines meat and cheese for a rather special taste. While these dishes are generally above average, some even excellent, true consistency seems lacking throughout the general operation. One feels that the service personnel are simply going through the motions, and that Turci's simply has lost much of its spirit and forcefulness.

VERSAILLES

2100 St. Charles Avenue   524-2535
Very Expensive

When owner-chef Guenter Preuss transitioned from the hotel (Fairmont) side of the food business to open the Versailles in 1975, he knowingly conceded the hard times ahead. After long and arduous years, Preuss' hard work and expertise have vaulted his establishment into pre-eminence among New Orleans' truly superior classic restaurants. Moreover, Preuss and his staff have emerged as the city's premiere hosts for small and medium-sized dinner parties and special occasions.

German-born Preuss is a veritable master of freshness, and the discipline he imposes on both himself and his staff make his presentations things of great beauty. Waiters here are visible and audible personalities, ultra-professional and polished to insure perfect dining encounters. Along with Commander's Palace and the neighboring Caribbean Room, the Garden District restaurant trio is the best one-two-three combination outside the French Quarter. As far as specific dishes, the Versailles' localized Bouillabaise is interesting and provides an insight into local ingredients. The classic Steak Avec Bernaise is elegant and perfectly suited to such an opulent setting. Rear door parking makes the Versailles even more convenient to those interested in truly regal dining. Closed Sundays.

YE OLDE COLLEGE INN

3016 S. Carrollton Avenue   866-3683
                            Moderate

Another marvelous old time-honored Uptown tradition which produces inexpensive food in a most unpretentious setting. This Carrollton landmark's Chicken Fried Steak sandwich has been its most note-worthy food item for many years and is still hailed by College Inn's vociferous customers. The Chicken Fried Steak is a Texas creation, but reaches major heights under College Inn's special handling. Another delightful menu selection is a well-prepared Oyster loaf.

While there are numerous dinners available, these take a back seat to the more convenient menu offerings. Traditional New Orleans Red Beans and Rice, a mainstay in any true neighborhood business, are well-soaked and spicily prepared. It is a safe bet that practically any of College Inn's specialties are well worth trying. It is just that sort of restaurant. It is cozy, relaxed and just plain fun. As in many New Orleans neighborhood restaurants, no credit cards are accepted here.

Valbon Puts The Mystery Back Into Wine Buying

VALBON. You sniff. You taste. At around $3.50, you realize you've discovered an extraordinary wine value. But where is it from? The label can't tell you. It's against French law.

But we can give you a clue. At the bottom of the label, in fine print, you'll find a number — 21202. It's the French zip code for the town where Bouchard Pere & Fils has bottled its classic Burgundies for 250 years. Wines that cost ten times the price of Valbon. So Valbon is from Bouchard P & F, blended and bottled in the most famous winery in the most famous town in the most famous wine region in all of France.

A contradiction? Not at all. Valbon is offered proudly, for those occasions when one of Bouchard's classics would be inappropriate. A perfect everyday drinking wine for the serious wine buyer. In either the crisp white or the robust red, you can enjoy Valbon without compromising your taste standards.

And to clear up the mystery: If you'll send us a stamped, self-addressed envelope, we'll send you free a Zip Code Directory for France, and you can look up the proud home of Valbon. In the meantime, zip down to your liquor store for a truly remarkable wine value.

Valbon
Bouchard Pere & Fils

Nine Generations of Wine Making at the same address…France 21202.

MID CITY

CHEZ HELENE

1540 N. Robertson Street   947-9155
Moderate

Owner-Chef Austin Leslie has been winning accolades with this modest establishment for the last decade. Whenever international chefs visiting New Orleans eat out in the city, chances are their hosts will eventually suggest Chez Helene. The reason is quite simple, for Chef Leslie consistently manages to produce the finest Negro/Creole food in the entire area.

Since much in Creole cooking has its origins in Negro culture, the preceeding statement needs some amplification. The type of food Leslie prepares is closely akin to the food blacks of the city choose to eat today, and is not a style of food designed to appeal to Chez Helene's large white following. His food is peppery, zestful and crammed full of spices and herbs which produce distinguished results.

His famous stuffed bell peppers, artfully conceived and seasoned, are a meal in themselves. Leslie's special Fried Chicken gives locally renowned Popeye's something to shoot at. Chez Helene's success comes from meticulous food seasoning that is a throwback to the era of great plantation tables. France's premiere Chef du Cuisine Paul Bocuse once found Chez Helene's food "encraibe" and that certainly says it all. The atmosphere is comfortable and relaxed, and prices are moderate. This is one of the real "musts" to anyone truly interested in definitive New Orleans cooking.

CHRISTIAN'S

3835 Iberville Street   482-4924
Expensive

When owner Chris Ansel moved his facility from suburban Metairie to a former church in New Orleans' Mid-city section, the site was indeed a first for city restaurants. Christian's has always been a very serious French and Creole restaurant and its chef Roland Huet is a Lyonnaise practitioner of the first magnitude.

The new church location seems to be the conduit which has provided success for the operation, and we do mean success. Christian's popularity has risen to the extent that, at times, it is truly one of the most difficult places in the area to obtain a reservation. Much of the success must be attributed to Huet, whose creative hand consistently produces a myriad of delicate concoctions which possess regional authority and classical vigor.

Christian's also has a fiercely loyal clientele who consider Ansel and his place the finest restaurant in the city. The staff is solicitous and cooperative and its convenient location is but an easy 5-minute drive from downtown. Huet's forte lies in the rich quenelles (a form of dumplings, but a great deal more involved) and regional dishes such as the Redfish with Green Peppercorns. The menu is adventuresome and should be tried on successive visits. Owner Ansel runs the place deftly, as befitting his family's years of local restaurant experience. Closed Sundays & Mondays.

DOOKY CHASE

2301 Orleans Avenue   822-9506
                          Moderate

Forget the neighborhood and dive right in when you see Dooky Chase, one of the truly great Negro restaurants in the city. The guiding genius here is Mrs. Leah Chase, who brings several generations of experience and a great deal of personal expertise toward providing a marvelous Creole eating experience. Just about all the food served at Dooky Chase is excellent, so it is difficult to pick out dishes which are really distinctive.

The sausages, for starters, are magnificent. Hot sausages are indeed HOT, while the smoked variety are at their best. Mrs. Chase's seasonings might seem a bit heavy at first, but real balance and sophistication soon become apparent. Her great Creole Gumbo, always a true insight to a thorough Creole kitchen, is peppery, appetizing and artfully prepared.

Dooky Chase has long been an "in" place, for both blacks and whites. Its food is consistent, prices more than reasonable, and its management absolutely wonderful. Would there were more like Dooky Chase around. The city of New Orleans would be much better for it.

EMPIRE ROOM
(Fountain Bay Motel)

4040 Tulane Avenue   486-6111
                      Moderate/Expensive

This unimposing evening dining room located within one of New Orleans' well-established motel properties features a la carte continental menu. The kitchen is among the better as far as motel properties go, and is capable of producing some outstanding fare.

An exceptional hors d'oeuvres plate contains, among its offerings, shrimp salad, stuffed eggs, a choice of chicken and potato salads and artichoke hearts. It is almost a meal unto itself and quite rewarding. The Shrimp and Crabmeat Salad Louisianne departs from the usual with creative success. The daily Soupe de Jour is remarkably well defined and pleasant to the taste. The regular salads are, if anything, simply too large when served with other items. The Redfish Meuniere stands out among the seafood entrees, and the Medaillons of Veal, a la Fontainbleu is another successful dish fashioned with simplicity and good taste.

Prices at the Empire Room are moderate and service is somewhat laid back and relaxing. There is excellent entertainment nearby and several well stocked bars to check out after dinner. The Fountain Bay (formerly the Fontainbleu) has been around for quite some time, and caters to a family trade.

GENGHIS KAHN

4035 Tulane Avenue

482-4044

Moderate

It is surprising that Korean food and Korean restaurants haven't proved to be more popular. At this writing, Genghis Kahn is New Orleans' only true Korean food spot which has become popular with local food lovers. Located in the Mid-city section of the city, Genghis Kahn offers an exciting variation from the horde (literally) of Chinese restaurants which have cropped up over the past few years.

Genghis Kahn's version of Korean cuisine tends to be quite spicy, and is not too far removed from the peppery Cajun cuisine of Southwestern Louisiana. There also exists a subtleness within Korean food which elevates it to the realm of the finer international cuisines. The fare appears similar to Chinese in most American minds.

A marinated beef dish, Bulgogi, provides a hint of sesame, and is finished off on the broiler which enhances its taste and effect. A Mongolian Special Hot Pot utilizes noodles and vegetables as a base, then combines deft spicing to achieve a most rewarding taste experience. Side dishes have unusual names and in some cases surprises (Kimchee, a marinated cabbage, is really hot), but most are well worth trying. Genghis Kahn is an adventure in unusual Asian dining and should be sampled by the true gastronomist.

MANDINA'S

3800 Canal Street   482-9179

Inexpensive

There should be a wonderful niche like Mandina's in every great restaurant city; a place devoid of embellishments and so in tune with the needs of its customers as to be considered practically everyone's favorite neighborhood restaurant. Mandina's is indeed among the highest-trafficked restaurants in the area and is located in the Mid-city section directly across from New Orleans' palacial funeral parlor Schoen's.

Mandina's is the original fun place to both eat and drink. The crowd at the bar (there's always a crowd, day or night) is clamorous, sport-oriented and at times conspicuously outspoken. Food is pure New Orleans/Italian at prices which have defied inflation for a number of years. The Paneed Veal Cutlets are from an old recipe as are the Red Beans and Rice of Monday's special fame. A heaping tasty Shrimp salad is enough for a full meal, and the French Fried Onion Rings go great with a cold beer. They are crispy, well-battered and maintain the true flavor of the sweet bermuda onions.

Waiters here have years of experience and fit the place well. There is little real service flow. The help is part of the party and that's what makes Mandina's so successful. Don't kid yourself, Mandina's isn't a classic restaurant and it doesn't claim to be. In a word, it is Mandina's! No credit cards here, it's cash which counts. Closed Sundays.

MONTE'S

4200 Canal Street   488-7207

Expensive

This recently-opened upbeat restaurant should not be confused with many of the neighborhood spots which dot the Mid-city section of New Orleans. Smallish (seating around 85), Monte's is attractively set with a combination of raised dining levels, booths and tables which divide the room into cozy conversation nooks.

The menu is a mixture of Creole, pure New Orleans and, of course, continental Italian dishes. From the appetizer selection, an enterprising Shrimp Monte brings together shrimp, crabmeat and mushrooms with a tangy cheese and spiced Italian breadcrumb topping. Shrimp Barbara is a finely seasoned Stuffed Shrimp entree, which is rich and appealing. Veal Isabelle is a classic Paneed Veal sauteed with mushroom caps. These dishes illustrate the kind of finesse available from Monte's kitchen.

As in most new restaurants, there are still minor problems in service, menu "outs", etc., but Monte's is a good pick for lunch or dinner. Closed Sundays.

RUTH'S CHRIS STEAK HOUSE

711 N. Broad Street   482-9278
Very Expensive

Continually the finest steak house in New Orleans for the past fifteen years, Owner Ruth Fertel's secret is her highly selective meat cuts which she imports directly from a location out-of-state which she chooses not to reveal. The menu is completely a la carte with a limited selection of side dishes and a usable wine list. Were the accompaniments on a par with the meat selections, Ruth's Chris' three locations would receive an even higher rating.

Among the steaks, a gigantic T-Bone and an equally impressive Filet are cooked in Ruth's Chris' butter sauce mixture to produce an impeccable taste sensation. One comes to Ruth's Chris to eat fine steaks and little else. The potatoes au gratin are commonplace and of no particular note as are the canned asparagus. Service at most of the locations is dependable, but not on a par with really top area restaurants.

Ruth's Chris has been the steak leader for many years locally and has maintained its quality standards admirably despite some inherent problems. Prices tend to be high by New Orleans standards, but in our opinion, the quality meat served make the prices fully justifiable.

SAXONY

1717 Canal Street   581-4466
Moderate

The Saxony Restaurant has always been predominantly a catering operation specializing in convention activities and private parties. It also operates a small capacity daily luncheon room which is open to the public and also quite convenient to downtown New Orleans. Just off the Canal Street/Claiborne Avenue intersection, the Saxony's menu combines some standard seafood items and a nice selection of steak items. Trade is from the business community and men outnumber women by a large ratio.

From the luncheon menu, The Crepes de Mer are outstanding, served in a rich cream sauce with large amounts of shrimp and crabmeat and covered with a thin pancake. The Shrimp New Orleans features an excellent breadcrumb filling and a mild taste which is pleasing. Shrimp Scampi tends to get lost in an overabundance of garlic, and the Barbequed Redfish seemed too vinegary to suit.

Steaks are consistent and prepared to order and usually come with french fries and a salad. For something different, try the Chicken Embassy, a stuffed breast of chicken in an orange-brandy sauce which is totally unique in New Orleans. Overall, the Saxony is a tidy operation, with consistent food at reasonable prices. Closed Saturdays & Sundays.

LAKEFRONT

Map, pg. 170

BRUNING'S

West End Park   282-9395

Moderate

Bruning's is the grand old dame of Lakefront seafood restaurants and traces its origins back over 120 years. Classic New Orleans fried seafood might easily have originated here, and the crowds which still patronize it are testimony to its former greatness.

But the Bruning's of the 1980's is a far cry from the marvelous establishment many of us grew up with and loved. Many of the faces are the same, but the food has gone its own commercial way. Gone are the great fried seafoods, shellfish, and the magnificent fried crawfish which helped build the Bruning's legend. In actuality, the boiled seafoods rate higher than the fried, but it seems a shallow victory due to the overall low quality of the foods presented. Closed Wednesday.

FITZGERALD'S

West End Park   282-9254

Moderate/Expensive

For what seems like close to a century, Fitzgerald's has been a local institution for seafood lovers who annually treked to West End Park to enjoy fresh New Orleans seafood. Maurice Fitzgerald has long departed the area and most of the old place's real creativity and consistency seem to have departed with him. Fitzgerald's real allure lies in the fact, superficially, that little has changed to remove the spot from the minds of those who grew up with its goodness and helped to build its reputation.

As always, the emphasis at Fitzgerald's is slanted toward heavily fried seafood, but the kitchen's real flare for frying has gone. The fish and shellfish are still fresh, but the servings are commercial in nature and generally unappetizing. The entire area of West End Park has undergone a renaissance of sorts lately, and there is hope that Fitzgerald's will be able to improve and rejoin the ranks of top-level seafood establishments. Everyone wishes it well.

IMPERIAL PALACE

125 Robert E. Lee Blvd.   283-3066
Moderate

This unpretentious Lakefront spot continues to provide the most consistent Chinese food in the entire area. It should not be confused with the opulent Imperial Palace Regency restaurant, which at one time owned both locations. The Imperial Palace is strictly for less formal consumption, with an experienced kitchen and service staff which really makes one feel at home.

The food is a combination of Szechuan and Cantonese styles, with a few Hunan dishes thrown in for good measure. The Moo Goo Gai Pan is a most exotic dish, served in the traditional Chinese pancake. Sweet and Sour Pork is another excellent dish and the Mandarin Duck leaves little to be desired. Host Roy Walker is gracious and has in the Imperial Palace an impressive oriental jewel. Closed Mondays.

MASSON'S LA FRANCAISE

7200 Pontchartrain Blvd.   283-2525
Expensive

This Lakefront tradition has been an award-winner for the past two decades. The restaurant, although relaxed, is able to maintain a basic formality which tends to set it apart from its other lake area neighbors. As the name implies, the emphasis here is French provincial, but a smattering of regional Creole menu items balances the food selection nicely.

Masson's crowd tends to be older New Orleans natives who have come to expect a certain style of food and service. Masson's kitchen is stable, with Chef Robert Finley having wielded the ladle for quite some time. During his tenure, Masson's kitchen has developed a high degree of consistency. Regulars prefer the etoufees and gumbos, but we have always thought the fish specials were the real strength of the menu.

There is also the Almond Torte, an exquisite dessert that provides an insight into what is possible with the correct combination of creativity and natural ingredients. The Torte is among the city's best desserts and definitely Masson's best single effort. Valet parking is available.

TONY ANGELO'S

6262 Fleur de Lis Drive   498-0888
Expensive

You are either a great supporter of Tony Angelo's Italian restaurant or not. It's just that simple, Tony himself has become something of a local kitchen legend, and he is tremendously innovative in his approach to food. From his extensive menu, one can glean a most rewarding insight into true Sicilian/Creole cooking and artistry. Tony's kitchen possesses a most balanced hand, ably demonstrated in dishes such as Italian Sausage and Peppers and a classic Veal Parmigiana, a specific creation without local equal. Tony Angelo's lasagne is at its rich, full best at any occasion, and a wonderful fried Calamari ranks as his finest single creation.

One hardly thinks of dessert at an Italian restaurant, but this establishment's special Lemon Ice Box Pie is a taste treat worth remembering. Reservations here are among the tightest in the suburbs, and weekends present even more difficulties. Due to the fact that many of Tony's regular customers tend to spend inordinate amounts of time at the table, even reservations are sometimes given to rather long waits. The food however, makes the wait worthwhile. Closed Sundays and Mondays.

WINDJAMMER

8550 Pontchartrain Blvd.   283-8301

Expensive

This restaurant, set in an authentic nautical atmosphere, has developed a large local following in recent years. The winning combination of a relaxed atmosphere, good stiff drinks and a varied menu has made the Windjammer a forerunner in local leisure dining. The decor utilizes soft woodtones to good effect. The large open dining area adds to an overall air of congeniality which permeates the dining experience.

Featured on the menu are some incredible BBQ Honey Ribs prepared outdoors on an open fire. Oysters Windjammer and a longtime menu item, Trout Supreme, are winners from the seafood side.

Windjammer seldom disappoints, and small and large private parties are welcome. To avoid the rigors of downtown dining, Windjammer is an excellent Lakefront alternative.

METAIRIE

AGOSTINO'S RISTORANTE ★★

4100 Jefferson Hwy. 835-3349

Expensive

Agostino and Estella Mantia are native-born Sicilians who bring first generation Sicilian cooking to a city mainly influenced by assorted versions of Sicilian foods which have been passed down through generations of Italian-Americans. Agostino's is the pure thing, and it invites curious comparison.

Located as it is on surburban Jefferson Highway, it is a jaded nook among culinary establishments. Food authenticity is unquestionable—many ingredients are still received directly from Palermo. As one would expect, veal dishes and freshly made pastas are the specialties of the substantial menu. Sauces reach a zennith here: vibrant utterly rich and luxurious, and of course, spicily fulfilled. Agostino's greatness lies in the fact that the food tends to transcend its surroundings, all the while providing an euphoric insight into modern Sicilian cuisine.

The Mantia's too, offer an insight into the personality and warmth of the great Southern Italian island. They have literally built their restaurant with their own hands, and part of their character is served with each dish. A dinner at Agostino's is a very, very nice way to spend an evening. Closed Mondays.

ANDREW MARTIN'S CAJUN CUISINE

3530 Village Drive 837-2152

Moderate/Expensive

This widely-Advertised Metairie eatery with its spacious high ceilings and attractive decor, simply does not live up to expectations. Its natural hardwood flooring makes for horrible acoustics and undue noise which disturbs the concentration on the meal. Martin's ceiling fans are run at extremely high speeds which make for discomfort to those seated directly below. The service staff is quite amateurish and unable to keep up an even pace when serving. Given the aforementioned problems, a good showing from the kitchen could conceivably still save the day. Sadly, this just does not happen.

The Gumbo is thick, relatively absent of real seasonings, and reminescent of a dish left on the steam table for too long. Other featured dishes, such as the broiled or fried trout are lifeless and lacking in real inspiration. The

Crabmeat au Gratin, long a standby, is a mere imitation of some of its more rewarding cousins. Freshness is supposed to be Andrew Martin's byword, but this is only important when the kitchen performs. While the food served is abundant, the overall degree of reliability is just too low for the restaurant to be taken seriously.

BUTCHER SHOP

3322 N. Turnbull Drive   454-2666
                        Very Expensive

When restaurateur Frank Occhipinti revived this three-time restaurant-loser, many eyebrows were raised. Occhipinti repostioned his place with a steak-oriented menu, limited side orders, and an expanded wine list. Time has proved Occhipinti's decision a correct one, and The Butcher Shop is now solidly established and more than capable of giving the Ruth's Chris Steakhouse locations a real run for their money.

Needless to say, only Prime Beef is served here, and the cuts tend to be large to mountainous, and practically unfinishable except for the heartiest eater. The Rib Eye is charbroiled to near perfection as is a wondrous Filet Mignon. Special steak sauces (at an additional cost) are available (Amergia is a favorite) to further compliment the meats. For side dishes the Panee Artichoke is well conceived and prepared, as are the French Fried Pepper Rings, a superby adaptation of one of New Orleans' favorite treats, green bell peppers.

There are other entrees available, but stick to the meat selections. The Butcher Shop is an important new addition to the suburban restaurant community and more importantly, the best pure steak operation to come along in many years. Closed Sundays.

DELERNO'S

619 Pink Street   831-3176
                        Moderate

This unpretentious location in the Old Metairie section is family-oriented, moderately priced and one of the most consistent small kitchens in the entire area. During crawfish season, Delerno's revels in the limelight of its famous Crawfish Festival Platter, which features six assorted crawfish specialties. The dish has drawn raves from local crawfish connoisseurs since founder, J.B. Delerno introduced it prior to his death several years ago.

Another Delerno innovation, a magnificent stuffed artichoke is a menu pleaser which can also be taken home and enjoyed later. The traditional seafood platter, the dish on which Delerno originally built his culinary reputation, and some startling Italian departures such as the deep pan Sicilian pizza make this spot incredibly popular. Delerno's serves an innovative crawfish topas, an appetizer whose popularity has become widespread.

Among members of the restaurant community, J.B. Delerno was a very respected personality. His sons have preserved their fathers' insight into the intricacies of regional and local cooking. Their performance has prompted The Insider's Guide to award Delerno's the co-honor (along with Bozo's) as the **Best Suburban Neighborhood Restaurant;** a two-star designation. Closed Mondays.

AUGIE'S RESTAURANT

3837 Veterans Highway   455-7181
Expensive

Of all the newly opened restaurants located in Metairie, Augie's has proven to be the most successful. Owner Augie Lopez was formerly associated with the very popular Sal & Sam's as executive chef and later at the Windjammer as chef and part-owner. Augie's is Lopez's initial restaurant venture as sole owner, and to this point in Augie's evolution, Lopez has done well. He attempted to recreate a bit of French Quarter ambiance in the suburbs, and the idea has paid off.

By combining several menu items, Augie's seems to have caught everyone's dining fancy. The Augie's Delight (soft-shell crab, Veal Augie and a petit Filet Mignon) is dependable and delicious. A mixed seafood appetizer tray has also proven popular as has an excellent Veal Pontchartrain (Veal Medaillons covered with hollandaise sauce and fresh asparagus).

Augie's employs several Lopez family members who seem dedicated to good food and large portions. The bar area at Augie's is one of the area's largest, and it is adjacent to the dining room. On weekends, and during lunches, this proves to be noisy, but no one seems to mind. Augie's best food is undoubtedly his daily special which he changes quite often. It's a fun place and Augie is a fun guy. What more can we say?

BOZO'S

3117 21st Street   831-8666
Moderate

To those of us who remember Bozo's old mid-city location, Chris Vodanovich's new suburban Metairie establishment is like seeing a page out of a decorator's handbook. Some businesses lose something when transferring quarters, but this is not the case with Bozo's. If anything, the food benefits from an enlarged kitchen.

Old favorites like Catfish (absolutely the finest in the entire city) and delicate Fried Oysters are still available, not to mention the superb

Seafood Platter which includes a half-dozen fried oysters, catfish, a stuffed crab and french fries. And don't forget the masterfully light potato salad, not really Germanic, but rather a Yugoslavian/Italian concoction which substitutes olive oil and lemon for mayonnaise with delicious effect.

Two new items, marinated crabs and crawfish (in season) are real show stoppers, once again making expert usage of olive oil, garlic and lemon. The reason for Bozo's new-found success in Metairie continues to be the hand of Vodanovich, who daily labors in his new kitchen. His staff tends to be relaxed, yet always manages to meet the challenge of the crowds. In earning the designation **Best Suburban Neighborhood Restaurant** (along with Delerno's), Bozo's continues to improve and gain admiration from its many followers. Closed Sunday and Monday.

DRAGO'S

3232 N. Armoult Road   887-9611
Moderate

When Drago's moved from its Lakeview site to a new location in the middle of Metairie's Fat City section, its reputation as an excellent neighborhood restaurant went with the move. Today, Drago's is recognized as a major ethnic restaurant with an amazing ability to combine adventuresome Yugoslavian food with local Creole specialties.

That Drago's has been able to establish and maintain a true Eastern European food identity is remarkable in a city notably lacking in quality ethnic restaurants. True to the Yugoslavian background, most of the appetizers at Drago's are of the marinated variety and well worth sampling. Marinated squid and fish are the best, but all are quite well received. The Yugo Platter and the stuffed squid are best among the entrees which include both fried and broiled seafood selections. Portions at Drago's tend to be enormous, which in other places, is not always a plus, but here quantity and quality are happy equals.

Yugoslavian Strudel is Drago's most memorable dessert. A complete Yugoslavian wine list compliments the menu well. Parking is extremely limited in this area, so it is advisable to come early. Closed Sundays.

ESPANA

2705 Jefferson Hwy.   835-1502
Inexpensive

Even though New Orleans is a city heavy with Spanish influence, it is interesting to note that the Espana is the only valid Spanish restaurant in the area. This Jefferson Highway location is Espana's second local home, and happily this larger space provides an oportunity for a business which seems much easier to control than its former cramped location. The air here is very casual and the clientele quite varied.

The food speaks loudly for itself. Traditional Paella is the mainstay of

Espana's kitchen, and it is remarkably smooth and consistent. The rice and seafood combines with chicken and expert spicing to provide a true taste adventure. Another fine innovation, an eye of round roast (Carne Sava) is stuffed with ham to provide an interesting meat combination.

Some of the lesser known dishes, most involving beans, sausages and other ingredients, are always great fun and should be tried if the spirit moves you. Senor Antonio Lopez runs a tight Spanish galleon and an even tighter galley with remarkably moderate prices. Ole! Closed Sundays.

ETIENNE'S

3100 19th Street   834-8583

Expensive

When Etienne's was a smallish Uptown eatery, we were always well satisfied with the performance of its kitchen. Since moving to Metairie some years ago, it is sorry to say that much of this culinary mastery has been forgotten and left behind. Dishes now lack any real creativity and the portions are sometimes micronized.

The place has been popular enough, particularly around lunchtime, so Etienne's specific style of food must be inviting to some. We are not overly fond of commercial food and this is exactly how Etienne's menu strikes us. Save your time and effort, as there are far better places around to satisfy your palate. Closed Mondays.

GOLDEN DRAGON

4417 Veterans Blvd.   887-6081
Metairie   Moderate

When Houng You Liu left Formosa as a Colonel in Chaing Kai Sheck's army, he and his family migrated to New Orleans and opened this tiny nook across from the Clearview Shopping Center. Business was good, so Mr. Liu and his son expanded to Lafayette and left the fate of the Golden Dragon to his wife and daughter.

The Golden Dragon specializes in Szechuan and Hunan regional dishes which bear similarities in seasoning to many local Creole and Cajun dishes. Golden Dragon requires one day's notice for Peking Duck, but the inconvenience is well worth the wait. The final product served in the traditional pancake is a truly outstanding example of classic Chinese fare at reasonable prices.

Golden Dragon's old standbys continue to be their most effective dishes. The Sweet and Pungent Whole Fish (served with head attached) is Fried. Shrimp Balls never disappoint, nor does the service or attitude of the staff. Closed Monday nights.

HIRED HAND SALOON

1100 S. CLEARVIEW
ELMWOOD SHOPPING CENTER
HARAHAN, LA 70123
734-0590

IMPASTATO'S

3400 16th Street   455-1545
Metairie   Moderate/Expensive

When little Joe Impastato left Moran's Riverside several years ago, after over 20 years of service, his legions of friends and supporters wished him luck. More than that they supported his new restaurant venture which has become one of Metairie's most successful locations. Impastato's success lies within the cooking, which is hearty Sicilian and laced with smatterings of New Orleans Style and Creole cuisines.

Best items are Sicilian. The Cannelloni appetizer is light, flavory and a most delicate taste treat. A magnificent house salad, named in honor of local oilman, Jim Bob Moffett, is a wonderful creation which includes greens, artichoke hearts, Genoa Salami and other choice tidbits. The creamy Italian/Blue cheese house dressing sets off the dish perfectly. Entree-wise, a delicious Osso Buco, baby veal shank in a wine sauce served over a bed of rice, was tender and most rewarding. Trout Marianna is an adventure in richness. The trout is paneed, and then topped with an artichoke and mushroom sauce literally swimming in butter.

Impastato's overcomes some minor problems such as woeful acoustics and heavy decor, but its staff is attentive and professional, and promises long term success. Closed Sundays & Mondays.

LA RIVIERA

4427 Shores Drive   888-6238
                                Expensive

This pleasant restaurant is located just off Clearview Parkway (near West Esplanade) in suburban Metairie and it outshines many area Italian restaurants in food, service and style. The elegant Italian setting is perfect for intimate dining and is especially welcomed in the suburbs. Many elegant restaurants of this type tend to be cold and impersonal, but La Riviera has warmth and charm.

Owner Goffredo Fraccaro is respected by his fellow restauraneurs with good reason. His scampi is a classic work of art which brings generations of Italian flavorings to the tip of your tongue. Graccaro's Ravioli stuffed with crabmeat in a white cream sauce recently won a culinary award in San Francisco competition and is a great taste experience. Pastas tend to be rich and are generally accompanied by fine sauces. Best are the fettucine and tortellini which are variants on the classic dishes and well worth trying.

Goffredo cooks both Northern and Sicilian Italian cuisines, but he seems more suited to the richer reds of the South. La Riviera has a large following which makes tables somewhat hard to come by, especially on weekends and during special holiday times. Closed Sundays.

LIDO GARDENS

4415 Airline Highway   834-8233
                    Moderate/Expensive

When Betty and Tony Mangiot crossed back over the Mississippi River to open the Lido Gardens, they left behind a stable business and a large West Bank following. (See Lido Restaurant for associated review). At his old location, Tony always performed as head chef, so it was reasonable to assume his food would lose nothing in the transition. Safe assumption, Lido Garden's cuisine is every bit as good as before.

Of special interest is a superb Manicotti and a wonderfully light Ravioli which is fixed with a distinctive Italian sausage. Perhaps the finest single dish is the classical Lasagne, which tastes as if a slight amount of anise has been added at some point producing a sweetish finish and memorable palate taste. Among the beef dishes, the Bruchelloni is without local parallel, and the rich and perfectly cooked Meatballs and Spaghetti are hard to beat.

Tony's wife Betty is a master of service and personality and makes even the casual diner feel welcome and at ease. Like their West Bank counterpart, entrees at the new Lido Gardens are reasonable and well worth the price. The Airline Highway location is an excellent one, with no real ethnic culinary competition nearby. The Mangiots should do very well here, for they are true professionals and deserve success. Closed Sundays.

LITTLE CAJUN CUISINE

3201 Houma Blvd.   455-7600
                         Moderate

Ever since this charming nook moved into larger quarters some time ago, the "Little" part of its name seems slightly out of context. The move was necessitated by the business' tremendous success which, happily, has continued unabated at this convenient Metairie location.

Owner Elmo Sonnier is from Lafayette, the Southwestern Louisiana heart of Acadiana, the city so synonymous with Cajun life and folklore. Elmo's insight into the mysteries of Cajun cuisine is profound, and it is directly responsible for his success. Seasoning of Little Cajun's dishes is the embodiment of correct Cajun cooking and bears close scrutiny by the ever-present Sonnier. Particular emphasis is given shellfish dishes, particularly crayfish (in season January through May) and shrimp. The popular Crayfish Etoufee is hearty, brisk and available year round. Shrimp selections are ideally simple.

Prices are reasonable and the wine list is well-attuned to the style of food served. Atmosphere tends to be casual and quite relaxed, with a large number of families enjoying the surroundings. Reservations on weekends are definitely recommended.

PEPPERMILL

3524 Severn Street   455-2226

Moderate/Expensive

The Peppermill is undoubtedly one of the better quality suburban operations to have opened during the past five years. Owner Josie Riccobono has made the best transition from home cooking (and home recipes) to professional standards of any restaurant owner within memory. Her cooking embodies a marvelous blending of her native Sicilian cuisine and old-style New Orleans. It has won the Peppermill a large and enthusiastic following. Mrs. Riccobono's treatment of fish and seafood dishes is quite deft.

Peppermill's specialty is an elegant seafood crepe, delicately covered with Peppermill's delicious seafood sauce. Another excellent fish creation, Stuffed Trout Peppermill, is also prepared with a seafood dressing and topped with a nicely done classic meuniere sauce.

Meatwise, the best offering is a meticulous Veal Severn, where slices of baby veal are accompanied by a shrimp and brandy sauce. The unique taste sensation lingers on the palate for hours. A number of Peppermill's dishes are first pan-fried and sauteed which accounts for their uniform good flavor. The atmosphere generated by the tasteful interior is as pleasing to the mind as such innovative food is to the palate. Peppermill is an ideal place in Metairie for intimate dinner gatherings. Closed Mondays.

RED ONION

2700 Edenborne   455-6677

Expensive

This large suburban restaurant has been immensely popular since the day it opened in the early seventies. The food has always been surprisingly good and the portions generous. Although the Occhipinti family is no longer associated with the operation, the new owners promise to continue the things which have made the Red Onion popular. The menu is varied, but the real strength lies in the Italian and continentally-conceived dishes included on the list.

Both the Crab Bisque and Crab Salad are highly recommended and the Rack of Lamb must be singled out as well-presented and carefully attended by the chef. Artful attention to detail, such as in Shrimp Benjamin or the meticulous Veal Bienville, propels the Red Onion into star status.

If there is one drawback, the place seems too crowded, with a few too many tables and chairs. That minor complaint is a remarkable tribute to the Red Onion's unwavering popularity, which we mentioned has been steady since its opening. Reservations are an absolute necessity on weekends, and are recommended throughout the week. Closed Sundays.

SAL AND SAM'S

4300 Veterans Blvd.   885-5566

Expensive

Soon after opening, this suburban eatery received a restaurant review which was less than optimistic. In a bold move, Sal & Sam's owners turned the review around and established the term "Food With Character", and have been wildly successful ever since. Sal & Sam's is almost legend now, and their formula seems quite simple. According to owner Sal Saia, all his operation does is "stick to basics and provide his customers with what they want."

The atmosphere is cheerful and relaxing, even though waiters are formal and table settings quite elegant. There is noisy chatter from most tables and patrons seem to have much in common. The crowd is a sporting one and local athletic events and teams tend to garner much of the limelight. Food tends to be continental and the kitchen is far above average. One of the better Steak Diane's in the city originates here and also an excellent appetizer tray which could easily serve as an entree. The staff delights in mammoth Caesar Salads, and little side dishes like Stuffed Mushrooms are a pure joy to taste.

The location reeks with personality and the bar is tended by some of our favorite people. Make reservations early for this popular dinner and late night spot. No luncheons Saturday and Sunday.

SCLAFANI'S

1315 N. Causeway Blvd.   835-1718

Moderate

Sclafani's is one of the eternally-popular New Orleans restaurants which generations of New Orleanians have grown up with. Sclafani's is family-oriented and deals with an almost completely local clientele. A new generation of Sclafanis continues to enjoy a reputation which has thrived by serving a variety of seafood (which tends to more Creole than anything else) and Italian specialties (which are most definitely Sicilian).

Sclafani's is neither elegant nor sophisticated as restaurants go. What makes it work so well is relaxed atmosphere, and the consistency of its menu items. Pasta dishes are large and the red sauces are quite rich. Sclafani's mainstays are fresh seafood and shellfish, and in particular softshell crabs in season.

Old regulars swear by the house salad which is set off by a unique mustardy dressing. Little changes here, and that is the underlying secret to Sclafani's ongoing charm and success. Closed Sundays.

SMILIE'S

5725 Jefferson Highway 733-3000
Moderate

Just past the East Bank approach to the venerable Huey P. Long Bridge lies the blossoming town of Harahan and its finest restaurant, Smilie's. Due to its proximity to a major industrial park, Smilie's tends to be somewhat ambivalent as restaurants go. One facet of the location is cafeteria-style service which tends to be wildly popular, particularly during lunch. Smilie's other face is that of a regular sit-down, full-service restaurant which caters to a different, evening crowd.

Happily, the kitchen which fuels both operations is multi-talented and exhibits a decided Italian influence over most of its menu items. Enchanting dishes such as fried Calamari (squid) and homemade Lasagna are Smilie's real forte, not to mention a surprisingly delicate Veal Piccata. There is also a hearty Italian sausage prepared the old way, which maintains its myriad of flavors and tastes. There is also a good seafood gumbo and a fine variety of chicken and steak items for the less adventuresome, but the real strength of Smilie's is definitely Italian and that's what should be explored. Smilie's is unpretentious and more family-oriented than most establishements of this calibre. It is always relaxed and its prices are reasonable and more than justified. Closed Sundays.

VINCENZO'S

3000 Severn Avenue 888-5000
Moderate/Expensive

This happy place, located across from the Lakeside Shopping Center, produces excellent Italian/Creole cuisine. Vincenzo's is a family operation of the Timphony family. It has proved very successful due to strict adherence to a number of old family recipes carefully handed down over the years.

Milk-fed baby veal dishes here are remarkable. Veal Lemone is a meticulously sculptured combination of the superb baby veal in a light wine sauce. Veal Vincenzo is lightly breaded, spiced with cheese and Italian flavorings and finally sauteed in olive oil and wine. Side dishes are also deftly conceived and well-presented as in the case of Fried Zucchini.

Vincenzo's prices are incredibly reasonable and reflect owner Timphony's opinion that great food need not be expensive food. The loyal crowd who regularly attend Vincenzo's hails from the sporting world, so the place is usually warm and alive with activity. Reserve early on weekends for Vincenzo's isn't quite as large as one would imagine, and word about their marvelous food has spread. Closed for lunch Saturday and Sunday.

PROVINCIAL

CROZIER'S

7003 Read Lane   241-8220

Expensive

Gerard and Eveline Crozier are the young and agreeable couple who have made this newly enlarged spot Eastern New Orleans' best purely French dining location. Gerard was formerly Executive Sous Chef at the Royal Sonesta Hotel. He began his own restaurant operation in 1977. Crozier's is the epitome of a smallish, unencumbered French auberge where supreme emphasis is given to culinary pursuits. Gerard Crozier's menu is miniscule by some standards, but is perfectly attuned to Crozier's culinary skills.

He excels in soups, with a superb Gratinee which rivals many European counterparts. His daily specials are delightful. His Coq au Vin is masterful, a luxurious fantasy which is a study in simplicity. The Escalopes de Veau aux Champignons shows perfect veal cutlets immersed in a delicate white wine sauce laced with freshly sauteed mushrooms.

While Crozier's food is practically impeccable, the service aspect of the business still has some visible growing pains to overcome before achieving maturity. Prices are on par with top downtown restaurants and service should be also. Once the front side is able to equal Gerard Crozier's culinary assertiveness, Crozier's will then become a major factor on the New Orleans restaurant scene. Closed Sunday and Monday.

JADE EAST

7011 Read Blvd   246-5590

Moderate

In New Orleans' rapidly expanding Eastern quadrant, this top-flight Hunan-style Chinese restaurant has made an immediate and impressive reputation. Chef Yu-Mei Ying brings over 30 years of background with him from New York's famed Hunan East Restaurant, which has been long considered as one of the earliest citadels of pure Hunan cuisine in the United States.

Mr. Ying's classic cooking outstrips both the surroundings and service at Jade East. Decor seems Spanish of sorts and the service staff tends to run minutes behind due to Jade East's large volume. An exquisite Hot and Sour soup will start you off. Next, the superb Moo Goo Gai Pan is certainly tops around the city. Another classic dish, Moo Shoo Pork is at its tangy, succulent best. Mr. Ying works his vegetables with the dexterity of a circus acrobat on the high wire. His ability to meld together major food flavors, so important to true Hunan provincial cuisine, is most rewarding to even the inexperienced palate.

Since Hunan tends to receive more seasoning than other Chinese provincial styles, the end product resembles both local Creole and Cajun food varieties. This factor could explain in part the tremendous rise in popularity and number of Chinese restaurants in New Orleans. Among the newcomers, Jade East certainly rates near the top.

LA PROVENCE

Route #1, Hwy. 90   626-7662
Lacombe   Expensive

La Provence might easily be considered the best French Provincial restaurant in the United States. Proprieter Chris Kerageorgiou is a Rhone Valley Native of Greek extraction who knows his professional art like few do. Practically everything on the menu is made from scratch, from the fresh saussisson to the memorable finely-layered baklava which is Kerageorgiou's personal favorite. The baklava graces the dessert cart which is regally wheeled around the dining room after dinner. In between there is a substantial array of entrees including a marvelous Veal with fresh tarragon, a near incomparable Salmon Pate, and a most memorable Terrine de Trois Poission. Side dishes show French, Italian, Greek and even a smattering of regional Creole influences.

La Provence is one of those places which enamors and attracts everyone who traverses its portals. Wildly popular for the last few years, it is near impossible to find a slack period for casual dining. Members of the Kerageorgiou family fulfill various roles at La Provence and tend to make the time spent there a memorable occasion. Closed Mondays and Tuesdays.

RESTAURANT MANDICH

3200 St. Claude Avenue   947-9553
                              Moderate

Another fine neighborhood restaurant serving the city's lower ninth ward area. Here, as in most places geared strictly to local trade, the atmosphere is relaxed and convival. A large bar area adjoins the dining room which creates in itself, a truly tumultous situation. Despite the constant din (especially in early evening), Mandich's kitchen rises miles above its relatively innocuous surroundings.

Best items are the fresh fish and seafood dishes which are consistently satisfying and can easily be classified as nearly superb. The Broiled Trout Mandich is among the finest in the city and is best enjoyed when served in the company of a chilled glass of beer. The fish actually melts in your mouth and leaves your palate with an excellent buttery aftertaste. Fried oysters are light and delicious, and the tangy Shrimp Remoulade is a house specialty of distinguished proportions.

Prices are ridiculously reasonable and the wait for a table isn't generally longer than a few minutes. Be prepared for a whale of a good time, for Restaurant Mandich is that type of location. Closed Sundays and Mondays.

MAYER'S OLD EUROPE

2998 Pontchartrain Blvd.   649-1426
Slidell   Moderate/Expensive

Several years ago, a restaurant named Old Europe existed in the French Quarter which was quite good. Problems arose and its owners finally decided to close in the mid-1960's. Late last year, the son of Old Europe's original owners decided to revive the name with this highly-appealing intimate location in nearby Slidell. For George Mayer, the return to the restaurant business was something his background and expertise called out for him to do.

Mayer does most of the cooking himself, and he accomplishes much with his continental menu. The appetizer selection is varied, with a marvelous Herring in Sour Cream topping the list. A delicate Crab Bisque shows Mayer's Creole hand. It has a distinctive winey flavor which is rewarding. The entree list isn't long, but it covers the entire spectrum from fish through heavy meats. The Trout Meuniere is crispy and golden while the Chicken Parmigiana is sauteed to near perfection and topped with cheeses and a fine tomato sauce. Two veal items, the Paneed Veal, served with an excellent Fettucine Alfredo, and a traditional Wiener Schnitzel are the best items on the menu. Mayer's heredity is Czechoslovakian, Austrian and Brazilian, which gives him a variety of tastes to choose from and which influences his Beef Magyar, a marvelous Hungarian Goulash, the likes of which simply do not exist around New Orleans.

The desserts are also a wonderment, but the slightly bitter Tyrolean Chocolate Fan Torte and the incredible Bavarian Chocolate Mint (actually a mousse) are perfect compliments to a fine meal. Mayer's OldEurope is a cozy place, uncrowded, attractively furnished and well-staffed. Mayer's wife, Carolyn, acts as hostess to give the restaurant a definite home flair. Closed Sundays and Mondays.

MINACAPELLI'S

229 Cousin Street   524-7455
Slidell   Moderate/Expensive

Downtown Slidell has undergone a revival of sorts thanks mainly to this dinner theatre operation and its exuberant owner, Joe Minacapelli. Locally produced plays of surprisingly high quality are featured with family-style Italian buffet. The rustic setting reeks of personality and character. Mama Minacapelli handles all the cooking chores and tends to stick with old-time Italian family recipes with some interesting and surprisingly professional results.

The buffet assortment is quite large, and one can usually find a home-cooked Lasagna (lighter and cheesier than those found in most restaurants) or another major pasta along with an excellent assortment of fresh vegetables (the zucchini is wonderful) and a large selection of desserts.

Papa Joe maintains a definite "home" quality about his operation and this genuineness tends to rub off on everyone. Weekends are quite crowded depending on the popularity of the play being produced at the time. The drive to Slidell is a leisurely 25-minutes from downtown New Orleans through some scenic countryside. It is part of the evening's fun at Minacapelli's. Closed Monday, Tuesday, and Wednesday.

MITTENDORF'S

Highway 51-55   386-6666
Manchac   Inexpensive

Nestled comfortably on the thin slip of land which separates Lake Pontchartrain and Lake Maurepas at Pass Manchac is this regional seafood restaurant which is probably the finest example of country seafood cooking in the entire area. Mittendorf's is large, simply and tastefully decorated, and most importantly, busy all of the time. The finest catfish (fresh water variety) in Louisiana (and maybe the entire world) are fried here to a crunch, crackly perfection.

Mittendorf's is Mecca to catfish lovers and customers travel many miles to sample this local speciality which is often caught in Mittendorf's back yard. Service is strictly a no-nonsense affair from the start, for eating is paramount in the court of the catfish king. There are other menu items, perfectly good in their own right, but somehow unable to match the delicious fried catfish.

When approaching New Orleans from the west by car, detour north at the Laplace I-55 exit and a few miles in the distance you will reach Mittendorf's. From New Orleans, the drive takes in the neighborhood of thirty minutes, which is time well spent in the pursuit of gastronomic excellence.

NAVIA'S

3636 Pontchartrain Dr.   643-1816
Slidell   Moderate/Expensive

Greater New Orleans' eastward expansion has spurred several fine new provincial restaurants, and Navia's has emerged as one of the area's best.

Comfortably nestled in the burgeoning city of Slidell, this restaurant masterfully combines a number of cuisines which must be correctly classified as continental. Although owner Diego Navia is Columbian, his forte is for French and Creole classics. His sauces are light and delicate, and his entrees are well-conceived and masterfully orchestrated.

Navia's location assures an excellent source of seafoods, a prime resource for this serious food operation. Navia's famous crabmeat dishes have become legend as has the fresh Redfish Navia, the top item on the menu. From the beef side, a masterful Tournedos La Tour is consistent and well-flavored.

The 25 minute drive from downtown New Orleans is quite scenic. The food when you arrive is well worth the drive. Closed Sundays.

RIVERBOAT TCHEFUNCTA

Highway 22   845-2383
Madisonville   Moderate

The name of this gorgeously-set establish ment is a mouthful. Owner Rene Nicholas is a transplanted Frenchman from the Rhone Valley city of Avignon, well known for the world-renowned Chateauneuf du Pape wine it produces. Chef Rene opened the Riverboat in 1973, after a varied career spent in hotels and private clubs. As one could guess from the nautical setting, Riverboat Tchefuncta's menu is dominated by seafood, with a healthy smattering of Nicholas' classical French cuisine.

Of particular note are the fresh crab and trout selections which are rumoured to be but hours old when served, and some of the entrees from the menu's classical side. The Escargot Bourguignon, for example, are fixed to artistic perfection. Tournedos Napoleon Chef Rene is another masterpiece. The beef is sauteed in butter and served over toast with an excellent marchand de vin sauce and a topping of hollandaise. After artichokes and stuffed mushrooms are added as side dishes, the presentation assumes gigantic proportions.

Were Chef Rene himself able to do all the cooking, his spot would achieve even higher accolades. The drive over Lake Pontchartrain's causeway takes only 35 minutes and the scenery is lovely. Closed Mondays.

ROJE'S (POLDI'S)

6940 Martin Drive   246-6770
                                      Expensive

This establishment in suburban Eastern New Orleans is undoubtedly one of the best equipped in town. Its interior is magnificently chandeliered and the dining rooms are elegantly attired. Ro-Je's Executive Chef, Leo

Hirsch, is a proven professional who has been with Ro-Je's since inception. A steady kitchen staff compliments his creations. Hirsch's food has steadily improved and today rates on par with most of the better restaurants in New Orleans. He is most at home with elaborate classical-style cooking which is well-suited to Ro-Je's sophisticated environment.

Veal Oscar has always been Hirsch's best dish, and is probably among the finest in the area. Seafoods take a back seat to a complete continental menu which features a variety of selections, both meat and fowl. An established Cornish Hen is one of the best found locally. Escargots Forestiere, snails marvelously stuffed within large fresh mushrooms, is another dish worth of attention.

The only real criticism of Ro-Je's centers around the truly enormous portions which are presented by the kitchen. Too much food in such a setting tends to detract from the enjoyment of all the courses. It is a minor criticism, admittedly. Closed Sundays and Monday Nights.

TCHOUPITOULAS PLANTATION

6535 River Road   436-1277
Waggaman, Louisiana

Neatly hidden away on the old River Road (on the West Bank of the Mississippi) several miles upriver from Downtown New Orleans, this rustic plantation restaurant has stabilized its kitchen during recent years. Tchoupitoulas Plantation's present owners (the Emile Gennaro Family) opted to combine standard continental fare with old-time New Orleans classic selections, and the decision has paid off.

Appetizer-wise, a fine gumbo and excellent crabmeat and shrimp salads satisfy the palate's initial desires. A house specialty, Oysters Tchoupitoulas, smacks of deft wine flavoring and is immensely satisfying. Trout Supreme might be the best item on the entire menu. A delicate butter and crabmeat topping highlights a wonderfully fresh piece of trout, a taste which lingers for hours after eating. Breads and pastries are homemade. (Banana muffins are terrific.) The entire setting of the house typifies an era which dates to 1812. Well worth the time spent to reach here. Closed Saturdays and Sundays for lunch.

AWARD RESTAURANTS IN OTHER AREAS

For the purpose of comparing our taste and judgement concerning New Orleans restaurants with other establishments which may be familiar to our readers, here is a sampling of other spots that we admire around the country.

LA COLOMBE D'OR

3410 Montrose Blvd., Houston, Texas   713/524-7999

This veritable masterpiece of French Provincialism is undoubtedly Houston's premiere home of haute cuisine. Proprietor Stephen Zimmerman has carefully blended together a marvelously ambiant dining room within his micronized five-suite European guest hotel.

Cuisine is pure Provincial French, generously sprinkled with herbs and seasonings seldom found elsewhere in the Houston area. Best dishes are a marvelous **Carre d'Agneau** (Rack of Lamb) and an equally satisfying **Scampi Colomb d'Or**. La Colomb d'Or easily ranks alongside New Orleans' three-star selections in both style, satisfaction, and serene gastronomic fulfillment.

JACQUES & SUZANNE'S

30th Floor, 1st National Bank Bldg., Little Rock, Arkansas   501/376-7661.

A downtown highrise location seldom aids a serious restaurant in a city the size of Little Rock, but Jacques & Suzanne's is the exception to the rule. Blessed with a fine kitchen and a European-flavored service staff, the place would do well in practically any environment. In Little Rock, it simply rises to superior heights.

The menu is mixed, but the strongest suit comes from the continental side. **Emince of Veal, Zurichoise** is mouth-wateringly delicious while the **Souffle Grand Marnier** is superb. It is a shame that out-of-the-way restaurants do not receive the type of exposure their larger city counterparts do. They are truly deserving of such honors.

L'ENCLAVE

8325 Walnut Hill Lane, Dallas, Texas   214/363-7487

What impresses most about L'Enclave is the fact that everything comes together almost magically in the smallish continental restaurant just off the North Central Expressway in Dallas. Food and service are impeccable, with a low waiter-table ratio which makes for truly attentive service. Food is purely Continental with a polished **Chateaubriand** and a creative version of **Veal Picatta,** highlighting the menu. Top-calibre clientele and an atmosphere of professionalism permeate this Dallas establishment.

ANAQUA RESTAURANT
(Four Seasons Hotel)

555 South Alamo, San Antonio, Texas   512/229-1000

Seemingly misnamed, the Anaqua Restaurant is a French gem of culinary accomplishment set amidst San Antonio's Mexican-American background. It's cuisine tends to be Parisienne French in scope with eye-filling presentations and a totally attentive service staff adding to the lustre. Chef Jacques Benoit is most at home with veal and fine fish dishes. His deft hand assures seasonings which complement and accentuate his creations. Place yourself in the hands of the chef here, you will not be disappointed.

PAPRIKA'S FONO

Chirardelli Square, San Francisco, California   415/441-1223

Nestled high atop storied Ghirardelli Square, Paprika's Fono commands the most exquisite view possible of San Francisco Bay. When one adds the fact that some of the finest Hungarian food to be found in the United States is served at Paprika's, the combination is practically unbeatable. From the fine **Veal Paprikas** and the rich **Classic Hungarian Gulyas**, Paprika's Fono is a western jewel of Eastern European cuisine.

CHEZ MARCELLE ★★

120 North St. Julien Rd.   318/837-3100
Broussard, Louisiana (near Lafayette)

The first really topnotch restaurant serving the Lafayette Acadiana area. Great regional cooking in a setting which would make even Evangeline happy. Great gumbo, Oyster Pan Roast and fine daily specials. Save room for wonderful cajun deserts. Don't miss this place. Closed Saturdays and Sundays.

'Ya got the glass, now get the mix!

FOR MAIL ORDERS WRITE—

Franco's

P.O. BOX 23245
FORT LAUDERDALE, FLORIDA 33307

Available at better gift stores
throughout New Orleans

DRINKING IN NEW ORLEANS

New Orleanians have never had puritanical reservations about alcoholic beverages. Their attitudes have always been more Latin than American. It is not a coincidence that the "cocktail" was invented in the city that care forgot.

Tavern licenses were auctioned to the highest bidder as early as 1746 with the proceeds going to support the charity hospital. Early colonists under Spanish rule almost revolted when non-Spanish wines were forbidden. Their love for the better quality French wines was so intense that the government gave in and allowed the import of French wines duty-free. Even today, some of the finest wine cellars in America are in New Orleans.

The city's favorite liqueur has always been absinthe, and absinthe bars were common before the bitter, licorice-flavored beverage was outlawed about 1905. Pernod is now the general substitute for absinthe, and it appears in many drinks and recipes originated in New Orleans restaurants.

Toward the end of the colonial period a rum-like liquor called "tafia" was made as a by-product of the sugar industry. Some rather large stills were located on plantations, and thousands of gallons were consumed by working class people who could only afford this cheap, potent, non-subtle drink. It was often given illegally to Indians and slaves.

Today alcoholic beverages are available in New Orleans 24-hours a day, seven days a week. Carrying drinks in the street is legal, and police are very tolerant of well-behaved inebriates.

Here are some insights into the famous drinks of New Orleans.

THE SAZERAC

The Sazerac cocktail is to New Orleans what the martini is to Manhattan. The name derives from a French brandy, Sazerac-de-Forges, which was popular in the 1850's. The recipe traces its heritage back to Antoine Peychaud's original cocktail, and uses the liquid tonic that he called "bitters". Through the years, a series of Sazerac bars made the drink big business. The Sazerac House of 1872 Royal Street had a bar 125-feet long manned by 18 bartenders. Rye whiskey replaced the French brandy as the major ingredient for many years, and then under the influence of Owen Brennan, restorer of the Old Absinthe House and father of the founder of Brennan's Restaurant, bourbon replaced the rye. In

1949, the Roosevelt Hotel (now the Fairmont) obtained the franchise, and the Sazerac Bar was moved into the hotel.

The classic preparation of the Sazerac uses one small sugar cube, a few drops of Peychaud's bitters, ¼ teaspoon Angosture bitters, 1½ oz. bourbon, ¼ teaspoon Pernod, and a lemon peel. Chill an old-fashioned glass with ice. In another glass dissolve the sugar with a small amount of water, add both bitters, and whiskey. After adding several cubes of ice, **stir very gently.** Empty the glass that is chilling and swirl the Pernod to coat the inside. Now strain the whiskey mixture into the Pernod coated glass and give it a twist of lemon peel. No lemon peel or ice in the glass, please.

RAMOS GIN FIZZ

This is another drink associated with the Sazerac Bar. It was "invented" by Henry Ramos during the 1890's. He owned taverns and his places were famous for an assembly line approach to making drinks. Assistant bartenders may mix and shake, but only the master bartender could serve the finished creation. When the Sazerac Bar was acquired by the Roosevelt Hotel, the hotel paid royalties to the Ramos family for every Gin Fizz it served.

The drink contains 1½ oz. gin, 1 egg white, 1 teaspoon powdered sugar, ½ fresh lemon juice, ½ fresh lime juice, 1 oz. cream (or half and half), and 3 dashes (⅜ teaspoon) of orange flower water (or orgeat). Stir sugar, lime and lemon juices, and egg white together. Add cream, gin and orange flower water. Shake vigorously for an extended period. Shaking is the secret of the drink. Pour into a 6-8 oz. glass and add real siphon-produced fresh soda water just before serving.

ABSINTHE

Genuine absinthe was outlawed about 1905 when medical men claimed that the wormwood steeped herbal absinthol caused insanity, palsy, and convulsions. Switzerland had exported some three million gallons a year before it was banned, and the total industry was worth $100 million at the turn of the century.

The popular taste, a bitter licorice-flavor, has been duplicated sans wormwood by the Pernod formula, Jackquin's Liqueur D'Anis, and Herbsaint (a New Orleans product). These products are now used in drinks and recipes calling for absinthe.

The Old Absinthe House at 240 Bourbon Street is the traditional headquarters for absinthe drinkers. It was built in 1806 and served as a shoe shop, grocery, and coffee house before it became an absinthe room in 1861 when Cayetano Ferrer became the chief mixologist and installed an elaborate fountain. The fountain was filled with absinthe and adjusted to drip a drop at a time into a glass of ice placed under the tap. The slow dripping was reputed to enhance the power of the drink. By 1890 the dwelling had earned the title and reputation of "The Old Absinthe House."

Here are four absinthe-type drinks that are still enjoyed in New Orleans.

Absinthe Suisesse This drink is associated with The Old Absinthe House. Mix 1½ oz. Pernod, 2 dashes white anisette (¼ teaspoon), 1 oz. water, ½ teaspoon powdered sugar, and the white of an egg. Shake vigorously with cracked ice, or make frothy in a blender.

Absinthe Frappe 1½ oz. Pernod, ¾ oz. white anisette, 1 oz. water. Shake the 2:1 liquor ratio with ice and serve in a tall glass.

Herbsaint Francaise 2 oz. Herbsaint, ½ teaspoon sugar syrup. Special "drip glasses" are used to make this absinthe-type drink. The ingredients are poured into the drip glass which is filled with cracked ice. When the liquid filters through, the top glass is removed, and the bottom glass is served.

Ojen Cocktail Ojen is a Spanish liquor (pronounced "Oh-Hane") which has a distinctive Pernod-like taste. It is recommended as an eye-opener for the morning after. Mix 1½ oz. Ojen with 3 dashes of bitters and pour into a prechilled old fashioned glass. Add ice.

HURRICANE PUNCH

Pat O'Brien's, at 7118 St. Peter Street, serves over 500,000 Hurricanes a year. You get to keep the 24-oz. hurricane lantern shaped glass in the bargain. Pat O'Brien's now makes its famous drink from a mix especially prepared by Franco's Cocktail Mixes. 4-ozs. of the mix (available now in specialty shops) and 4-ozs. of dark, amber rum go into the crushed ice filled special glass. The garnish is orange slice and cherry, and it is drunk through straws.

FRENCH 75

This is an Arnaud's creation. When the "Count" was alive, he would send this drink to the tables of his favorite patrons. Dash of lemon juice, 1 oz. gin, ½ oz. Cointreau, champagne, and lemon peel are the ingredients. Shake lemon juice, gin and Cointreau with ice and strain into a champagne glass. Top with champagne and a twish of lemon peel.

MILK PUNCH

This is an especially appropriate drink for breakfast at Brennan's. It contains 1¼ oz. bourbon or brandy, 3 oz. light cream (half and half), 1 teaspoon superfine powdered sugar, and a dash of vanilla. Shake the ingredients well and top with nutmeg.

CAFE BRULOT

A gifted waiter can turn this after dinner flaming coffee into a great piece of showmanship. The trick is in pouring the flaming mixture from the ladle to the glass. A three-foot arc for a long armed, confident garcon is not uncommon. Cafe Brulot tastes like a very rich liquid fruitcake. It is both coffee and dessert. The ingredients are 1 cup cognac, 1 slice orange, 1 slice lemon, 2 large sugar cubes, 2 whole cloves, a vanilla bean, a stick of cinnamon and 1 cup of French coffee or espresso. Restaurants, and even individual waiters have their own variations of this recipe. In many cases the fruit rind and not the fruit itself is used. The presentation of a brulot bowl is the traditional place to mix the spices, fruit, and brandy. The bowl is heated, the brandy flamed and the coffee is slowly added. The waiter then demonstrates his unique skill in pouring the hot liquid into serving glasses. The individual serving may be topped with whipped cream.

PRALINE LIQUEUR

This unique "New Orleans Style Liqueur" captures the taste of pecans and vanilla, so familiar in the famous confection, in a forty proof drink that mixes well in both cocktails and foods. It's a bit of New Orleans in a bottle.

The Praline Emporium Company of New Orleans, which created the liqueur, offers a colorful free Praline Liqueur Food and Drink Recipe Book if you will write to: Recipes, Suite 3, 2615 Edenborn Ave., Metaire, LA 70002.

To sample its delights, you might try:

Pralines 'n' Cream 1½ oz. Praline Liqueur, 2 oz. cream combined in a tall glass with ice cubes. Top with soda and garnish with a cherry.

The Rex 2/3 cup chicory coffee, 1½ oz. Praline Liqueur. Serve in a mug topped with whipped cream.

The Mardi Gras 1½ oz. Praline Liqueur, 1½ oz. Vodka. Serve up or on the rocks.

FRENCH COFFEE

Creole coffee is a blend of Central and South American coffee beans that are dark roasted until they are almost black. Roasted chicory root is usually added as a flavor enhancer. It is a taste that was acquired during the post Civil War period when coffee was scarce, and chicory was used as a filler or a substitute for coffee. Creoles and Cajuns are serious about their coffee. It is a fuel to their culture and a staple ingredient of their hospitality. It has the body and color of espresso, but the taste is pure New Orleans. The "dark roast" coffee, with or without chicory, is available in grocery stores and specialty shops throughout the New Orleans area, and in the Cajun parishes of Southwest Louisana.

CAFE AU LAIT

Cafe au Lait is prepared with two pots. One contains hot, dark roast

French coffee, and the other hot milk. Equal amounts of each are poured into a cup usually simultaneously. The result is a light brown, hot beverage that is delicious. Even children love cafe au lait.

DIXIE BEER

In 1982, the Dixie Brewing Company celebrates its 75th Anniversary. The brewery has been at the same location on 2537 Tulane Avenue since it opened on November 1, 1907. Dixie survived Prohibition (1929-1933) as a company by manufacturing ice cream and soft drinks. Today, it is the sole survivor of many local beer producers in New Orleans, and it is one of only 25 small independent breweries still remaining in the United States. New Orleanians are loyal to Dixie Beer, and rightly so. It is a first class product.

Visitors are welcome at the Dixie Hospitality Center on the main floor of the brewery. The process of brewing beer is explained, and samples are offered. There is a gift shop offering a variety of mementos of the visit. Next door to the Hospitality Center, the Dixie iron gates open onto the Dixie Alleyway, a beer garden used for parties and banquets by groups of up to 500 persons.

In 1935, Valentine Merz, Dixie's founder, donated $50,000 to start the fledgling Audubon Zoo. It is fitting today that the impressive zoo includes a Dixie Beer Garden. A relaxing pause in the Garden is a must when visiting the Audubon Zoo.

△ ATTRACTIONS

1. Absinthe House, pg. 304
2. Shrine of Saint Jude, pg. 85
3. Beauregard Square, pg. 85
4. Municipal Auditorium, pg. 85
5. Louis Armstrong Park, pg. 85
6. Perseverance Hall & Jazz Museum, pg. 86
7. Theatre of the Performing Arts, pg. 331
8. St. Louis Cemetery No. 1, pgs. 86, 16
9. Saenger Theatre, pg. 102
10. Musee Conti Wax Museum, pg. 77
11. Jackson Square, pg. 53
12. International Trade Mart, pg. 97
13. River Cruises, pg. 25
14. Canal St. (Free) Ferry, pg. 97
15. Moon Walk, pg. 66
16. French Market, pg. 68
17. Old US Mint, pg. 84
18. Maison Blanche Dept. Store, pg. 321
19. D.H. Holmes Dept. Store, pg. 321
20. US Customs House, pg. 87

☐ ACCOMMODATIONS

1. Chateau LeMoyne, pg. 155
2. St. Louis, pg. 168
3. Royal Sonesta, pg. 167
4. The Monteleone, pg. 163
5. Royal Orleans, pg. 165
6. The Marriott, pg. 191
7. Le Richelieu, pg. 160

◯ RESTAURANTS

1. Arnauds, pg. 225
2. Broussard's, pg. 227
3. La Louisiane, pg. 235
4. Brennan's, pg. 225
5. Antoine's, pg. 224

See detailed maps of French Quarter streets Canal to St. Louis, page 70, St. Louis to St. Philip, page 158, and St. Philip to Esplanade, page 224.

FRENCH QUARTER AREA OVERALL

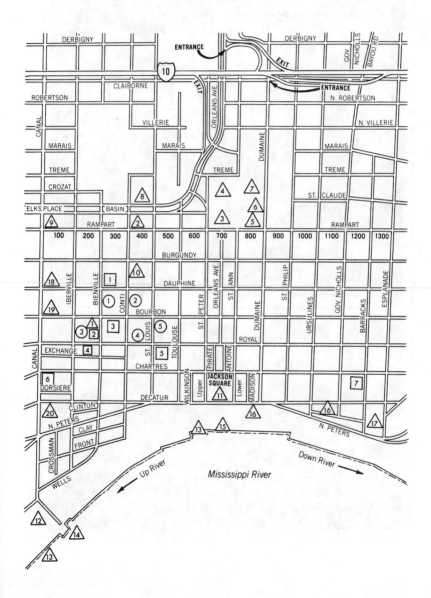

NIGHT SPOTS

AL HIRT'S BASIN STREET SOUTH

501 Bourbon Street   Map, pg. 159   525-6167

To many his music is incredible, but to New Orleans he is just plain "Jumbo." Blessed with a national reputation and marvelous personal style, Al is a wonder to behold. One show nightly, starting at 10:30, except on Tuesdays and Sundays. Check with Club and make reservations, for Al sometimes plays national gigs which take him from the city.

BLUE ROOM
(Fairmont Hotel)

123 University Place   Map, pg. 105   529-7111

Always considered one of America's premiere supper clubs, the Blue Room continues to provide name entertainment in its intimately styled showroom. Cover charge is $8 Mon.-Thurs. and $10 Fri.-Sat. Bandleader, Bill Clifford and his band are always available for dancing. Cocktails and dinner are served from 6:30 p.m. daily. Closed Sundays.

CAROUSEL BAR
(Monteleone Hotel)

214 Royal St.   Map, pg. 71   523-3341

A dark, intimate piano bar with stylish, sophisticated entertainment at the keyboard. (Lately Sylvia Johns) The circular bar within sight of the entertainment is actually a slow moving carousel. It has been a meeting landmark in the city for many years. Music 9-2, Mon.-Sat.

CHRIS OWENS CLUB

500 Bourbon Street   Map, pg. 159   523-6400

For the past few decades, Chris Owens has been the French Quarter's most celebrated female entertainer, and she shows no signs of relinquishing her title. Her club's atmosphere is a throwback to old-style nightclub reviews with theme settings and moveable sets. Chris performs twice nightly (three shows on weekends) except Sundays with a wonderful mixture of singing and dancing with a decided Latin beat. $7.50 admission covers the entire show and two drinks. Good professional entertainment in an intimate setting. Show times 10 and midnight.

COURT TAVERN

614 Bourbon Street   Map, pg. 159   522-7261

Newly reopened night spot featuring (what else?) classical Dixieland style music. No cover, and music starts daily from 9:30 p.m. and continues without interruption until the wee hours. It is located next to the Bourbon Street entrance to the Court of Two Sisters Restaurant. Groups change so a call ahead would be wise. Closed Sun.-Mon.

CRAZY SHIRLEY'S

640 Bourbon Street   Map, pg. 159   581-5613

Luther Kent and his Trick Bag (Wed.-Sat.) are the best part of this standard Bourbon Street operation. Drinks are ordinary as are the surroundings, but Kent and his group rise above these improbabilities. Extremely good listening if you enjoy Dixieland.

DUKES' PLACE
(Monteleone Hotel)

214 Royal Street   Map, pg. 71   581-1567

Remnants of the Original Dukes of Dixieland appear nightly in this appealing rooftop location which also provides an excellent view of Ole Man River winding past New Orleans. Four shows each night, starting at 9:30. Room enough for dancing. Top notch music, done in the exact style which propelled the Dukes to the top of Dixieland Jazz's heap. A swinging good time.

ESPLANADE LOUNGE
(Royal Orleans Hotel)

621 St. Louis Street   Map, pg. 159   529-5333

A really first rate food & drink operation which features an outstanding selection of hors d'oeuvres, pastries and desserts to compliment a fine bar.

Soft piano accompaniment from Rich Fullman tops off this sophisticated rendezvous. Open daily from 7:00 a.m. until 2:00 a.m. Very relaxing and sure to please.

FAMOUS DOOR

339 Bourbon Street   Map, pg. 71   523-9973

One of the traditional Dixieland spots, with nearly continuous music. Roy Liberto and his Bourbon Street Five alternate with Thomas Jefferson's Creoles, and both are quite good. Better than average drinks and a world of authentic atmosphere which adds to the experience.

HIRED HAND SALOON

1100 S. Clearview Pkwy., Elmwood Shopping Center   (504) 734-0590

Located in suburban Jefferson Parish in the Elmwood Shopping Center near the Huey P. Long Bridge, the Hired Hand Saloon has quickly become the area's top western meeting spot. With a large (1,700 square feet) dance area and the finest live western entertainment, the Hired Hand is a place not to be missed. Monday nights are special ladies nights (2-for-1 drinks from 7:00 till 10:00 p.m.) and free western dance lessons are held on Mondays and Tuesdays between 7:00 and 9:00 p.m.

LOBBY BAR—NEW ORLEANS MARRIOT

555 Canal Street   Map, pg. 71   581-1000

An unexpected treat in the downstairs Lobby Bar is musician Alvin Alcorn and his group. Alcorn is one of the few remaining Jazz pioneers. He also performs for the Commander's Place Jazz Brunch on Sundays. The style is mostly bluesy and oh so smooth. Ask Alvin about his travels and stints in the movies, he's a great personality.

LUCKY PIERRE'S

735 Bourbon Street   Map, pg. 159   523-0786

Local favorite Frankie Ford returns to his successful stint of the 60's and provides songs and patter at the piano bar. Old time hits and modern musical adaptations keep the patrons of this late night haunt happy. The drinks are good, and the atmosphere is very relaxed. Some of the Quarter's show people stop here for drinks, and breakfast in the back room. The music starts at 10 p.m. Tues.-Sat.

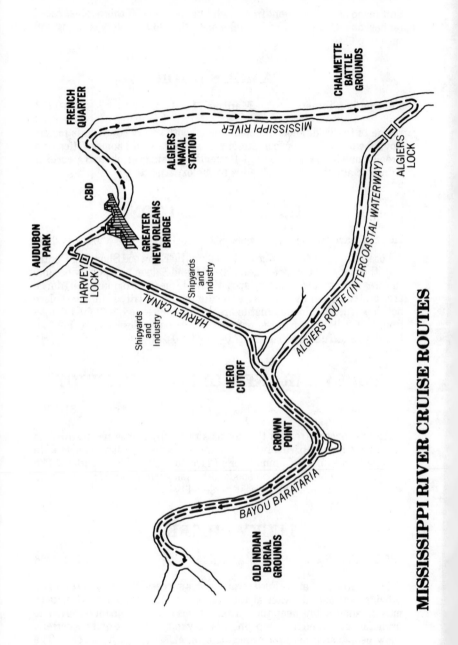

MISSISSIPPI RIVER CRUISE ROUTES

MAISON BOURBON

641 Bourbon Street   Map, pg. 159   522-8818

Better than average groups in a less than average setting which seems a lot like open air entertainment. Lou Sino and the Bengals have played here as have Murphy Campo and the Jazz Saints. Continuous live music from 11:00 a.m. daily until 4:00 a.m. Wed.-Mon. The real beneficiaries of Maison Bourbon are those passers by who are too tight to spring for a drink and opt instead for a free view from the sidewalk. Mon.-Wed. hours 9-2.

MYSTIC DEN
(Royal Sonesta Hotel)

300 Bourbon Street   Map, pg. 71   586-3000

Perhaps the most ambiant night spot in the French Quarter and therefore the entire city. Singer-Virtuoso Guitarist Elario is featured in the Mystic Den and has become New Orleans' most popular individual entertainer. The Den's decor mirrors Mardi Gras and carnival time with imbedded doubloons on the tables and plaques commemorating the different carnival Krewes who paraded when the Mystic Den was first opened in 1969. Drinks tend to be expensive ($3.75), but Elario's greatness (His Fiddler on the Roof comes to life as if you were on Broadway) overcomes the pricings. The Den is crowded, especially on weekends when Elario's faithful sit out his whole group of sets. Shows Tues.-Sat. at 10 p.m.

NATCHEZ STEAMBOAT

Toulouse Street Wharf   Map, pg. 159   586-8777

Entertainment has always been secondary aboard the Natchez, and rightly so. Lately however, this authentic steamboat replica has added some name acts (Pianist Bill Bachmann and His Jazz Filé are great) for her two hour cruise and the prospects for even cozier cruising seem brighter. The Natchez boards at 6:00 p.m., departs at 8:30 p.m. and returns to her morrings around 10:30 p.m. Good fun on a practically spotless boat. Tues.-Sun.

NEW BLUE ANGEL

225 Bourbon Street   Map, pg. 71   523-1011

Superb trumpet playing by George Finola is the whole show at this newish (as Bourbon Street goes) Dixieland Jazz spot, and he is also the hottest jazz talent in town. Along with his group, The Chosen Few, Finola performs the late evening set, both on weekdays and weekends. Not much atmosphere, the Blue Angel's blatant commercialism nearly overcomes Finola's marvelous artistry. Drinks are average also, but one doesn't mind when George and his boys are on stage. Shouldn't be missed. Music 9 to 2:15 a.m. daily except Sunday.

OLD ABSINTHE BAR

400 Bourbon Street   Map, pg. 71   561-9231

This famous meeting place is visibly loaded with memorabilia and personality. It is truly a New Orleans French Quarter landmark which features mostly local talent in a strictly laid back setting. A minor $1.00 admission is charged, in all probability designed to keep the street people out of this hallowed setting. Great drinks, pure authenticity and memorable fun. The music continues almost until dawn, 6 a.m. on some weekends.

OLE MAN RIVER'S

2125 Highway 90   Map, pg. 170   436-3000
Avondale

Immensely popular West Bank nightspot, not far from the Huey P. Long Mississippi Bridge. Entertainment is topnotch, from Ramsey Lewis jazz to Country and Western stars. While Ole Man River's caters to a younger crowd, the shows are well done and certainly worth the 30-plus minute drive from downtown. Check weekly show listings, for acts change regularly.

PADDOCK BAR & LOUNGE

309 Bourbon Street   Map, pg. 71   523-8939

For classical Dixieland Jazz purists, the Paddock Lounge is a Bourbon Street landmark which has withstood the test of time and hasn't changed a wink in two decades. At the Paddock, Jazz is a no-nonsense affair which tends to elevate the entire music scene. Drinks are quite reasonable, atmosphere is relaxed and the music is fast moving. The music goes from 9 to 2 on weekdays, and 10 to 3 on weekends.

PAGODA BAR
(Imperial Palace Regency Restaurant)

601 Loyola Avenue   Map, pg. 105   522-8666

Neatly attired bar area within the city's most fabulously done Chinese Restaurant. A good sized dance floor provides a welcome relief from the rigors of French Quarter walking and socializing. Generous drinks, and Henrietta Boggs provides a warm and personable piano for the weary. Tues.-Sat., 8:30-1.

PETE FOUNTAIN'S
(New Orleans Hilton)

Foot of Poydras Street   Map, pg. 105   561-5000

The mellow sweet tones of Pete Fountain's magic clarinet bring joy to Fountain's legions of admirers. Pete performs one show Tuesdays through Fridays at 10:00 p.m. and on Saturdays at 9:00 p.m. While the club itself is somewhat ritzy and slightly cold, Pete's music warms the chilly air in its own incredible manner. Reservations are a must during busy times and particularly on weekends. Don't miss Pete, he is a truly gifted musician. Closed Sundays & Mondays.

PRESERVATION HALL

726 St. Peter Street   Map, pg. 159   523-8939

Started in the early 60's to provide a permanent home for some of New Orleans' original jazz musicians, Preservation Hall has emerged as the dominant spot for true jazz in the city. No reservations, no credit cards, practically no seats to speak of. You sit where you can and that's part of the Preservation Hall experience. Artists change from time to time, but all are guaranteed to please and meet the 8:30 opening set. Upon leaving, a $2.00 donation to preserve Preservation Hall is expected. It is well worth the price. Be prepared to stand in line on weekends as the crowds gather early.

STEAMER PRESIDENT

Foot Canal Street & River   Map, pg. 309   586-8777

A wide variety of entertainment is offered aboard the President, a local seamark for decades, which attracts primarily the younger set for its entertainment cruises. Good drinks here and an excellent way to enjoy the evening as New Orleans' storied waterfront slides silently and smoothly by. The President's cruise is a nice long one, which boards at 9:00 p.m. and departs promptly at 10:00 p.m. Ship returns around Midnight to its Canal Street wharf. Weekends only.

TIPITINA'S

501 Napoleon Avenue   899-9114

This neat (if a tad seedy) nightspot on Napoleon Avenue just off Tchoupitoulas Street is the best attraction in the Uptown section. Music is always live with smallish ($2-$4) cover charge depending on just who's performing that night. Range is from Reggae to blues and Tipitina's sometimes books up-and-coming local acts. Large (and always crowded) dance floor and a really relaxed atmosphere. The music starts at 9:30.

TOP OF THE MART
(International Trade Mart)

2 Canal Street   Map, pg. 105   522-9795

Whirl around New Orleans at the dizzy speed of two miles per hour. Actually, you travel three feet per minute and are provided with a marvelous panorama of New Orleans which is a treat in itself. Drinks are of the commercial variety and a small combo or organist provides soft background music. A nice, out of the ordinary meeting place.

TOULOUSE THEATER CAFE BAR

616 Toulouse St.   Map, pg. 159   522-8684

This small room comes alive after the final curtain for **One Mo Time,** the musical comedy about a touring group of black nightclub entertainers. The show attracts many international visitors and musicians who stay to patronize the cafe bar. The featured jazz musician is often joined by members of the show cast, or by passing musicians who sit in for the fun of it.

TYLER'S BEER GARDEN

5234 Magazine Street   891-4989

An impressive list of top flight entertainers stops at this well-attended spot near Audubon Park. Wide variety of music, and everyone is musically serious. Tyler's is more than just music, however, and the food here is better than you would expect. Oysters on the Half Shell are ridiculously inexpensive and add to the fun. Shouldn't be missed if you enjoy good music. Music starts at 9 p.m. weekdays, 10 p.m. on weekends.

PAT O'BRIEN'S

718 St. Peter St.   Map, pg. 105   525-4823

Long considered the most colorful of the Quarter's watering holes, Pat O'Brien's remains the city's top visitor attraction, especially after dark. A fixture between Bourbon and Royal on the otherwise quiet St. Peter Street, "Pat's" is the home of the often copied Hurricane (see page 305), and many other satisfying alcoholic fantasies.

Piano sing-a-longs are non-stop in the main bar area where the ribald lyric flourishes. A more sedate long bar, and an impressive outdoor patio and fountain area offer escapes from the rigors of the Quarter. There always seems to be a line at the door to Pat O'Brien's during special events, like Tuesdays! Film personality Pat O'Brien has no affiliation with this New Orleans institution. The bar may be more famous than the star.

WOODY HERMAN'S

601 Loyola Ave.   Map, pg. 105   522-8788

This grand new night spot within Poydras Plaza features one of America's true jazz legends in a major showcase setting. Woody Herman's 16-piece band performs nightly (except Sunday) with a mixed folio of classic Swing, and modern Herman arrangements. Between Woody's sets the Heritage Hall Jazz Band, with 24 musicians on stage, raises the roof with Dixieland standards.

This top flight entertainment attraction is the best recent addition to the galaxy of stars who make New Orleans their home. The $20 cover charge includes two well made drinks, and an invitation to dance. Reservations can be made direct, or through the adjacent Hyatt Regency Hotel. Group rates available.

SHOPPING

THE FRENCH QUARTER

One of the joys of the Quarter is browsing its hundreds of galleries, antique shops, and specialty stores. Royal and Chartres Streets are the major shopping avenues, but all the side streets near Jackson Square are worth exploring.

Popular items include China Carnival masks, posters with Carnival and jazz themes, and gift boxes of pralines. Serious collectors will appreciate the furniture and decorative art showrooms, and the many galleries offering original paintings, sculpture, and fine prints. You will also find civil war bullets and antique firearms, hand crafted ceramics, armies of toy soldiers, handmade dolls, locally made perfumes, jewelry, fashions, and Creole food delicacies. The list, of course, could fill a catalog as large as your imagination. The Quarter is not just for souvenir shopping, it is a discovery experience of things elegant and grand.

CANAL STREET

The city's major department stores are within four blocks of each other on Canal Street convenient to the French Quarter and the Central Business District.

Godchaux's and the **D.H. Holmes Company** are considered the better line of stores for fashions. **Maison Blanche** and the **Krauss Company** are also full service stores. The **Sears** store at 201 Baronne can be seen from Canal and Dauphine. The downtown stores are generally open between the hours of 10 a.m. and 5:45 p.m.

MAGAZINE STREET

This street stretches six miles from the foot of Canal Street, and is the boundary street that separates the Garden District from the Irish Channel. Magazine Street has undergone a rebirth in recent years primarily due to the concentration of antique shops and dealers along its route. At last count, there were over 75 stops for the antiquer. If there is an undiscovered furniture or decorative treasure left in New Orleans, it is probably hidden among the cluttered shops and warehouses on Magazine.

The largest concentration of dealers and shops is from the 1500 block to the 6000 block at the foot of Audubon Park. The Magazine Street public bus is a good way to reach the Park and see the shops at the same time.

The shops range from the palatial and exquisite to the quintessence of junk, with all the descriptive variations in between. If you have ever had a case of bric-a-brac frenzy, or antique fever, Magazine Street will reinfect you.

UPTOWN SQUARE

This is a new shopping center near Audubon Park at 200 Broadway and Perrier near the river. If you are visiting the Park, this might be an interesting detour.

The Square is a maze of two-story structures resembling connected Spanish villas. There are plazas, courtyards, fountains, towers and turrets to reinforce this design effect. D.H. Holmes, Kreeger's and Godchaux's have large branch stores here with an emphasis on fashions. Both stores have been serving New Orleans, by the way, since the 1840's. There are about 50 individual stores and shops in the complex including a cafeteria with balcony seating.

This is where cosmopolitan New Orleans shops for fashions.

RIVERBEND

If you are riding the St. Charles Streetcar, it might be convenient to ride to the end of St. Charles and exit for a browsing of this Dublin Square shopping area. There are interesting shops along South Carrollton Avenue, and down Hampson Street leading to the square. A former residential area has been given over to specialty shops where the goods run from fashion spotswear to gourmet cookware. Where the streetcar turns at Riverbend, you are less than half a block from the levee and the river.

YOU BOUTIQUE

8131 Hampson St.   Map, pg. 118   865-7491

Yvonne La Fleur traveled the fashion world before she came home to New Orleans to establish what is now the city's largest boutique. After having her own label and showroom on New York's Seventh Avenue, she patterned her exclusive boutique after a store in London called Biba's. The contemporary style of You Boutique was created for "ladies who are discriminating, well-educated, affluent, and very much aware of how they want to look."

The Riverbend area store features Yvonne La Fleur's own designs and personal selections from New York and Paris. She personally creates custom millinery, and also offers shoes, cosmetics and fragrances, party wear, accessories, sportswear, and even furs in her large salons.

Her knowledge and design expertise in hats has been employed on several films. She worked on the "Great Catsby", and "Pretty Baby", and received the screen credit for the millinery that she created for "Chanel Solitaire", a French movie about the life of designer Coco Chanel.

Shopping at You Boutique is an elegant experience. Gift selections may be modeled by one of the beautiful sales ladies, and if Yvonne La Fleur is on the floor, you can discuss the last word in fashion that may be only hours old. Yvonne buys for You Boutique, and often brings the goods back on the jet that returns her to New Orleans.

CURRENTS FINE JEWELRY

8120 Hampson St.   Map, pg. 118   891-9800

Terry Widert, a native of New Orleans with a fine arts background has a unique shop which specializes in the custom design of gem stones. The bi-level showroom is contemporary Art Deco in decor. The stained glass and the special lighting effects make for a romantic atmosphere.

Weidert's partner is Robert De Luca who operates their Vale, Colorado store. Their design concept is for personalized, individual jewelry. They work with their resident goldsmiths in creating rings, bracelets, necklaces, tie tacs, watches, and even cigarette lighters. Semi-precious stones such as amethyst, citrines, garnets, and tsavorite are used in addition to diamonds, emeralds, and other precious gems. A stop at Currents should be part of a visit to the elegant shops in the Riverbend area.

MIGNON FAGET LIMITED

710 Dublin St.   Map, pg. 118   865-1107

A restored two-story cottage on Dublin Street in the Riverbend area is the design studio and retail shop for one of New Orleans' most innovative artists. Mignon Faget's jewelry is displayed in the Kruger Gallery of New York. Recognition has also come from Women's Wear Daily, W, Vogue, Harper's Bazaar, and Glamour. She has been commissioned to create sterling and 14K gold jewelry collections for a variety of cultural groups including the New Orleans Museum of Art.

Ms. Faget often uses nature as models for her designs. Since 1970, when she first designed a silver belt buckle from a sand dollar, the collection has grown under the title of Sea and Earth to include sea snails, scallops, ark clams, acorns, and even red-beans. For whimsy, there are "animal crackers" of silver. The full color catalogue of Mignon Faget originals includes elegant and tasteful designs for pendants, earrings, belts, necklaces, lapel pins, bracelets, rings and award winning cords to be tied at the neck.

Ms. Faget is another native New Orleanian who has achieved international recognition as an artist, but who choses to stay in the city that she loves. See her collection if you have the slightest interest in distinctive jewelry.

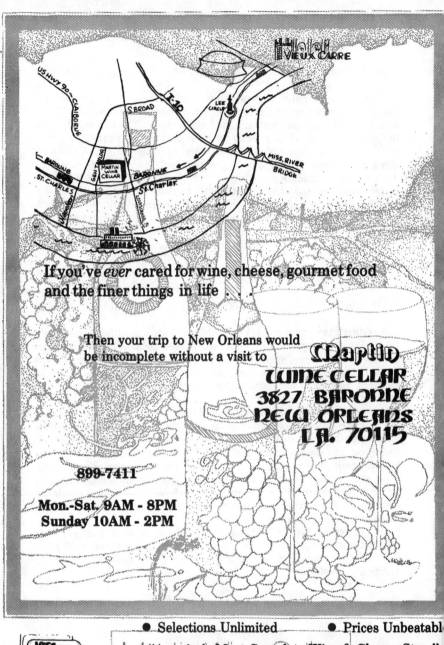

If you've *ever* cared for wine, cheese, gourmet food and the finer things in life . . .

Then your trip to New Orleans would be incomplete without a visit to

**Martin Wine Cellar
3827 Baronne
New Orleans
LA. 70115**

899-7411

**Mon.-Sat. 9AM - 8PM
Sunday 10AM - 2PM**

WINE SHOPS

If you are visiting from a part of the country where the fruits of the vine go unrecognized, New Orleans offers a welcome opportunity to shop for your wine rack. The demand for fine wines at restaurants and home dinner parties in the city is a tradition that dates from colonial days. Retail shops are thus well supplied with good wine selections in all price ranges to satisfy their discriminating wine buying public. Here are some good places to browse.

MARTIN WINE CELLAR

3827 Baronne St.   899-7411

Perhaps the finest retail wine store in the South if not in the entire country. Complete selection of fine wines, brandies, ports, and liqueurs. Martin's is complemented by an excellent cheese section and a newly-opened delicatessen which also features enjoyable sandwiches and specialty items. Spectacular selection of gift baskets and extremely low prices make Martins' the bellwether in local wine circles. Do not miss this place.

UPTOWN SQUARE WINERY

200 Broadway   866-2791

This attractive wine and cheese location has emerged in recent years as a truly complete gastronomic center. Excellent selection of culinary and beverage items in a most attractive and easy-to find setting. Plenty of parking and friendly sales personnel.

THE WINE MERCHANT

5000 Prytania   891-5014

This smallish retail store specializes in French Bordeaux Chateaux and provides knowledgeable wine expertise to its customers. The owner is an agreeable chap who goes out of his way to accommodate his customers.

FRENCH QUARTER WINE CELLAR

700 Dauphine   523-5969

This is perhaps the most accessible wine and spirits location in the French Quarter hotel area. Although the shop is small, it has a surprisingly large stock. Proprietor Greg Pembo is thoroughly knowledgeable and his selections are well chosen. Good values, too.

WINE & CHEESE SHOPPE

3305 Severn   888-6910
Metairie

Suburban Metairie's top retail store directly behind the huge Lakeside Shopping Center. Good selection of wines covering the entire European/California spectrum. A nice cheese selection is also available and some well-priced gift packs add to the allure.

BAKER'S WINE GALLERY

445 Terry Parkway   362-6955
Gretna

The West Bank's only real wine selection which sometimes surprises its clientele with excellent specials.

OCCHI'S WINE & SPIRITS

850 Veterans Hwy   831-9463

This suburban wine, spirits, and deli shop is just what the doctor ordered for busy Veterans Highway. Frank Occhipinti and his seasoned staff offer a truely representative selection of imported and California wines. The deli section has been expanded to perform catering, and to offer special party trays. Open 10 to 10 daily.

New Orleans fashion designer Yvonne LeFleur puts her emphasis on femininity at You Boutique.

ANNUAL EVENTS

SPRING FIESTA

When the bells of the St. Louis Cathedral sound the hour of seven on the first Friday after Easter, the colorful April pageant of the Spring Fiesta repeats a social and cultural tradition that dates back to 1937. Jackson Square is filled with lights, music, and the court of the Fiesta Queen and her hoop skirted attendants. The coronation is followed by "A Night In Old New Orleans" parade. Floats, decorated horse-drawn carriages, and marching bands tour the French Quarter. Following the opening night of revelry, homes in the Vieux Carre, and Garden District, and plantations along the Great River Road are opened for tours.

This is one of the few times of the year when private homes are open to the public, and with the azaleas in full bloom, it is an especially beautiful season to view their gardens. The Vieux Carre Patios by Candlelight tour reveals the hidden gardens with romantic highlights. All tours are hosted by costumed beaux and belles who relate their history with enthusiasm. Reservations are required. Tour tickets support the non-profit association which produces the 19-day schedule. In-city tours are about $8.50 per person. Plantation tours by bus are about $30. For a complete schedule and details, write or call Spring Fiesta at 529 St. Ann St., N.O. La. 70130, (504) 581-1367.

NEW ORLEANS FOOD FESTIVAL

This culinary arts show and tasting event occurs in early July when city chefs and country cooks come together to celebrate the love of good food, and elegant presentations.

Festival goers can purchase sample portions of the cuisine, see the grand displays, and attend the gourmet dinner which climaxes the annual event. For more details on the upcoming festival events, write or call the festival at P.O. Box 2410, N.O. La. 70116, (504) 529-2906.

JAZZ AND HERITAGE FESTIVAL

This New Orleans rite of spring spans two weekends in late April or early May when countless music and food hungry citizens flock to the Fairgrounds Racetrack for an open air festival. Food booths set up by local organizations offer all the things New Orleanians love to eat: shrimp, crabs, oysters, crayfish, gumbo, jambalaya, fried chicken, po-boys, and much more. Craft stalls and demonstrations help to emphasize the heritage aspects of the festival and add to the community fair flavor of the event.

And then there is the music ... traditional jazz and all its cousins on bandstands, and open spaces all over the Fairgrounds. Cajun bands, gospel, blues, pop, and Dixieland at every turn. During the weekdays the music spills over into other parts of the city with street parades and big name concerts.

The Fairgrounds scene is an unstructured people event which often turns into a melee of bodies. Show up early to get your turn in the lines to the food booths, and bring your waders if there has been any recent rain. To obtain the schedule of the upcoming activities, write or call P.O. Box 2530, N.O. La. 70176, (504) 522-4786.

FESTA d'ITALIA

The Piazza d'Italia on Poydras and Tchoupitoulas becomes an old Italian marketplace and town square every Columbus Day (2nd Monday in October) as American Italians demonstrate pride in their Italian heritage. The Festa d'Italia is sponsored by the American Italian Federation of Louisiana, and its events run throughout Columbus week.

There is usually an enthusiastic parade, celebrities, and great Italian food delicacies to sample. Italian music, arts and crafts add to the festive celebration. Everyone is welcomed. For more information, write the Federation at 2810 Napoleon Ave., New Orleans, La. 70115.

DIRECTORY

EMERGENCY NUMBERS

FIRE **581-3473**

POLICE **821-2222**

EMERGENCY MEDICAL SERVICES **821-3232**

AUTO POUND **586-5095**

POST OFFICES

Vieux Carre Station, 1015 Iberville 589-2256

ITM Station, International Trade Mart.....................589-2269

Main Post Office, 701 Loyola Ave.........................589-2201

UNIVERSITY SPORTS

The Sugar Bowl Classic is played in the Superdome on New Year's Day. Tulane University plays its football schedule in the Superdome, and College basketball games are played in the city by Tulane, the University of New Orleans, Southern University of New Orleans, and Xavier University.

PROFESSIONAL SPORTS

The New Orleans Saints NFL football team played its first season in 1967. Its home games are played at the Superdome.

GOLF AND TENNIS

CITY PARK
Four 18-hole golf courses................................283-3458
Tennis Center 482-2230

AUDUBON PARK
18-hole golf course.....................................861-9513
Tennis Center 861-2537

PERFORMING ARTS

THE NEW ORLEANS SYMPHONY

203 Carondelet St., Suite 903   524-0404

The symphony season runs from October through May with as many as 16 concerts featuring guest conductors and touring artists. Performances are held in the New Orleans Theatre of the Performing Arts in Armstrong Square. Chartered bus service is provided for concert goers in four New Orleans suburbs. Individual and season tickets are available.

BROADWAY SERIES AT THE SAENGER

P.O. Drawer 51540   525-1052

The restored Saenger books hits of the season on Broadway. Sandy Duncan has flown on this stage in "Peter Pan", and Elizabeth Taylor, Richard Kiley and other top performers schedule New Orleans on their national tours.

COMMUNITY CONCERTS

921 Canal Street   523-6891

This October to May series sponsored by the Community Concert Association offers an eclectic collection of six events by international touring companies and individual artists. Opera, dance, music spectaculars, and instrumental virtuosos are represented. Performances are held in the Theatre of the Performing Arts. Tickets available at Maison Blanche Canal Street store.

INDEX